CW00482283

'With a corporate career spanning four continents and a recent pivot into entrepreneurship and venture investing, Alan Rosling is ideally placed to make sense of the current entrepreneurial boom in India. This book is a definitive guide to the hot-growth companies in India, and it provides highly valuable lessons for would-be entrepreneurs, investors and policy-makers. I thoroughly recommend it!' – **JULIAN BIRKINSHAW, Deputy Dean and Professor of Strategy and Entrepreneurship, London Business School**

'An important and necessary book. It comprehensively covers the evolution of business in India and captures the pulse of entrepreneurial energy sweeping the country today.' – **ADI GODREJ, Chairman, Godrej Group**

'This is a very upbeat view on India's entrepreneurial future, from an old India hand. Alan Rosling writes perceptively, with insights born of personal experience and observation. He also points out that while Indian entrepreneurism is at an exciting stage, it requires effective action to reap its full potential. Hence the question mark in the title. An excellent read, and a welcome guide for entrepreneurs and policy-makers.' – **ANAND MAHINDRA, Chairman and Managing Director, Mahindra & Mahindra**

'[Alan] Rosling has conducted an in-depth study of the entrepreneurial scene in contemporary India using 100+ interviews with entrepreneurial ecosystem players. This book adds tremendous value to those who wish to become entrepreneurs.' – **NARAYANA MURTHY, Founder, Infosys and Catamaran Ventures**

'India's time is now; the opportunity at hand is immense with the strength of our 800 million youth. From his months of interactions with young India and a lifetime of his own experience, Alan [Rosling] paints the promising state of the nation, as it is. The best way to understand what entrepreneurship could mean for India is to hear it from the entrepreneurs themselves and that is precisely what this book is about...' – **BHAVISH AGGARWAL, Co-founder and CEO, Ola Cabs**

'Today's India is defined by new-age, bold entrepreneurs, and this book is an insider's [account] of these change agents of our country.' – **VIJAY SHEKHAR SHARMA, Founder and CEO, Paytm**

'Alan Rosling's three-and-a-half decade long romance with India has taken many guises – that of the corporate insider, the investor, the entrepreneur, all after a stint with the British prime minister. I recommend with enthusiasm this entirely readable romp through the frontlines of India's entrepreneurship revolution.' – **TARUN KHANNA, Director, South Asia Institute, Harvard University, and Jorge Paulo Lemann Professor, Harvard Business School**

'A highly engaging account of the evolution of Indian entrepreneurship and the pivotal forces of change that have shaped the economy over the last few decades. Alan [Rosling]'s deep-rooted personal engagement with India, which enables him to relate to the changes easily, makes the book special.' – **SUNIL BHARTI MITTAL, Founder and Chairman, Bharti Enterprises**

'*Boom Country?* is an entertaining, inspiring and important book. It documents and explains India's remarkable entrepreneurial turn in the 21st century, and is full of insight and colourful detail, often in the words and from the perspectives of the entrepreneurs themselves. Alan Rosling combines an outsider's objectivity with the insider's passion to bring us a great book – a potential business classic.' – **JAIDEEP PRABHU, Jawaharlal Nehru Professor of Business and Enterprise, University of Cambridge**

'From brave entrepreneurs to fearless start-ups, Alan Rosling's narrative on India's entrepreneurial evolution is compelling and captivating.' – **KIRAN MAZUMDAR-SHAW, Chairperson and Managing Director, Biocon**

'Everyone looks at the success story of an entrepreneur at his/her peak. Alan [Rosling]'s book captures some of the subtleties of the driving forces behind the people who made considerable sacrifices to build a business. There's a wave of entrepreneurship in India and this new ethos deserves documentation. Alan [Rosling]'s definitive account of this explosion of start-ups speaks to India's core of entrepreneurship, innovation and the evolution of a nascent ecosystem.' – **NAVEEN TEWARI, Co-founder and CEO, InMobi**

BOOM COUNTRY?

The New Wave of Indian Enterprise

Alan Rosling

hachette INDIA

First published in 2017 by Hachette India
(Registered name: Hachette Book Publishing India Pvt. Ltd)
An Hachette UK company
www.hachetteindia.com

1

Cover design by Bhavi Mehta

ISBN 978-93-5195-080-6

Hachette Book Publishing India Pvt. Ltd
4th/5th Floors, Corporate Centre,
Sector 44, Gurgaon 122003, India

Typeset in Minion Pro10.5/14.5
by InoSoft Systems Noida

Printed and bound in India by
Manipal Technologies Ltd, Manipal

To five boys, who have given me joy,
1.3 billion Indians who welcomed a firangi,
and the one begum with whom I share it all.

'The opening up of new markets, foreign or domestic, and the organizational development from the craft shop to such concerns as U.S. Steel illustrate the same process of industrial mutation – if I may use that biological term – that incessantly revolutionizes the economic structure from within, incessantly destroying the old one, incessantly creating a new one. This process of Creative Destruction is the essential fact about capitalism.'

Joseph A. Schumpeter, *Capitalism, Socialism and Democracy* (1942)

'All new small businesses have many factors in common. But to be entrepreneurial, an enterprise has to have special characteristics over and above being new and small. Indeed, entrepreneurs are a minority among new businesses. They create something new, something different; they change or transmute values.'

Peter Drucker, *Innovation and Entrepreneurship* (1985)

CONTENTS

INTRODUCTION

An Entrepreneurial Pivot

'I think people like him [Ratan Tata] giving [their] time is very important for entrepreneurs of my generation because most of us are still building. It's still very early in our journey and the early parts are not just [about] the excitement of fast growth and phenomenal opportunities but are about building lasting businesses. That's what I think we can learn from traditional industry in India like [the] Tatas.'

Bhavish Aggarwal, Co-founder and CEO, Ola Cabs

'That is not a good idea,' Ratan Tata told me.

He spoke deliberately, his deep voice hinting at time spent in America. Tall and imposing, elegant in his tailored double-breasted suit, his dark eyes stared at me from under craggy brows. Silence filled his office. I sat on the modernist leather and chrome sofa, aware of the light flooding in from the balcony garden outside, feeling completely deflated.

It was 2003 and I had gone to the man I respected most, the doyen of Indian business, to ask for his help and advice. After 20 years of working for large companies I wanted to become an entrepreneur. As I explained to Ratan, my idea was to create an advisory firm to help foreign companies navigate the opportunities in and complexities of India, in partnership with my friend Sujit Gupta, the retiring chief Tata representative in Delhi, and Shardul Shroff of Amarchand & Mangaldas & Suresh A. Shroff & Co., one of India's leading lawyers.

I had spent five years as Country Chairman in India of the Jardine Matheson Group, the noble house from Hong Kong whose history is deeply connected with India's historic China trade. Jardines's most important investment in India now was a 20 per cent stake in Tata Industries, the smaller holding company at the heart of the Tata Group, India's largest and most revered industrial group. I had been the only non-Indian non-executive director of one of the holding companies of the Tata Group, a foreigner representing Jardines, and so had been privileged to watch the internal workings of the house of Tata just as many of the changes Ratan had initiated since becoming Group Chairman in 1991 began to yield significant results.

I had just completed an intense and stressful restructuring and sale of one of Jardines's operating companies, Concorde Motors, a joint venture (JV) with Tata. After a short period of welcome decompression following a mad period of doing two jobs – the group role and being Managing Director at Concorde – and living in three cities, Bombay, Bangalore and Calcutta[1] (where my family was based), I was now contemplating my next career step. I felt it was time to address the nagging urge I had suppressed for years to set up something of my own. After all, most of my friends from business school, 15 years out, were already entrepreneurs.

Ratan's stare softened and he smiled at me. He broke the silence. 'I have a better idea than your Delhi venture with Sujit and Shardul,' he said. 'Why don't you join us?'

It was an offer I could not refuse. My entrepreneurial urge was buried again and I spent the next five years as the first foreigner on the board of Tata Sons, the main holding company of the Tata Group, charged with driving the imperative to internationalize. I thought I knew India and the Tata Group well, but trained in Western management thinking and used to process-driven and financially oriented international companies, I had much more to learn about how to get things done and contribute to building a business of scale in and from India.

---

[1] I have used the most common colloquial names in English for Indian cities, even where officially the name has changed: so Mumbai remains Bombay, Bengaluru is Bangalore and Kolkata is Calcutta, though Chennai has taken over from the earlier Madras. Where an interviewee has used Mumbai or Bengaluru or Kolkata, rather than Bombay, Bangalore and Calcutta, then I have not changed it. This holds for names of institutions as well.

'The thing we need to learn from China,' Ratan had once said in a board meeting, 'is a level of ambition. In India, we have never thought big enough.' From $2.4 billion of international sales in 2003, we grew to $38 billion outside India, or 61 per cent of total group sales, by 2009, the year I left and finally became an entrepreneur.

In August 2016 I went to meet Ratan to interview him for this book. Appropriately, it was my one hundredth interview. His new office in Elphinstone House, to which he had moved on retirement, seemed a replica of his old one in Bombay House, the Edwardian headquarters of the Tata Group in south Bombay's crowded business district, known as Fort. It had the same minimalist and modern feel, the same sense of light, the same leather sofa. Ratan trained as an architect at Cornell University and his style is distinctive, American modernist in part, but also Japanese in its simplicity. He told me once on a flight together that in retirement he was looking forward to returning to his first love, design and architecture. He would, he said, set up a studio.

Now retired for nearly four years and approaching his seventy-ninth birthday, Ratan seemed aged from when I had last seen him some months earlier. In hindsight, given the dramatic events that were about to unfold in the Tata Group, I now realize that he must have been weighed down by his growing concern for the direction of the group and the security of the Tata legacy under his successor as Chairman, Cyrus Mistry. The removal of Cyrus, abruptly executed at the Tata Sons board meeting on 24 October 2016, would have been under consideration. Ratan revealed nothing of that to me.

Until his brief resumption of the group chairmanship on an interim basis during the transition in leadership, and instead of returning to design and architecture as he had earlier contemplated, Ratan spent much of the first years of his retirement becoming India's most prominent angel investor. On his retirement as India's most iconic business leader after 50 years with Tata, and more than 20 years as Chairman, instead of spending more time on his hobbies, his dogs and cars and planes, sitting on grand boards globally, or focusing entirely on the philanthropy of the Tata Trusts, Ratan has dedicated much of his time and resources to supporting young entrepreneurs in India. He has pivoted from the world of international big business to the growing ecosystem of Indian start-ups. He even dresses differently; his habitual smart suit and bright Italian silk tie has been replaced by a blue button-down shirt and chinos. So far, he has made 34 investments in small or growing companies, including Snapdeal, Ola Cabs, Paytm, CarDekho, Zivame, Urban Ladder and BlueStone. As he began to speak of the young entrepreneurs and new ideas that now engaged him, an intense enthusiasm and youthful interest in the possible shone through.

Ratan's pivot towards supporting young entrepreneurs encapsulates the theme of this book – that something new, different and exciting is happening in India in entrepreneurship. I asked Ratan how his interest in supporting early-stage entrepreneurs had developed. He replied that he had always been keen to help young, ambitious people but had been constrained by lack of time and potential issues of conflict of interest while he was working full-time with the Tata Group. But he also admitted that he had been slow in recognizing the scale, depth and extent of the current entrepreneurial boom. He told me, 'There was a certain trigger that took place that accelerated the depth of my interest in this area [start-ups] and that was the realization that the smartphone was going to revolutionize the spread of merchandising in India, the flow of two-way information and the reach of the customer who could not previously access the traditional brick and mortar networks that existed in India. I realized this probably much later than I should have.'

Ratan has invested in businesses whose technology and team appeal to him, but he also has a bias for supporting entrepreneurs who might otherwise struggle to gain support from traditional equity investors. Deeply interested in science and technology, and with a strong commitment to social responsibility, the investments that his firm, RNT Associates, has made have been across a wide spectrum of Indian start-ups. Ratan explained, 'I have very little interest in those entrepreneurs who are running after valuation and are looking to flip quickly; I've stayed away from them. The guys who attract me are the smaller segment who are looking at where they can make a difference to the vast manpower base that India has, to the length and quality of life and dealing with ailments, illnesses and hardships.'

Here was the leading business figure of recent times, a man soon to be in his eightieth year, talking with the animation and excitement of a college student about the potential for change in India, and the technology and people enabling that change.

As I listened to his words I realized I too had failed to appreciate early enough, while I was employed in large companies, the profound nature of the changes and development taking place in the entrepreneurial culture of India. I have for long believed that India enjoys considerable competitive advantages over many other countries and has the potential, until recently only partially delivered upon, to achieve rapid growth and positive social change. I chose to focus my career on India because I saw this huge potential, but tended to think of it in terms of the opportunities for large companies, both domestic and foreign. Once I became an entrepreneur myself, on leaving Tata, I began to appreciate the growing vibrancy of the start-up culture and the new enthusiasm for entrepreneurship among India's young.

My Indian journey began as a callow student in 1982. I woke up on the morning of my twentieth birthday on the grubby floor of a room in a cheap hotel named Step Inn somewhere in New Delhi, another slumbering body next to me in a sleeping bag and two more in the bed. Four of us had decided in a frivolous moment to spend part of our summer holiday after our second year at Cambridge, or 'Long Vac' as it is known, travelling around northern India. As a history student I had read much about India but knew virtually nothing and absolutely no one. Unlike many British families, mine had no historical connections with India except a great-uncle who had spent some years there in the Royal Air Force (RAF) Regiment during the Second World War. On arrival in the foggy murk of a warm August night, off the ex-servicemen's bus service from Palam Airport in Delhi (known as the Indira Gandhi International Airport since 1986), we had been persuaded by an auto-rickshaw driver to go to Step Inn. So started a relationship with the country, an intense engagement of love and exasperation, excitement and frustration, that has lasted 35 years so far.

My obsession with India only grew with time. It was another 16 years before I finally moved to Bombay in 1998, but in those years I learnt much. After Cambridge I started my working life as a banker with S.G. Warburg & Co. I took three months off before going to Harvard Business School (HBS) in 1986 and travelled around west and south India on my own.

After business school I sought a real management job in manufacturing and joined Courtaulds Textiles to run a unit manufacturing knickers and bras for Marks & Spencer. The fall of Mrs Thatcher in 1990 resulted in an opportunity for me to join the staff of the new prime minister, John Major, as Special Advisor in the Policy Unit at 10 Downing Street. I was focused on domestic issues such as rail privatization and the growing demand in Scotland for devolved government, but still took an active interest in the economic reforms that started in India in 1991.

Much against the wishes of the Foreign Office I inveigled myself into the planning of John Major's visit to India in January 1993 when he was invited to attend the Republic Day celebrations in New Delhi as the Chief Guest. The visit schedule was redesigned to put the business relationship between India and the UK at the heart of the programme and we insisted on a trade delegation, that filled the rented jumbo jet, be taken along. I sat in on the prime minister's meeting with his Indian counterpart, P.V. Narasimha Rao, who hardly said a word (as they said of Rao's customary expression through all events and on all occasions, 'If in doubt, pout'). I helped put together, overnight, the Indo–British Partnership Initiative to give the two prime ministers something to announce at their joint press conference as the bilateral meeting had not yielded much. I wrote the speech to businessmen that my boss delivered in the ballroom of the Taj Mahal Hotel in Bombay, a place I have subsequently grown to love.

After Downing Street, I joined Guinness's subsidiary United Distillers (UD), then the world's leading spirits company, as Strategy Director, and India loomed as an important opportunity as the economy began to emerge from the Nehruvian ice age. Despite being the second largest whisky market in the world, India had been closed to imports since the early 1970s. As the economic reforms gathered pace from 1991, these restrictions began to be eased, initially through permitting the bulk import of Scotch for local bottling. Before I joined, UD had agreed to a joint venture with Vijay Mallya's United Breweries Group (UB Group) to relaunch imported Scotch, starting with Black & White and VAT 69. The joint venture did not go well and in my last year at UD I focused full-time on a breakthrough strategy for the Indian market. I hoped this would be my ticket to move to India. We negotiated a deal with UB to buy all of their major brands such as

Bagpiper, McDowell's and Blue Riband, 12 million cases per annum in total, leaving UB to supply the locally produced brands on long-term contract. Term sheets were agreed upon and the contracts painfully hammered out. However, a short time before the contracts were due to be signed in June 1997, the merger of our parent, Guinness, with Grand Metropolitan, owner of our biggest competitor, International Distillers & Vintners (IDV), was announced. This was the deal that created Diageo. As a consequence, my deal and my passage to India were off.

I cast around for another way to get to India, and later in 1997 accepted the role of Jardine Matheson Group's Country Chairman, based in Bombay. Jardines had a number of businesses in India already. Jardine Fleming was then one of the leading international financial institutions in the country. Jardines was also pioneering modern retail in India with approvals to set up the first joint ventures in supermarkets, drugstores and car retailing. But, beyond the potential to do much more in our operating businesses, the real attraction of the job for me was that my predecessor, John Mackenzie, had negotiated partnership arrangements with both the Tata Group and HDFC, two of the finest companies in India. I was going to India at last, with the opportunity to work with Ratan Tata and India's most respected banker, Deepak Parekh.

Five years at Jardines led to five years at Tata, during which I witnessed a dramatic amount of positive change in the Tata Group. Tata Consultancy Services (TCS) vaulted to a formidable position in global IT services, Tata Steel and Tata Motors made major acquisitions internationally, and genuine innovation began to spread across the group, best symbolized by the affordable car, the Nano. Business is about choice and risk, and not everything the group did in those years worked out as planned, leaving issues which Cyrus Mistry was trying to address when he was unceremoniously removed as Ratan's successor as Group Chairman.

The Tata Group is the corporate icon it is in India because of its values, rather than purely because of its size, strategic ambition or business performance. I learnt a huge amount from working for the group and for Ratan, but my biggest insight was that it really is possible to make a positive impact on society and do good through good business. I remember one occasion when we were debating a decision. I presented the hard business logic of one option. Ratan had sat quietly through the discussion until he suddenly said that, despite the economic case for the option I recommended, we were going to take a different course because that was morally the right thing to do. No Western company I have worked with would have made such a call based on what was right rather than what was more profitable, of course assuming that both options were legal.

By 2009 I felt I was finally ready to take the first step away from the corporate world and into the exciting freedom offered by entrepreneurship. A central role in the Tata Group had been tremendous and a privilege, but I now wanted the latitude to build something of my own and the freedom to work for myself. I had also been too often frustrated with dealing with the complex politics of Bombay House, the lack of clarity in so much, and the loose and ill-defined relationships with the sprawling group companies. I could not see myself staying in a similar role until retirement as most of my senior colleagues seemed set to do. I was 46, and directors were then allowed to stay until they turned 75.

At first on leaving Tata I created my own advisory business, Griffin Growth Partners, to assist clients in complex emerging markets including India and the rest of South Asia. Very soon I was drawn into co-founding Kiran Energy together with my old friend, Ardeshir Contractor. The Government of India was finally becoming serious about addressing climate change, and the tumbling cost of solar modules meant that in the long run it would be solar energy, rather than wind energy, that would be the appropriate renewable technology for India, given the high levels of insolation. By the summer of 2010, we had raised $50 million from three US-based Private Equity (PE) investors and secured our first 20 MW project in Gujarat. By the end of the year we had signed a joint venture with the Mahindra Group and won the first round of bidding under the Government of India's National Solar Mission for an initial 5 MW plant in Rajasthan. I led on business development and external relations, particularly with the government. I was walking dusty fields in rural India seeking suitable land, sitting in dark corridors outside the offices of bureaucrats in Delhi and multiple state capitals, trying to nudge policy and win power purchase agreements, and calling on every Indian corporate we knew to sell solar power. Almost by accident, I was a real Indian entrepreneur.

By 2013, we had built Kiran Energy into one of the leading renewable energy generators in the country with more than 100 MW in operation. I decided it was time to step back from my full-time executive role at Kiran Energy and develop other interests. I revived the advisory work through Griffin. I also found myself being drawn into more opportunities to work with start-ups in India.

It started with a meeting at a cocktail party at the Taj Hotel in Bombay. Arvind Kothari approached me and reminded me that we had met a few years previously while he was with TCS in Paris and had arranged my visit to the office. A few months later Arvind contacted me again to ask me to help him as he developed an idea for a cloud-based mini-ERP system for small kirana, that is, 'Mom and Pop' or local, stores in India. I worked with him for more than a year, but despite the impressive software he had created and the positive market reaction from kirana owners, we could not raise funding. Having run down his savings, Arvind did a deal with Reliance Industries and joined them to offer his product on Reliance's Jio data platform. A number of the Venture Capital (VC) funds to which we pitched the idea in 2013, who had then thought the concept would not work in India, subsequently invested in similar products in the boom of 2015. Timing is often crucial in fundraising.

Another chance encounter at a conference led me to agree to work with Rajeev Mantri as he developed his idea for Navam Capital. Rajeev had worked in New York for Lux Capital, a venture fund that invested in early-stage companies pursuing science-driven innovation. Rajeev came back to India in 2008 and began investing in similar science-based deep technology companies. He started with three businesses in Delhi: EnNatura Technology Ventures in organic inks, Vyome Biosciences in dermatological pharmaceutics and Invictus Oncology in cancer drug discovery. Rajeev was far more actively involved in these businesses than most VCs would be, playing a founding role at Vyome besides writing the first cheques to fund both Vyome and Invictus. I now sit on the board of Vyome, representing Navam.

These first encounters with the start-up world in India led to more. I spent many months working with my friend S. Suresh, whom I knew from Concorde Motors, on an idea to introduce self-storage to India. In focus groups consumers loved the idea of 'cloud storage for the clutter' in their homes but did not seem ready to pay a price reflecting the cost of real estate in Indian cities. We concluded it was too early and challenging to scale profitably. Mukesh Bajaj, Partner at CreditCheck Partners, introduced me to Srinivas Vishnubhatla as he was considering returning from the United States (US) to create Mosaik Risk Solutions. Mark Runacres, Director at SQN Partners, suggested I meet Manoj Nair who had just launched RedGirraffe.com with the intent to revolutionize property rentals in India. I found myself advising a range of Indian start-ups.

I have spent most of my time in India in the corporate world. Even Kiran Energy had been formed and financed and had grown as if it were an established business. Our logo is a conservative blue, we often wear suits to pitch for project debt from banks like State Bank of India (SBI) and the Infrastructure Development Finance Company (IDFC), and we have partnered with major companies such as Mahindra & Mahindra (M&M), Larsen & Toubro (L&T) and First Solar. My first encounters in the start-up world coincided with the sudden realization that an increasing number of people I knew or had worked with had become entrepreneurs. Friends at Tata, McKinsey & Company, Bain and Goldman Sachs mentioned an exodus of young talent, not to competitors, but to start-ups. We also lost a few of our young, commercial employees in Kiran who had been with us from early days of the company. Rushabh Desai left to set up a jobs portal and Siddharth Bhandari tried to create a roti home delivery business in Bangalore.

Suddenly, it seemed that everyone was talking about entrepreneurship in India, including the present prime minister, Narendra Modi, who launched the Startup India initiative in January 2016 as a flagship policy drive. There has been a sudden surge in the coverage of entrepreneurship in the newspapers at the same time, especially the business pink press. In 2016, up to September, 12,110 articles in the Indian media mentioned the word 'entrepreneur' compared to 8,316 articles in the whole of 2015 and 7,688 articles in 2014. The leading publications covering entrepreneurship were *Economic Times* (866 mentions in 2016 up to September across the print and e-edition) and *The Times of India* (838 mentions).[2]

---

2   LexisNexis

It became increasingly clear to me that the entrepreneurial boom was of deeper importance and potential than was being reflected by the sensational coverage in the business press of fundraising, valuations, personality clashes and exits in the e-commerce sector. The recent dramatic surge in entrepreneurialism in India bodes well for the future of the country in terms of economic growth, jobs and quality of life for the majority of India's people. India seems set to become a genuine boom country for new enterprise.

As this book chronicles, the rising tide of new enterprise in India has been enabled by the convergence of four main factors. First, advances in technology, especially information technology (IT), have been critical in opening up new potential and lowering barriers to entry. Second, attracted by the growing opportunities, a new availability of risk equity capital has enabled entrepreneurs without access to family money to launch businesses more readily. Third, government policy has played an important role in creating new opportunities through the faster economic growth triggered by the economic reforms of the past 25 years and by reducing the friction of regulation holding back business. Most important of all has been a change in culture and world view in India, particularly among the young, resulting from exposure to world-class education and international attitudes. Entrepreneurship is now 'cool' and socially acceptable, not just among peers but also many extended Indian families. Young people feel able to take risks their parents would probably have avoided. They want the freedom to design their own lives. Increasingly, they choose not to emigrate, or not to stay in the US after education there, as so many of the best in earlier generations did, but instead to apply their newly liberated thinking and great talent to the opportunities and challenges in India.

The substance of my argument in this book is derived from interviews with more than one hundred participants in the entrepreneurial ecosystem in India (see p. xxiii, 'Author's Note on the Interviews'). I have quoted extensively from these interviews so that the ambition and belief in the future shared by most of these risk-takers might shine through. Many of these entrepreneurs believe that they are contributing to the transformation of India, not just making money for themselves and their investors. What is clear from the interviews is the gathering pace of entrepreneurship in the country. Their narratives, taken together, paint a consistent and compelling picture of growing opportunities and the release of the brakes that have hitherto held back India's potential. This easing of the business environment is illustrated by a clear contrast in the stories of the older and more recent entrepreneurs I interviewed. The newer entrepreneurs have typically found the path to success to be swifter, risk capital more readily available and government hurdles lower than did those who started their businesses earlier.

The entrepreneurial scene in India, however, remains imperfect, patchy and volatile. The rejuvenated spirit of enterprise is much wider and deeper than just the e-commerce companies in Bangalore, which are all too often seen as the most prominent manifestations of the resurgent ambition to transform India through new business. More than a third of the entrepreneurs I interviewed were in IT or e-commerce, and about the same number in finance or services. Manufacturing and innovation-led enterprises are fewer in number, at least in part because they still face more challenges in India's complex operating environment and in raising funds. Furthermore, the new entrepreneurship of ambition is currently geographically and socially patchy, with hotspots in Bangalore, Powai in Bombay and Gurgaon next to Delhi. There are, of course, entrepreneurs of ambition in rural and small-town India, in addition to the millions of entrepreneurs of necessity, but their concentration and impact is much less so far. Equally, most of those I interviewed were drawn from a relatively narrow pool of well-educated, English-speaking professionals, many with international educational or career exposure, especially to the US. This much is clear: For the entrepreneurial revolution to achieve its full potential, the boom in new enterprise, with its supporting ecosystem, needs to spread further by sector, geography and social background.

While researching and writing this book in 2016 and early 2017, the positive mood in the market had deflated somewhat and funding sources tightened. I saw this as a natural correction of the over-enthusiasm during 2014 and 2015. Looking forward, no doubt the incoming entrepreneurial tide will be choppy, with reversals of fortune, failures and swings in levels of confidence. Nevertheless, it is clear that the underlying surge in new enterprise represents a gathering and seminal shift in the business culture of the country, which over time holds the potential of profound and positive outcomes for the economy and the people of India.

This book is organized in eight chapters. The first describes India's business landscape, both established corporates and entrepreneurs, and puts the Indian entrepreneurial ecosystem in the context of entrepreneurship internationally. The second covers the entrepreneurs I interviewed who started their businesses earlier than 2000, while the third compares and contrasts eight entrepreneurs who started after 2000. There are then four thematic chapters covering each of the four drivers of change: technology, the availability of equity capital, the role of government and cultural changes in Indian society. The final chapter identifies ways in which the entrepreneurial ecosystem still needs to develop and mature.

Interspersed between the chapters are nine short profiles with one exception of a single entrepreneur, chosen to reflect the points being made in the adjoining chapters. In most cases I have chosen entrepreneurs who are less well known than icons such as Narayana Murthy (Infosys and Catamaran Ventures), Sunil Mittal (Bharti), Sachin Bansal (Flipkart) or Bhavish Aggarwal (Ola Cabs). The profiles are of Vijay Shekhar Sharma (One97/Paytm), R. Ravindranath (Milltec), Sanjoy Roy (Teamwork Arts), Dhiraj Rajaram (Mu Sigma), Shashank N.D. (Practo), Srikumar Misra (Milk Mantra), Neeraj Kakkar (Hector Beverages) and Amuleek Singh Bijral (Chai Point), Mahesh Choudhary (Microqual Techno) and Aniruddha Sharma (Carbon Clean Solutions).

Author's Note on the Interviews

In the absence of quality data and research about the entrepreneurial process in India, I set out to meet and interview 100 entrepreneurs, investors and observers of the entrepreneurial ecosystem in India. I completed 105 interviews of 109 people (in four cases I did joint interviews), as listed in the Appendix. These busy people gave me their time, their stories and their views, often sharing intimate, difficult or embarrassing anecdotes and opening up to another entrepreneur as they might not have done to a journalist. Almost all of these interviews have been in person but a few, typically where I knew the person well, were by phone. Most interviews lasted an hour or two, but many were several hours and a few led to repeated interactions over many hours.

Where possible, I met the interviewee in his or her office – I believe the style of workplace also tells a story. Ajay Piramal's waiting room was hung with a stunning collection of works by the Bengali painter Jamini Roy; Ajay told me that initially he started buying art as an investment based on professional advice, but now he has come to truly love his collection. I met Ronnie Screwvala in his beautiful office in Worli, Bombay, overlooking the Arabian Sea, with books on film and fashion as well as novels lining the walls. Jaithirth (Jerry) Rao's office off Hughes Road in Bombay was also dominated by books, but in this case they were piled high in chaotic towers like in the study of an eccentric professor. Ajay Bijli's PVR office in Gurgaon was cinema-themed with film posters on the wall, popcorn offered at reception and reclining chairs taken from a movie hall. Ashish Goel of Urban Ladder met me in his office furnished with products from their online catalogue. Pranay Chulet's new Quikr campus is in an old textiles factory refurbished into a spectacular open-plan office full of open spaces and walkways, and throughout there are mementos of his father's career as a mining engineer with Hindustan Zinc.

A number of the interviews were with people I have worked with, and in some cases still do. These include Ardeshir Contractor, my co-founder at Kiran Energy; Anand Mahindra, our joint venture partner in Mahindra Solar One; Arvind Kothari; Rajeev Mantri; Shiladitya Sengupta; Nelabhotla Venkateswarlu (N. Venkat); Mukesh Bajaj; Srinivas Vishnubhatla; Vijay Reddy; and Manoj Nair.

I sought a balance of more experienced entrepreneurs and more recent entrepreneurs, those who have succeeded, failed and are still trying, men and women, and from different backgrounds and regions. I recognize that the list has an urban, English-speaking bias and that voices from rural India and small towns are largely absent. Small entrepreneurs of necessity and those who speak only an Indian language are not represented. I developed the list largely through contacts and relationships, as is the way in India, and I acknowledge the resulting slant.

Most of those I approached agreed to meet in a generosity typical of Indian hospitality and manners. Only a few declined or struggled to give time. Of course all are busy people and talking to me offered no real upside for them. Dilip Shanghvi of Sun Pharma politely declined, given his travel schedule. Anil Agarwal of Vedanta regretted, perhaps feeling the timing not good given the downturn in the commodity cycle. Nikesh Arora said no, and his departure from Softbank a few months later might explain this. I was amused by the initial response of Kunal Bahl of Snapdeal to my request to meet. I had a working title for the book of *The New Banias* ('bania' is a trader from a traditional business community) and Kunal regretted that he could not meet me as he was not a bania, and I should instead meet his partner Rohit Bansal, who was. Kunal and Rohit subsequently offered to meet me together, but the time they could give me on a visit to Delhi clashed with my appointment with Sunil Mittal and we were not able to find another slot. Snapdeal, Zomato and Hike are three of the current nine recognized Indian 'unicorn'[3] companies that I did not meet. The others are covered: Flipkart, One97/Paytm, Ola Cabs, ReNew Power, Mu Sigma, InMobi and ShopClues.

Of the 109 people I interviewed, I counted 92 as first-generation entrepreneurs, defined as being a founder of a company in India. The other 17 include government policy-makers, investors, academics, journalists and other observers.

The 92 entrepreneurs are heavily skewed towards relatively recent starters. I defined a first group of entrepreneurs who started prior to 2000, 21 in total, as 'Manmohan's Children'. While a few started in business prior to the 1991 reforms, they all benefitted and grew in businesses boosted by the liberalization unleashed by prime minister P.V. Narasimha Rao and his finance minister, Manmohan Singh, and extended by the BJP government

---

[3] 'Unicorn' is commonly used to describe an unlisted start-up company that achieves a valuation of $1 billion or more. Valuation of private companies is often not straightforward, fluctuates over time, and is based on reported valuation ascribed by investors. CB Insights publishes a constantly updated list on a global basis at https://www.cbinsights.com/research-unicorn-companies. China, by contrast to India, currently has 42 unicorn companies listed by CB Insights. Also, Quikr had earlier been included in the list of companies from India.

of Atal Bihari Vajpayee from 1998. Seventy-one interviews were with entrepreneurs who started after 2000, and many after 2010, the group I have called 'The New Generation'. Their stories differed markedly from those of the earlier entrepreneurs, reinforcing that something of real note has changed in India.

An academic might caution about the robustness of the data set given the sample size and my methodology of selecting interviews. Only six are from the eastern region, the others broadly split between north, west and south India, though the north is relatively more important (34 per cent) among the New Generation than among Manmohan's Children (24 per cent). Women are heavily under-represented at six of the 92. While India does quite well relative to many Asian and indeed Western countries on gender balance in certain sectors (the public sector, the professions, banking), in business women are generally poorly represented. There are some signs that in the younger generation this is correcting to some extent with a number of well-known female entrepreneurs. However, 6 per cent may not be far off the proportion of women in the entrepreneurial world.

An even more sensitive topic in India, particularly for a foreigner to broach, is the question of background, community and caste. We foreigners lack the easy ability to read the nuances of Indian identity. I observe my Indian friends automatically placing people they meet based on name, language and background. With this caveat, as well as I can place my 92 entrepreneurs, 25 per cent come from a traditional trading community (notably Marwari, Gujarati, and Sindhi), 24 per cent are Brahmins, only three are Muslim and none are Dalits or tribals. The predominance of those from traditional trading communities and Brahmins is slightly lower in the later group than the earlier one, suggesting that the virus of entrepreneurial zeal is spreading from traditional business backgrounds to wider groups in India. However, there is clear under-representation in entrepreneurship of people from eastern India, women, Muslims and those from less advantaged social backgrounds.

Two other themes that consistently emerged from the interviews are supported by analysis of the backgrounds of the 92 entrepreneurs. The first is the transformative impact of education. All of the entrepreneurs featured here are graduates, almost all engineers. Many spoke of the importance of their time in college in opening up their minds to the possibilities of business life and entrepreneurship in particular. Twenty-seven per cent of the 92 are alumni of the Indian Institutes of Technology (IITs), more than 13 per cent attended the Indian Institutes of Management (IIMs).[4] The proportion who graduated from an IIT is broadly unchanged between the earlier and later groups, but the representation of IIM alumni is higher (16 per cent) in the later group.

The second, and even stronger, common theme is the importance of exposure to the US, either for education or for employment. Forty-two per cent of the 92 had spent time in the US, and this was slightly higher among the New Generation (44 per cent) than among Manmohan's Children (38 per cent). Further, a number of the entrepreneurs who had not lived in the US had been exposed to American business thinking by working for multinational companies (MNCs) in India, and of course all have been immersed in American culture through the media and the Internet. Hence my contention that the story of the rise of entrepreneurship in India is in good part the story of the opening up of – or, in the most positive sense, 'the Americanization of' – the Indian mind.

There is another group among the New Generation who were not represented among Manmohan's Children: Foreigners. There were six foreigners among the second group, including two Non-Resident Indians (NRIs) who have returned to create businesses. Two of them, both non-Indian, now possess Overseas Citizens of India (OCI) cards by marriage and so have in some way become Indian.[5] Clearly, six out of 92 is over-

---

[4] One of Prime Minister Jawaharlal Nehru's lasting legacies was to create the Indian Institutes of Technology and Indian Institutes of Management. There are now 23 IITs (of which the institutes at Kharagpur, Delhi, Bombay and Madras are probably the best known) and 20 IIMs (of which those at Ahmedabad, Bangalore and Calcutta are generally thought the leaders). Gaining admission in these institutions is an intensely competitive affair.

[5] India does not permit dual citizenship. Indians living overseas have long been termed Non-Resident Indians (NRIs). More recently, the government has formalized their status by issuing 'long-term visa' documents, initially termed Persons of Indian Origin (PIO) Cards, and more recently Overseas Citizens of India (OCI) Cards.

representation and reflects my own network and background. However, this attraction of India to non-Indian nationals illustrates the growing relative importance of India not just as a market for investment but also as a place to create a great business. I am another member of the caste of foreigners who believe that India is a tremendous place in which to live and do business.

A Long Struggle Rewarded
VIJAY SHEKHAR SHARMA

We were sitting in Starbucks in Greater Kailash in Delhi when Vijay Shekhar Sharma, founder and CEO of One97 Communications, told me about his meeting with Jack Ma, the founder of Alibaba. Now said to be the world's largest retailer, surpassing Walmart on some measures such as having operations in 190 countries, Alibaba's Initial Public Offer (IPO) in September 2014 valued the company at $231 billion. The outcome of the meeting was an investment of $680 million into Vijay's Paytm from Alibaba and Ant Financial in 2015. 'My life story has had a lot of rough patches. Jack told me that if Alibaba is to grow in India, he needed partners who are entrepreneurs like me. Not a large company like the Tata Group because large companies have a number of things to do, while for me this was the one thing. He said that successful companies could be made by many entrepreneurs, but extraordinary companies are made by those who have gone through real hardship in their lives.'

Vijay has certainly come a long way, faced many challenges and tried many different businesses before One97 and its subsidiary, Paytm, took off. His nadir was in 2004 when he was not generating enough cash from One97 to pay himself and had to freelance outside the company to earn extra money. He was scrounging off friends to eat, and often went to bed after having had just a Coke and a Britannia Bourbon biscuit.

Vijay is from a small town near Aligarh in India's largest state, Uttar Pradesh. His father was a teacher and his grandfather a well-known ayurvedic doctor. He told me, 'In the social environment we come from, there is nobody who is a businessman. People normally take a job. Businessmen are looked down on as they are more or less traders, and traders are not considered to be good people. They are not [perceived as] straightforward, sincere.'

At the suggestion of a relative, Vijay applied to the Delhi College of

Engineering, but found the course very hard because his English was poor. Naturally reclusive, he retreated to the computer lab, where he discovered the Internet. He learnt about the world of technology from magazines in the library and those he picked up second-hand at a Sunday market. By the time he left college he had already created an Internet business offering web-hosting services.

For a brief time after college he worked for an American company. Then, in 1998, he set up another business providing content management services, which was successfully sold in 2010. Vijay was just 21 at the time and suddenly had more cash than his family had ever seen before. In 2001 he created One97 to offer marketing services to telecom companies who were not adept at exploiting the data they had available. It was a high-growth business but capital intensive because the sheer volume of data involved required heavy investment in computing power. Telecom customers were also somewhat slow to pay, hence Vijay's acute cash flow headaches in these years.

By 2004 there was mounting family pressure to close One97 and get a good job, not least so Vijay could get married. His mother told him that people thought he worked for himself because he could not get a job. When an arranged marriage became a possibility, his prospective father-in-law, who worked in the Rajasthan State Finance Corporation sanctioning small loans, audited Vijay's financial position. This included a visit to inspect the company's books, arranged by Vijay's father without his knowledge. Vijay was rejected as a suitable boy, and it was a year later that the marriage finally took place.

In 2008, he secured his first VC investment from SAIF Partners and Silicon Valley Bank, who put in $18 million in tranches. Vijay credits Ravi Adusumalli of SAIF not just as a supporter and friend, but also for effectively being a co-founder of Paytm. In 2011 Vijay proposed to his board that the smartphone revolution was changing India so radically that One97 needed to pivot towards becoming a mobile payments service. The majority of the board opposed the proposal. As Vijay recalled: 'On the board call they said, "Vijay, we know you are a great technology guy, we know that you can predict technologies much in advance, but you do not know how to build a consumer brand. It's about 24×7 customer care and branding." One board director resigned because we were going to get into a regulated business.'

After the meeting, Ravi called Vijay and asked him to explain in detail his logic for pushing the mobile payment idea so hard. Vijay ran him through his thinking, especially that there was no easy way for Indians to shop online because there was no secure payment system. 'India didn't yet have PayPal. E-stores, game stores, iTunes and Google Play Store would all need a payment system.'

Between them, SAIF and Vijay controlled 80 per cent of the company. Ravi told him to try out the new payment business with ₹5 crore ($757,000) and prove the concept. They launched Paytm a few months later. By the year end they needed more cash for the rollout of Paytm and Ravi agreed to an immediate cheque, with paperwork to follow later, over-ruling his colleague who was the acting Chief Financial Officer (CFO) of the company.

Vijay believes strongly that working with investors like Ravi, who take a long-term view and have a feel for the business, is essential, rather than those more financially oriented investors who are often seeking an early exit. He finds Alibaba, his strategic investor from 2015, to be a great partner because they are able to support Paytm with technology, product and insights as the marketplace subsidiary, Paytm E-Commerce, develops in competition with Flipkart and Amazon. In early 2017, Alibaba was reported to have invested a further $177 million in the e-commerce business, taking its stake in Paytm's marketplace operation to a majority. 'My learning has been that the best part about strategic money is there is no exit cycle. I have so much respect for the Chinese. If you want to see what is happening in technology and especially mobile Internet in the world, you don't go west, you go east. There is no better place than China.'

Vijay's latest venture is to launch a fully-fledged payment bank as a separately regulated entity, so in future he will compete against SBI and Citibank, not just Snapdeal and Amazon. Paytm's digital wallet appears to be one of the major beneficiaries of the 'demonetization' of large denomination bank notes in India, announced unexpectedly by Prime Minister Narendra Modi on 8 November 2016. The abrupt withdrawal of ₹500 and ₹1,000 notes seems set to push the economy away from working so heavily with cash and towards electronic payments through systems like Paytm.

Vijay concluded our interview by saying, 'I think I am building a timeless company. I wish to build a $100 billion company, a 100-year-old company.' With great courtesy and enthusiasm, he insisted I join him at the NDTV studio to watch him being interviewed for a show on new entrepreneurs, then offered to drive me back in the sleek BMW that reflects the sudden upturn in his wealth, not least based on the influx of capital from China. He has certainly come a long way from a small town near Aligarh, and a life of Coke and a Bourbon biscuit for dinner.

CHAPTER 1

A Land of Entrepreneurs

'There are entrepreneurs all around us, but I think the scale at which you operate matters. I meet entrepreneurs in India, unbelievable entrepreneurs, every week...but at the scale at which they are operating there is not much impact. You can't imagine the entrepreneurship that is there.'

Kishore Biyani, Founder and CEO, Future Group

'The key point is, there are a hell of a lot of people out there,' asserted Gurcharan Das waving his hand towards the darkening trees that framed the Lodhi Gardens in Delhi as we walked together at pace. The cacophony of birds among the greenery and ruined monuments almost drowned out his voice. 'India is a country of entrepreneurs. Don't dismiss the ragpicker as not being an entrepreneur. A large percentage of the population is classified as self-employed and these guys do some remarkable things.' Gurcharan, a well-known figure in intellectual circles in Delhi since he took early retirement from being Chief Executive Officer (CEO) of Procter & Gamble (P&G), India, to focus on writing,[1] acknowledged the greeting of another evening walker passing by in the gathering gloom. Gurcharan is editing a series of books on the long history of Indian business, including volumes on the Marwaris, Tamil traders, the East India Company and the emergence of Indian-owned managing agents to rival British-owned

---

[1] Gurcharan Das's best-known books are *India Unbound: From Independence to the Global Information Age*, New Delhi: Penguin Books India, 2000, and *India Grows at Night: A Liberal Case for a Strong State*, New Delhi: Penguin Books India, 2012.

companies.[2] He went on, 'And the Dalit entrepreneurs you should not ignore; they have a Chamber of Commerce of their own, with 3,000 or 4,000 entrepreneurs.'

Any encounter with India leaves a sense of millions of small traders, service providers and suppliers of everything conceivable. It seems that everyone is scrambling to make a living, trying to survive, seeking an opportunity to make money, offering something for sale, looking for an angle. There are some 12 million small stores, called kirana shops, across the country selling groceries and everyday items. Indian streets are replete with the shops and stalls of traders of a vast array of commodities, often clustered together so that vendors of paan (a favourite Indian digestive that combines betel leaf with areca nut and often other spices or tobacco), saris, sports goods and jewellery are located next to each other. A home in India is offered scores of specialized services by people often carrying on the trade of their fathers – the milk or vegetable vendor, the collector of waste paper and empty bottles, even the man who winds clocks. Each of them is a small entrepreneur. Each transaction appears entirely flexible, slightly ill-defined and all-too-often requires negotiation and time invested to establish a personal relationship. The skills still exist in small shops to stitch clothing, to order or repair anything from a television to a broken buckle. India is a country of artisans, hustlers, merchants and small traders. It seems that in this country the business gene is more honed, the mental arithmetic quicker, the sales patter more voluble.

Nandan Nilekani, one of the co-founders of Infosys[3] and now an investor, remarked entirely aptly, 'India is a nation of entrepreneurs. Every farmer is an entrepreneur. He is taking complete risk. If the rain fails, he is gone; if the crop fails, he is gone. Every small shopkeeper is an entrepreneur. The lady selling vegetables in a basket at the junction of Haji Ali [in Bombay] is an entrepreneur.'

While such small entrepreneurs of necessity are everywhere in India, the business culture has traditionally been more concentrated both socially and

---

[2] The Story of Indian Business series, edited and introduced by Gurcharan Das, published by Penguin Random House India.

[3] Infosys is one of India's most respected and valuable companies, and a leader in IT services.

geographically. Socially, business has been more prevalent among certain castes and communities, while geographically commerce has tended to be more acceptable and intensely developed in certain areas, especially in the western part of the country.

Adi Godrej, Chairman of the Godrej Group,[4] offered an explanation. 'Not all parts of India have been equally entrepreneurial. I would say that parts of western India have been extremely entrepreneurial for many decades, but that is not necessarily true of parts of eastern India.' Adi went on to suggest that this regional variation might have arisen from geography and climate. Western India is drier, making agriculture more difficult. Hence, trade with the rest of the country, the Gulf and Africa became more important in this region where life was otherwise tough, in contrast to an area like Bengal which is well-watered and intensely fertile and where securing a comfortable life dependent on local resources was consequently easier.

Differences in the appetite for business are not just geographic, but also social. India is a complex mosaic of different communities and identities defined regionally, linguistically, by caste, faith, tribe, class and education, sometimes clustered but also frequently fragmented and dispersed widely. Certain communities in India have a deeply embedded cultural proclivity for business, most obviously the Marwaris, Sindhis, Gujaratis, certain Muslim groups like the Bohras, and in the south the Chettiars. Arvind Kothari, now an entrepreneur again after a period spent at Reliance Industries working on the launch of the Jio data network, explained the family expectations derived from his upbringing as a Marwari in Ahmedabad: 'I was the first guy from my entire community, from both my mother's side and my father's side, to do a job. The traditional view is that you should be the owner of your own time and do what you want instead of working under someone else. After all, you can't leave a job to your children.'

A number of the people I interviewed from these trading communities described how their fathers began to teach them business from a very early age, taking them into the shop or office to allow them to imbibe the business of trade. 'I think it goes back to a deep cultural thing in the family system

---

[4]   The Godrej Group is one of India's larger and respected family groups and operates in furniture, locks and safes, consumer products, engineering and real estate.

and [is] linked to the joint family concept,' remarked Uday Kotak, one of India's most successful financiers and founder of Kotak Mahindra Bank. 'As a boy, I spent time in the family business in the cotton trade and that was great learning. But I also faced the challenge of dealing with 14 family members in one office.'

The flipside of this proclivity for business among traditional trading communities has been a long-rooted strand of distrust of such banias, as traders or merchants are called, in many places in India. Vijay Shekhar Sharma voiced some of this attitude among Brahmins in Uttar Pradesh. I witnessed it strongly among the so-called *bhadralok* Bengalis (the dictionary meaning of the Bengali word being 'prosperous, well-educated people') in my years in Calcutta, particularly against Marwaris who had migrated from Rajasthan and come to dominate many industries in the east, including tea and jute. Jerry Rao, founder of Mphasis, the software company he sold to Electronic Data Systems (EDS), and who is now focused on building affordable housing, observed, 'If you go back and look at the Bollywood movies of the 1950s and 1960s, the trader is always portrayed as the bad guy. The mill owners were seen as demons. But today I think it's no longer quite that stark as making money in business has become more acceptable.'

India's current complex and sophisticated business culture has developed from these ancient trading traditions, leavened by the impact of colonialism and the advent of foreign multinational companies from the early twentieth century. In western India, from the mid-nineteenth century, a number of entrepreneurs made the jump from trading success to more formal corporate structures and investment in manufacturing assets. Foremost among these was Jamsetji Tata, the founder of the Tata Group, who like a number of others first invested in the cotton textile industry. In eastern India, British dominance of most formal enterprise lingered longer, especially in industries like tea and jute. Omkar Goswami's book *Goras and Desis: Managing Agencies and the Making of Corporate India*[5] chronicles how, from the 1920s, Indians, especially Marwaris, began a progressive takeover of these industries previously controlled by British managing agencies. This long handover

---

[5] Goswami, Omkar, *Goras and Desis: Managing Agencies and the Making of Corporate India*, New Delhi: Viking, 2016 (part of The Story of Indian Business series, edited and introduced by Gurcharan Das, published by Penguin Random House India).

accelerated in the 1960s but was only complete following Indira Gandhi's imposition of controls on foreign investment in 1973.

After India achieved Independence in 1947, the process of evolution and development of India's formal business community accelerated and spread socially and geographically. Harish Damodaran documented in his book *India's New Capitalists*[6] how there has been an increase in entries into formal business and the organized boardroom from many communities and backgrounds, not just from traditional business communities, often enabled by education. The bania trader communities were the first to make the transition from informal, family-based and typically trading business to modern, corporate entrepreneurship. The Birlas are the best-known example of a bania family transforming into modern industrialists. Damodaran identifies three main routes into formal business: bazaar to factory among the traditional trading castes; office to factory among well-educated groups, especially Brahmins, Khatris and Bengalis; and field to factory among wealthier agriculture-based castes such as Kammas, Reddys or Jats. However, Damodaran notes, certain social groups, especially Dalits and tribals, appear not to have succeeded so far in taking advantage of opportunities to create formal businesses of scale and hence transform from entrepreneurs of necessity to entrepreneurs of opportunity.

Another economic consequence of Independence, and the socialist thinking of India's first generation of political leadership, most especially Prime Minister Jawaharlal Nehru, has been the size of the corporate public sector. Nehru set out to achieve public control of the 'commanding heights of the economy', reserving multiple sectors for state undertakings. Many of India's largest companies even now are state-controlled, including in banking (especially the massive State Bank of India, SBI), steel (Steel Authority of India, SAIL), utilities (National Thermal Power Corporation, NTPC), and oil and gas (Oil and Gas Corporation, ONGC).

By contrast, and in spite of governmental hostility to foreign capital from the 1950s to 1980s, India has substantial, successful and respected MNCs operating in its mixed and variegated economy. These include companies

---

6   Damodaran, Harish, *India's New Capitalists: Caste, Business, and Industry in a Modern Nation*, London: Palgrave Macmillan, 2008.

that have been in India long enough to become almost fully indigenized, such as Hindustan Unilever, Siemens, HSBC and Madura Coats. Since economic reforms started, a new wave of foreign companies have entered and some, such as IBM, G4S and General Electric (GE), are now among India's largest employers.

India's rich and complex economic history has therefore resulted in the depth, variety and vibrancy of its corporate and business make-up today. Sitting atop the traditional small-scale traders and entrepreneurs of necessity, India has developed a more evolved and modern business environment than might be expected in an economy with a per capita gross domestic product (GDP) only now approaching $2,000. There are world-class and world-scale companies in multiple sectors, including software services, metals, pharmaceuticals and engineering. More than most emerging economies, India has a well-developed 'soft infrastructure' of a market economy, including regulators, lawyers, accountants, advertising agencies, bankers and consultants. The Bombay Stock Exchange (BSE) is the oldest in Asia and lists more than 5,500 companies with a combined market capitalization of some $1.6 trillion, while in more recent years the National Stock Exchange (NSE) has emerged as a more modern, technically advanced rival. The publication of the annual *Forbes* list of billionaires[7] is reported with the relish reminiscent of cricket commentary as the number and relative position of the growing number of Indian tycoons is picked over. In 2016, Mukesh Ambani (Reliance Industries), Dilip Shanghvi (Sun Pharma), Azim Premji (Wipro) and Shiv Nadar (HCL) were among the top 100 billionaires globally, each estimated to be worth more than $10 billion.

A feature of the Indian corporate scene is that many businesses are extremely diverse in the sectors in which they operate. Often family-controlled and managed, large groups such as Tata, Reliance, Mahindra and Godrej have grown as much by diversifying as scaling their core businesses. Tata, in particular, spans the economy covering basic industries like steel, engineering (notably vehicle manufacturing), consumer products and retailing, and newer businesses like software. This unusual degree of

---

[7] http://www.forbes.com/billionaires/

diversification has multiple causes. Indian business families often have a number of members active in the business and each family participant is given an area of responsibility. Conservatism and risk mitigation also encourages multiple business lines. The heavy regulation of private business introduced by Prime Minister Jawaharlal Nehru following Independence meant that lateral growth by securing new licenses in a different sector was often easier than scaling in a core business. Professor Tarun Khanna of Harvard Business School (HBS) has convincingly argued that in emerging markets in which there are multiple institutional failures, diversity is a more cogent strategy than in a developed market with more efficient markets for information, money and people.[8]

In the past 25 years, a raft of new, first-generation entrepreneurs have launched themselves into this complex business environment. Today many of India's most exciting companies are relatively recently formed. These new entrepreneurs are the focus of this book. In their ambition and outlook, they differ from the millions of entrepreneurs of necessity but also India's more established business leaders. They might come from the traditional business communities, but often do not. They typically focus on one sector and drive for scale in that business, unlike many of the older Indian groups. They represent a palpable new departure in the Indian business scene and encapsulate much that is hopeful about the future of the country.

History matters

'This was always a very mercantile country,' observed Saurabh Srivastava, one of the early leaders of the IT industry, co-founder of NASSCOM, the influential IT industry body, and now an investor in start-ups directly and through the Indian Angel Network group, which he co-founded. 'Three hundred years ago India was 25 per cent of the global GDP, the same as China.'

Through most of recorded human history, India has been one of the two largest and advanced economies in the world. This was based both on its size and natural resources, agricultural and mineral, but also on the trade

---

[8] Khanna, Tarun, and Krishna G. Palepu, 'Why Focused Strategies May Be Wrong for Emerging Markets', *Harvard Business Review*, 1997.

both eastwards and westwards from very early times. India was a key stage on the maritime silk and spice routes and had trade relations with Europe from Greek and Roman times. When the Portuguese arrived in India in the sixteenth century, and the British and French followed in the following century, they found an economy of far superior sophistication and wealth compared to early modern Europe. The size of the cities, the opulence of the imperial court, the technical skills of the producers of textiles and steel, the evolved commercial and financial systems, all impressed just as much as the opportunities for acquiring sought-after trade goods.

Most of the history of the Indian economy from that point to very recently has been a tale of relative, and sometimes absolute, decline. Saurabh points to two culprits for this abject performance of the Indian economy over many decades, at least until recent years, despite the vibrant tradition of teeming entrepreneurs: First, colonization by the British and second, particularly since Independence, the government.

The impact of British rule on the Indian economy and Indian business is still hotly debated by historians. The first Indian member of the British Parliament, Dadabhai Naoroji, elected from Westminster in 1892, was among the first to accuse the British of damaging the Indian economy. Many historians have followed him by pointing to low or static economic growth under the East India Company and the Raj, a dramatic decline in real wages of both artisans and many farmers, a balance of payments deficit and unhelpful tariff structures designed to encourage imports from Britain but not exports from India. Shashi Tharoor has recently updated this argument in his hard-hitting book, *An Era of Darkness*,[9] in which he paints an unforgivingly negative picture of the record of the British in India in economic, political and moral terms.

While the British came as traders, and indeed British India was run by a for-profit company until 1858, the colonial encounter clearly discouraged modern industry in India and engendered an anti-business bias among the educated groups, like the *bhadralok* of Calcutta, who collaborated most closely with the Raj. To these well-documented facts, Saurabh added a different spin: 'The biggest loss of the 200 years [of colonial rule] wasn't

---

[9]   Tharoor, Shashi, *An Era of Darkness: The British Empire in India*, New Delhi: Aleph Book Company, 2016.

the Kohinoor, it was self-confidence. When you are colonized you lose self-confidence.'

From the late nineteenth century, notwithstanding the unhelpful policies of the Raj, modern industry began to develop in India. Jamsetji Tata, the founder of the Tata Group, was a firm nationalist and attended the first meeting of the Indian National Congress in 1885. He established his textile mills and sought to develop a steel industry in part as a step towards self-determination and often very much against the instincts and policies of the British-run Government of India. It is said that Tata set up the Taj Mahal Hotel in Bombay to best global standards after being denied entry to a British-owned hotel. Sir Frederick Upcott, the chief commissioner of the Great Indian Peninsular Railway, summed up British attitudes to the idea of advanced manufacturing in India when he promised to 'eat every pound of steel rail the Tatas succeed in making'.

Whatever the impact of the British on the Indian economy and business culture, the first decades of Independence made matters worse. Jawaharlal Nehru, heavily influenced by the Fabian socialism he had imbued in Cambridge and the apparently successful Soviet planning model in Russia, introduced state planning of the economy, nationalization of key industries and complex licensing of the private sector most particularly through the Industrial Development Regulation Act of 1951. This was extended and made even more restrictive by his daughter, Indira Gandhi from 1966. As Adi Godrej of the Godrej Group explained, 'A lot of the entrepreneurship in India was diminished considerably during the socialist years, from 1947 to 1991. There was so much socialism that a lot of the entrepreneurial spirit was suffocated. And then many people with entrepreneurial talent emigrated and stayed on after their education in the West.'

This was the India I first encountered in the 1980s and first tried to do business with in the 1990s. At that time, foreign investment and imports were restricted and strictly controlled. A large number of sectors were either nationalized or reserved for small-scale industries. Licenses were required for most private sector activities and the government specified who could make what, where, and dictated the terms of its sale. However well-intentioned, the impact of this nightmare system on Indian business was profoundly pernicious. As Saurabh Srivastava said, 'If you had the money then you just went and bought a foreign collaboration, manufactured and sold at cost-plus, so there was no need to innovate, there was no need to do research and development (R&D). We made the worst products in the world.'

In about 1990 I visited the Hindustan Motors plant at Uttarpara near Calcutta. Up until the foundation of Maruti in 1982 by Sanjay Gandhi, Indira Gandhi's younger son, there had been two car manufacturers in the country: Hindustan Motors making a derivative of the 1950s' Morris Oxford and Premier Motors making a version of the 1960s' Fiat 1100. Imports of other vehicles were severely restricted. New entrants into the industry were denied, despite repeated attempts by Tata to secure permission to make cars. Customers paid up-front to get onto a waiting list for either of the two available vehicles, then waited months for delivery. Opportunities consequently abounded for secondary markets in cars sold at a premium to the sticker price, preferential allocation for the connected, and corruption. There was no competitive pressure to offer quality, customer service or innovation.

The tour of the factory at Uttarpara was a shocking experience. The plant was enormous, employing thousands, and almost fully integrated, from screws and bolts to engines, with enormous negative implications for complexity and cost competitiveness. The level of investment, productivity and working conditions were Dickensian. I witnessed body panels being hand-beaten with hammers, body shells being manually painted and half-finished vehicles being moved between manufacturing shops on hand carts. Dazed, I sat for lunch with the senior management and asked how Hindustan Motors planned to survive the rapid growth of Maruti – which was selling an excellent small car, the Maruti 800, based on a modern Suzuki design – and the impending competition from foreign majors like Ford, General Motors and Toyota who were seeking entry into the market.

'The Ambassador will always have a place in India,' I was told. 'It is perfect for Indian roads and usage, unlike these foreign cars. A whole Indian family can be accommodated [in it]. It can be repaired at thousands of workshops across the country.' My interlocutor smiled, about to produce his trump card. 'We have employed McKinsey. We have a strategy.' I asked if that included new models, new investment and better service.

'We will have a new engine, Japanese design. And go-faster stripes on the body.'

The lumbering Ambassador, with or without go-faster stripes, symbolized the state of the Indian economy by the early 1990s. While the tiger economies of South-East Asia achieved miracle growth rates, and China introduced reforms from 1979 that transformed its growth prospects, India persisted with the mindset of a protected and controlled economy. The consequence was a so-called 'Hindu rate of growth'[10] of some 3.5 per cent on an average over three decades, and a growth per capita of only about 1.5 per cent. This poor performance had nothing, of course, to do with Hinduism and everything to do with the failure of a planned, socialist economy. Rajiv Gandhi tried to modernize the economy when he unexpectedly became prime minister in 1984 after the assassination of his mother, Indira Gandhi. He achieved some success but did not have the political will to overcome the vested interests and socialist dogma that prevailed among the powers that be in Delhi.

It was a foreign exchange crisis in 1991 that finally triggered profound reform. By mid-1991 India's balance of payments deficit had ballooned after the rise in oil prices following the first Gulf War. The rupee had depreciated sharply and the nation's foreign exchange reserves had diminished to only three weeks of cover. The country teetered on the brink of bankruptcy. The government, led by P.V. Narasimha Rao, authorized the export of India's bullion reserves to the Bank of England as security for emergency loans. The depth of the humiliation was encapsulated for me by a story later related by a senior advisor in the Ministry of Finance. He recounted how at least one of the trucks in the convoy carrying 47 tonnes of gold to the Bombay airport late at night for the chartered flight to London, broke down en route. India was bankrupt and was not even able to transport its gold reserves to the airport without mishap. A new approach was desperately needed.

---

[10]   The 'Hindu Rate of Growth' was a term coined by the Indian economist Raj Krishna and was popularized by Robert McNamara. It had nothing to do with Hinduism, but rather contrasted the low rate of real growth achieved in India, lower on a per capita basis, with the much higher rates achieved by the export-oriented economies of East and South-East Asia. As such, it was an implied criticism of the under-delivery of Nehruvian socialism.

The crisis, at last, gave the government the resolve and political cover to push through a major liberalization of the economy, building on the earlier efforts of Rajiv Gandhi. Industrial licensing was abolished in most sectors, import duties cut, private capital permitted into previously reserved sectors, and foreign investment courted. Coca-Cola and IBM, both of which had been driven away from India in the 1980s for refusing to comply with the increasingly draconian rules for foreign investors, were welcomed back along with other foreign investors. India had stepped out of its Alice-in-Wonderland socialistic isolation and rejoined the world economy.

Reform and restructuring

The results of the liberalization of the Indian economy over the past 25 years have been dramatic and today's India differs profoundly from the closed, slightly shoddy place of 1990. GDP growth rates have accelerated; India's compound growth rate was 7.7 per cent from 1990 to 2015,[11] still behind that of China in these years but one of the fastest among major economies globally. The Ambassador has been replaced by a plethora of modern cars, and production of the car at Uttarpara has stopped. In 1990 there were 19 million vehicles, including motorbikes, on Indian roads; by 2013 there were 182 million.[12] Foreign consumer brands are now freely available throughout the country. Starting from a world of rationed and unreliable telephones from a single government provider, India crossed 1 billion mobile phone subscribers in 2015.[13] The number of air passengers in India, which was 8.9 million in 1991, had by 2015 burgeoned to 80 million.[14]

Inward foreign investment was one of the drivers of these changes, but much less so than in China. From $4 billion in 2000–01, foreign direct investment (FDI) inflow increased to $45 billion in 2015–16.[15] Most MNCs are now present in India to sell, manufacture or source offshore services and

---

[11] http://data.worldbank.org
[12] https://data.gov.in/catalog/total-number-registered-motor-vehicles-india
[13] http://www.itu.int/en/ITU-D/Statistics
[14] http://data.worldbank.org
[15] http://dbie.rbi.org.in

have contributed significantly to India's competitive business environment and the training of the country's deep talent pool. While global quality manufacturing is possible in India, as companies like Larsen & Toubro (L&T), Reliance Industries, Hero and JCB illustrate, India has not developed like China as a major manufacturing hub for international markets. This is largely due to the continuing poor infrastructure, high input costs and persistence of complex regulations especially over employment of labour. Rather, India's relative competitive advantage has been derived from its pool of talented people, and hence its most competitive export industries have been in sectors such as services, software and engineering exports, where the elements of external friction, largely related to government action or inaction, are less important.

While foreign- and government-controlled companies have led the surge of growth in China, at least until recently, India has enjoyed a more vibrant domestic private sector. Enterprise, and the soft infrastructure that underpins it, survived the Nehruvian ice age and business flourished once the shackles were eased. However, to survive in a newly competitive and open environment, with increasing foreign and domestic competition, established Indian businesses needed to restructure and renew themselves. Some traditional business houses succeeded in reinventing themselves for a reformed world, but others did not and have been replaced by new competitors.

To demonstrate this process of renewal and replacement, Harish Damodaran analysed the leading 50 corporate groups in India based on sales and assets for an article in *The Hindu BusinessLine* in 2014.[16] The largest groups among the top 50 at that time were Tata, Reliance, Birla, Vedanta, Essar, Mahindra, Jindal, Adani, Bharti and Infosys. In 2014, only 11 of the top 50 in 2014 had been on an equivalent list for 1964, 50 years earlier, and 17 had been in the top 50 in 1990, just before the reforms. Some of the largest groups had managed to recreate themselves and survive over this period of time, including Tata, Birla and Mahindra, but at the same time India's leading companies had seen a large turnover of old names

---

[16]   Damodaran, Harish, 'Crony Capitalism? Really?' *The Hindu BusinessLine*, 18 March 2014.

and the emergence of new winners, typically more focused competitors in new sectors, including Infosys (software), Bharti (telecom), Dr Reddy's (pharmaceuticals) and Kotak (finance). The founders of a number of these companies have been interviewed for this book.

The reinvention of the Tata Group following the reforms of 1991 is a proxy for what a good proportion of Indian industry achieved in order to survive and then flourish in a newly open and competitive world. Other industrial houses like Birla, Mahindra and Godrej went through comparable rethinking and restructuring. Moreover, as the largest industrial undertaking in the country, both at the start of the reforms and now, the fate of the Tata Group mattered more. I was witness to the latter part of the process from 1998 onwards.

Ratan Tata became Group Chairman in 1991 just as the reforms were initiated. At that time there was considerable doubt whether this private and often retiring person would succeed in preserving the sprawling and very loose group left by his distant cousin, J.R.D. Tata, who had been chairman for 53 years. In the year to March 1991, the aggregate group revenue was ₹11,002 crore ($6.1 billion at the then exchange rate). In the year in which Ratan retired, 2012, the Group's turnover had increased to ₹527,047 crore ($96.9 billion), a rupee-based compound growth rate of 19 per cent. In the same year, 2012, the group's combined market capitalization was $95.4 billion, which had grown at a rate of 16 per cent compound in rupee terms and 13 per cent compound in dollar terms over the period of his chairmanship.[17]

Ratan's success over these 21 years was based on four strands of persistent effort.

The first was governance. Ratan had to gain managerial control of the group, increase the shareholding percentage from the group centre and improve oversight and management processes without damaging the culture of strong ethics and a dedication to nation-building that the group had stood for since its foundation. In 1991, Birla owned more of Tata Steel stock than did Tata, and the incumbent Chairman of Tata Steel, the pugnacious and colourful Russi Mody, ran a campaign to wrest control away from Tata.

---

[17] Sourced from Tata Sons Limited.

Similar battles were fought, perhaps less publicly, with other *satraps*[18] who, under J.R.D. Tata's very loose group culture, controlled the major operating companies including Tata Chemicals and Indian Hotels.

One of my most poignant memories of my Tata days was a birthday dinner given by Ratan for me in the Chambers Club at the Taj Hotel, probably in 2000. That morning I had bumped into Ratan going into Bombay House and he said that everything was arranged for the evening. I had no idea what he meant until I received a call from his office to invite me to dinner that night. It turned out that he had been tipped off that it was my birthday and that I would be alone in Bombay. Noshir Soonawala, the Group Finance Director, Ishaat Hussain, his successor, and Jamshed Irani, the Managing Director of Tata Steel, made up the party. More than the cake and kindness, what I remember is the long evening of reminiscences of early corporate battles: Politically motivated strikes in Tata Motors in Pune; crisis management during communal riots in Jamshedpur, including Ratan smuggling a Muslim employee out of the factory in the boot of his large American car; anecdotes of Russi Mody's flamboyant lifestyle; resistance to calls to lobby for protectionism as part of the so-called 'Bombay Club' of industrialists who opposed a more open economy; and rejection of the pressure to 'do business' with greedy ministers, political parties and militant unions.

The second strand of Ratan's success was a rigorous drive to improve the operations of group operating companies to achieve competitiveness domestically and then internationally. This is best illustrated by the story of Tata Steel's becoming the lowest-cost steel producer in the world. Jamshed Irani told me much about this transformation through a series of steady improvements and critical investments, but centring on the careful management of energy with waste heat being cycled back into the plant. Ratan used to tease Jamshed by arguing that Tata Steel's key competitive cost edge resulted more from captive raw materials (iron ore and coal) rather than operational excellence, and that the process of steel-making lacked recent innovation and had not really changed from Bessemer's day.

---

[18]   The term used for a provincial governor in the Persian empire, now used to denote an over-mighty manager controlling an associate company.

Comparable cost reduction and productivity programmes in key companies such as Tata Motors and Tata Chemicals, often deploying Japanese management thinking, played a key role. Much of this was institutionalized in the Tata Quality Management System (TQMS), originally based on W.E. Deming's Total Quality Management model, which Ratan embedded across the group.

The third strand was portfolio strategy, which included resource allocation decisions. While older companies in the group, such as Tata Steel, Tata Motors and Tata Power, grew well, if cyclically, the real winner was TCS, founded in 1968, well before the other Indian IT majors. TCS now represents more than 60 per cent of the group's market capitalization of $128 billion.[19] The cash generated by TCS while it was a division of Tata Sons up to 2004, and its dividends after the IPO that year, sustained the group's investment plans. Before being appointed Chairman, Ratan had developed a growth strategy he termed 'The Tata Plan', much of it conceived while sitting beside his ailing mother's hospital bed at Memorial Sloan Kettering Cancer Center in New York. The strategy identified a number of growth areas in which the group should invest including telecom, auto-components, materials and financial services. Later, other growth opportunities developed in real estate, defence and retailing. More controversially for the Tata culture of loyalty and continuity, Ratan also exited a slew of businesses, including Tomco, the oils company sold to Unilever in 1993, a series of joint ventures, including with IBM, Lucent and Honeywell, and finally managed to close the last textile mills in Nagpur and Bombay that had been the group's genesis.

The final strand, in which I had a ringside seat from 2004, was making the group global. By around 2000 most Tata companies had responded to the competitive challenges of liberalization, addressed weaknesses from the days of Government 'license raj' around cost, quality and service, and were benefitting from the more rapid growth of the Indian economy. We thought that there were some sectors in which the group operated whose economics were local and national, such as retailing and real estate, and these should remain domestic. Some sectors offered the possibility of

---

[19] Sourced from Tata Group, as of 18 August 2016.

international-scale economies, such as hotels and power, and these we would take to foreign markets selectively and in niches. But other businesses had true global scale requirements and in these we needed to internationalize aggressively in order to survive long term. Despite being smaller scale compared to global majors, we often enjoyed a competitive cost edge for the time being, largely derived from the cost of our people and skills, being India-based. These sectors included IT (TCS), materials (Tata Steel) and engineering (Tata Motors).

I recall an early board meeting in 2004 when I presented my first thoughts on a group strategy for internationalization. It included data on our then overseas presence which previously had never been put together, but amounted to some $2.4 billion or about 7 per cent of sales. Based on the inputs of the operating companies, overlaid by top-down analysis, I proposed which companies should be taken international and which should be our priority target markets. I also suggested a 10-year target of achieving 50 per cent of sales outside India, but that was felt to be too ambitious and was scaled back to 30 per cent. As it turned out I underestimated both the speed of our international expansion, because I had not factored in large acquisitions, and the weight we would achieve in Western markets, especially the United Kingdom (UK). I had expected a major thrust of our growth to come from regional markets and large emerging markets such as China, Brazil and South Africa, but that took longer to achieve. The Tata Group's sales in China, $8.7 billion in 2015,[20] has more to do with sales of Jaguars and Land Rovers, now produced locally in a joint venture with the Chinese automaker Chery in Changshu, than with organic growth of other group companies.

Coming from a Western background I was consistently amazed by the commitment, growth orientation and ambition of most Tata companies and their employees. In many ways the group was demonstrating traits of true entrepreneurship, despite its size, long history, occasional conservatism and unenviable reputation for central bureaucracy. Ratan was taking the group back to its roots, and the original philosophy of Jamsetji Tata, as a long-term risk-taker seeking opportunities to create businesses of impact that would contribute materially to economic growth. The flip side of this

---

[20] Sourced from Tata Group.

was that I was frequently taken aback by the lack of clear process, paucity of data and analytics and occasional over-reliance on the key decision-takers, particularly Ratan himself, to determine everything. When I first got involved with Tata Industries in 1998 the largest new investment was in telecom, with both mobile and fixed line licenses in Andhra Pradesh. The plan was being developed and then overseen by a few smart but inexperienced young managers, members of the coveted Tata Administrative Service (TAS), with limited telecom expertise but enjoying the confidence of and access to the Chairman. It was hard for me to understand how such major commitments could be made in this somewhat buccaneering fashion. After working for foreign MNCs, with their stronger planning, finance and control processes, I needed to reset my thinking about how best to plan and manage in the rapid growth and ambiguity of an emerging market.

In 1999, Jardines had the opportunity to invest in Titan Company Limited, then seen as a fringe operation within Tata. I spent time with the extrovert Managing Director, Xerxes Desai, and recommended that we should make the investment. However, I proposed the condition that the plan to enter jewellery, Tanishq, should be dropped as I could not understand how a disorganized sector with traditional buying patterns and trade practices could be consolidated by strong design, professional retailing and brand building. How wrong I was! We did not make the investment. Titan, including Tanishq, has been a huge success in the years afterwards and now enjoys a market capitalization of ₹29,000 crore ($4.4 billion).

The competitive imperative in which the Tata Group had not made adequate progress by the time I left in 2009, in my view, was in the fostering across the group of an ability to innovate consistently. I thought that competitive advantage based on cost would erode as Indian salaries increased, competitors developed their own footprints in India and the group globalized. Hence, innovation would become an increasingly important muscle for success across group companies. There were, of course, examples of both incremental and disruptive innovation, such as the $2,000 car, the Nano, or TCS's global delivery model. But these were too few in number and not all worked out successfully. Most importantly, despite its clever design and engineering, the Nano has never achieved a fraction of its potential.

Despite all of the Tata Group's successes in these years, not all of the ambitious plans for expansion under Ratan's leadership worked well, as is the nature of risk-taking in business. The Tata telecom business has struggled for years to turn cash positive, and the launch of Reliance's Jio service at such low price points will not make matters easier. The acquisition by Tata Steel of Corus in the UK turned out to have been made at the top of the commodities cycle. Tata Steel modelled the impact of credible downside cases for steel prices, but nothing we contemplated was near as bad as things turned out, with historically low steel prices and relatively high iron ore prices. Tata Motors has struggled in the domestic vehicle market, notwithstanding the phenomenal international success of Jaguar Land Rover. Tata Power's ambitious bid to build a 4GW power plant at Mundra in Gujarat under the government's ultra-mega power policy went awry when the government of Indonesia imposed minimum export prices on coal, thus escalating the cost of imported fuel for the plant which could not be passed through in the tariff for electricity.

Ratan's successor as Chairman, Cyrus Mistry, inherited these legacy issues and failed, despite good intent, to address them before he lost the confidence of the largest shareholder in Tata Sons, the Tata Trusts, which in turn are still chaired by Ratan. After Cyrus refused to step aside gracefully, we have witnessed the drama of a Chairman of Tata Sons removed at board meeting in October 2016, effectively at the behest of his predecessor, the return of that predecessor as Group Chairman on a temporary basis pending a new long-term appointment, accusations of poor governance tossed both ways, and a series of board battles for control at the major listed operating companies. None of this is good for Tata or India and has been distressing for those who believe strongly in what Tata represents.

The appointment of N. Chandrasekeran (Chandra) as the new Chairman from February 2017 is very positive for the Tata group. Chandra is a highly intelligent, hard-working and decent person with much relevant experience from his successful years at TCS. While the bitterness of Cyrus's defenestration may linger, not least in residual legal challenges, Chandra commands respect internally and in the country, and has the personal character and ability needed to resume a momentum of change in the group while maintaining its values and cherished traditions. He will face challenges with strong parallels to those which Ratan himself took on in 1991. He will need to reimpose control and discipline across the group and hold to the highest standards of ethics and governance. He will need to tackle the most pressing issues in Tata Steel Europe and the domestic telecom business, lift the operating performance of the group as a whole and reduce its dependence on the recent stellar performance of TCS and Jaguar Land Rover. He will need to recraft a corporate growth strategy that enjoys the support of the shareholders, most particularly the Tata Trusts, and which will include tough resource allocation decisions over which opportunities to invest in and which to exit. Above all, he will need to balance hard business and financial decisions, including challenging restructurings and exits, with the strong ethical culture that makes the Tata Group what it is.

The reinvention of the Tata Group since 1991, as the liberalized economy presented pressing challenges of increased competition as well as exciting opportunities at home and abroad, can be seen as a proxy for the overall success of large Indian business in this period. Looking forward, past success and size is no longer sufficient to guarantee the future as technological change accelerates, markets become yet more competitive and expectations of governance standards become more exacting.

India today

India is in an entirely different and stronger position today than ever before. Moreover, relative to other economies, in both the developed and emerging worlds, India looks to have enormous potential for growth in the coming decade and more.

The reforms of 1991 opened up the economy and created a step-change in growth. With GDP growing at 7.9 per cent in the year to March 2016,[21] India looks set for a period of stronger growth in the next few years. Notwithstanding the recent slow-down triggered by demonetization of large currency notes, most economic indicators are moving positively, whether it

---

[21] Government of India, 'Provisional Estimates of Annual National Income 2015–16 and Quarterly Estimates of Gross Domestic Product, 2015–16', 31 May 2016.

be GDP growth, fiscal and trade deficits, inflation or levels of investment. Underpinning much has been the rapid development of urban centres, both large and small, and the rise of middle-class consumption.

Two factors bode well for continued growth. First, India has a well-developed private sector with a growing number of world-beating companies. Second, it has a very favourable, young demographic profile and a deep pool of skilled but affordable manpower. It is this young, competent, ambitious and affordable workforce that really underpins the competitive success that a number of Indian companies have enjoyed on a world stage.

Politically, there is also much to be optimistic about. For the first time since 1989 there is a government in Delhi that commands a majority in the lower house of Parliament, the Lok Sabha. Despite a slow start from 2014, the government has shown itself capable of long-term thinking and tough decisions. To date, its most concrete achievement is legislation to introduce the unified Goods and Services Tax (GST), to be implemented from July 2017, that promises to simplify trade across the country and is expected to add 1–2 per cent to GDP in so doing. There are signs of solid progress on other priorities such as improving the ease of doing business, building better infrastructure and encouraging manufacturing.

IT Services has been the poster child of India's economic success on the global stage. Saurabh Srivastava, the IT veteran we met earlier, observed, 'This industry broke the shackles. I think a lot of entrepreneurship growth came from this industry. Partly because we had no choice and there was no domestic market, we had to go global and be global in quality and practices.' NASSCOM, the industry body, estimates[22] that in the year to March 2016 the IT industry had a turnover of $143 billion (up from $1 billion in 1991), employed 3.7 million people and was responsible for 9.3 per cent of India's GDP. The impact of this industry is wider than simply these staggering statistics. IT boosted the self-confidence of millions of Indians, provided role models, generated wealth that is now being reinvested, and changed the perception of India internationally. In my experience most Chinese officials and business people are sceptical, at best, about India.

---

[22] NASSCOM, *The IT-BPM Sector in India: Strategic Review 2016*, February 2016.

However, the one industry in India which impressed China's National Development and Reform Council (NDRC) was software services. NDRC invited Indian software companies to propose a joint venture in China, and in 2005 selected TCS along with Microsoft to create the JV along with Chinese government entities. TCS now has six delivery centres in China.

Unfinished business

The declared intent of the Government of India from 1991 onwards has been to encourage growth broadly through competitive and open markets and private sector investment. However, it is unfortunately true that much of the explanation for India underperforming its potential for Chinese levels of growth is connected with issues caused by, or not addressed adequately by, the government. It is, therefore, a major bull point for the prospects for India that the current government has set out to address many of these issues.

Business people, whether domestic or foreign, from large- or small-scale enterprises, would quickly agree on a long list of the issues they face, and where India has lagged behind developed markets or China. The key issues are poor infrastructure; remaining areas of restrictive policies; complex and poorly managed regulations; consequent pressures for corruption; and excessive, uncertain and convoluted taxation. Many of these can be summarized as 'ease of doing business', now a critical policy focus of the government. The World Bank publishes an annual Ease of Doing Business Index[23] based on 10 attributes from ease of starting a business to closing a business. India still ranked number 130 out of 189 countries in 2016, below the West Bank and Gaza and Iran, and all the other so-called BRICS nations. This was, however, an improvement of 12 rankings over 2015, and further strides are expected given the focus of the central government, as well as welcome efforts by state governments.

I can vouch from repeated experience how difficult it can be to do business in India, how illogical various regulations can appear, how much

---

more costly things can become due to delays, taxes, unclear licensing requirements, obdurate customs officials or poor roads. I have felt, too often, in my 30 years of doing business in the country that my last boss in London might have been right and that India really would undermine my career and sanity. Yet, it is also true that persistence and determination almost always delivers a way through, without having to resort to any improper methods or speed money. On one occasion while at Jardines, I was managing the disposal of a business that had failed and which we were handing over to a buyer for the grand sum of ₹100. The process was long and complex, especially securing a tax compliance certificate from the notoriously difficult Income Tax Department. Everything was finally done, except that, as a foreign invested company we had to demonstrate to the Reserve Bank of India (RBI) that the full sales proceeds, ₹100 or some $2, had been remitted back to the foreign investors. A new problem then arose. The sales consideration was below the minimum amount required for a foreign remittance, and cash could not be exported in the shape of a ₹100 note. After scratching our heads for some time a clever advisor realized that the RBI would be satisfied with the ₹100 being a charitable donation rather than a foreign remittance. It seems appropriate that the favourite God of many Indian businessmen is Ganesh, the elephant-headed remover of obstacles.

Economic growth is a means to the end of addressing two fundamental challenges for the country – poverty and job creation. First, despite the faster GDP growth in recent years, a large number of Indians still remain in absolute poverty. The World Bank estimates that in 2011, 259 million Indians (21 per cent of the population) were below a basic poverty level set at an income of just $1.90 per day.[24] This is a major improvement on 1993 when it was 424 million (46 per cent), but still a massive moral and social issue. Secondly, while the skew of the demographic profile of India towards the young (46 per cent of the population is aged less than 25 years)[25] is a major source of potential for growth, it is also a challenge.

---

[24] World Bank, http://povertydata.worldbank.org/poverty/country/IND
[25] CIA World Fact Book, https://www.cia.gov/library/publications/the-world-factbook/geos/in.html

It is estimated that 1 million job seekers will enter the economy every month in the coming years,[26] and India's record of job creation from economic growth has been far from stellar.

The present government, led by Narendra Modi, has identified boosting manufacturing as a critical way to create good jobs. The Make in India strategy, launched in September 2014, has a target of adding 100 million new jobs in manufacturing by 2022. However, this looks challenging given India's poor record in attracting investment in labour-intensive manufacturing and the likely impact of technology in boosting productivity, replacing labour and therefore reshoring to the West.

The critical contribution of entrepreneurship

India is a land of millions of entrepreneurs and has a deep tradition of business. That is fortunate, as the next phase of the growth of the economy will not be driven by state planning and the public sector – as attempted from 1947 to 1991 – or by investment from large corporates, whether Indian or foreign in origin, as was conceived from 1991 onwards. Increasingly, wealth will be generated, poverty will be addressed and jobs will be created by an explosion in entrepreneurship. This change – and the consequent renewed importance of entrepreneurship – is already well underway.

The Modi government has rightly prioritized the encouragement of start-ups and entrepreneurship as a key plank of economic policy through the Startup India and Stand-Up India programmes, mentioned earlier and discussed in detail later in the book. Much of this thinking was preshadowed in the 2012 report for the Planning Commission under the previous government, 'Creating a Vibrant Entrepreneurial Ecosystem in India',[27] which identified the important role smaller and newer companies play in economic growth and job creation. One of authors of the report, Jayant

---

[26] 'The Asia-Pacific Human Development Report 2016', United Nation Development Programme (UNDP).

[27] 'Creating a Vibrant Entrepreneurial Ecosystem in India', Report of the Committee on Angel Investment and Early Stage Venture Capital, New Delhi: Government of India, Planning Commission, June 2012.

Sinha, then an investor with Omidyar Network, became the minister of state for finance from 2014 to 2016 and drove much of the policy development in this area for the Modi government. The critical role of small and new businesses in economic growth is becoming better understood. Much of the recent economic research, especially in the US, has concluded that the real engine of job creation has moved from large companies to small and medium-sized enterprises (SMEs). David Birch[28] estimated that 82 per cent of new jobs created in the US in the six years to 1976 were generated by SMEs. Similar conclusions have been reached by other recent research. The Kauffman Foundation[29] concluded that in the US, between 1977 and 2005, existing firms shed 1 million jobs a year on average. By contrast, firms less than a year old created 3 million new jobs per annum on average in this period. Moreover, it was not all new firms but a few, successful 'gazelles' that created the bulk of new employment; one influential study found that 88–92 per cent of new jobs were created by just 4 per cent of firms.[30]

Despite these startling conclusions on the economic importance of start-ups, the quality and accessibility of academic work on entrepreneurship is surprisingly limited. The most readable remains the work of Peter Drucker, especially *Innovation and Entrepreneurship*.[31] Drucker's conclusion about the US in the 1980s could be applied confidently to India today: 'What is happening in the US is something quite different: a profound shift from a "managerial" to an "entrepreneurial" economy.' He went on to state that something had happened to young Americans' 'attitudes, values and ambitions'. Comparable things are happening to the attitudes of young

[28]   Birch, D.L., 'The Job Generation Process', Cambridge, Massachusets: MIT Program on Neighborhood and Regional Change, 1979.

[29]   Kane, Tina, 'The Importance of Startups in Job Creation and Job Destruction', Kauffman Foundation Research Series: Firm Foundation and Economic Growth, Ewing Marion Kauffman Foundation, 2010.

[30]   Birch, D.L., and J. Medoff, 'Gazelles', in Lewis C. Solmon and Alec R. Levenson, (ed.), *Labor Markets, Employment Policy and Job Creation*, Boulder, CO: Westview Press, 1994.

[31]   Drucker, P.F., *Innovation and Entrepreneurship: Practice and Principles*, New York: Harper & Row, 1985.

Indians today, as we shall see, which bodes well for the entrepreneurial boom that is gathering pace.

The best current research I have encountered on entrepreneurship is that of Amar Bhidé.[32] His survey of 100 start-ups in the US reveals much that will resonate with the typical entrepreneur, including those in India. Most start-ups, he concludes, are created for self-employment and the majority stay small. Bhidé shows that initially founders are usually capital-constrained and rely on 'opportunistic adaptation to unexpected events'. Most are created around replicating an existing business idea, with only about 10 per cent being based on a genuinely new concept. The majority are forced to turn a profit quickly. Most raise little or no formal capital initially, relying instead on boot-strapping and savings; only about 5 per cent raise money from VCs. Entrepreneurs tend to demonstrate a high tolerance for ambiguity and an ability to change course as circumstances and opportunities develop. What marks out those who break through to larger scale is often the 'exceptional execution of an ordinary idea' or the selection of an industry with 'significant change and flux'. Those who survive and grow often have to demonstrate a 'fundamental transformation' of their initial business model. Most do not. He found that 60 per cent of start-ups fail in six years and 70 per cent in eight years.

Bhidé's picture of typical entrepreneurs in the US will resonate well with many entrepreneurs in India, though in my interview group of 92 entrepreneurs perhaps more with 'Manmohan's Children' (the older group) than the 'New Generation' (the younger group). The older group demonstrated more struggle, flux and pivoting, and much less access to risk capital. Many of the newer stories I heard are more purposeful, better funded and based more on a pure idea. However, the great majority of small entrepreneurs in India follow the entrepreneurial pattern Bhidé describes.

Which brings us to a key conundrum. Despite its teeming population of entrepreneurs, until recently at least, India has been short of the high-aspiration entrepreneurs who create the 'gazelles' that research indicates generate job growth. As G.A. Anandalingam and Erkko Autio pointed out

---

[32]   Bhidé, Amar V., *The Origin and Evolution of New Businesses*, New York: Oxford University Press, 2000.

in an article in the *Economic Times* in 2015,[33] India has some 10 per cent self-employment (compared to Zambia at 35 per cent), which seems high. However, these are substantially low-aspiration entrepreneurs who generate limited value-add and jobs.

This phenomenon, common to poorer or developing economies, is described by a number of the contributors to Maria Minniti's *The Dynamics of Entrepreneurship*.[34] There is typically a U-shaped curve correlating income per head and self-employment. In poorer economies, self-employment is often high as a proportion of the working age population but the quality of activity is low as most are small entrepreneurs of necessity. As income per capita increases and formal employment opportunities develop, in middle-income countries, the proportion of the population which is self-employed tends to be lower. Then, beyond a point, self-employment increases again as the economy becomes more sophisticated and wealthier. Hence, there are often proportionately more self-employed people in very poor countries than more sophisticated economies known for dynamic start-up cultures. The reasons for this poor 'quality' of entrepreneurship in transition economies are many, but Minniti's contributors ascribe it to a lack of formal market-supporting institutions, institutional weaknesses including issues with the rule of law and corruption, poor access to finance and attitudinal issues such as fear of failure. Much of that list, if translated from academic-speak, would ring true for India.

The key data set on which Minniti's authors base their analysis is the *Global Entrepreneurship Index* (GEI), published annually by the Global Entrepreneurship and Development Institute.[35] The GEI is a composite index that seeks to measure the quality and scale of entrepreneurship across the surveyed countries. It covers 132 countries and combines survey

---

[33] Anandalingam, G.A., and Erkko Autio, 'Now, to let the genie out: India needs better, not more, entrepreneurs', http://blogs.economictimes.indiatimes.com/et-commentary/now-let-the-genie-out-india-needs-better-not-more-entrepreneurs/, 16 June 2015.

[34] Minniti, Maria (ed.), *The Dynamics of Entrepreneurship: Evidence from the Global Entrepreneurship Monitor Data*, Oxford: Oxford University Press, 2011.

[35] Ács, Zoltán J., László Szerb and Erkko Autio (ed.), *Global Entrepreneurship Index 2016*, Washington DC: The Global Entrepreneurship and Development Institute, 2016.

data and the use of other published indices. For India, the 2016 numbers are based on surveys of 3,360 people in India conducted in 2013–14, so are possibly somewhat outdated given the rapid development of the entrepreneurial ecosystem.

India fares poorly in the GEI despite its teeming millions of entrepreneurs and its exciting new cult of the young tech entrepreneur. In the 2016 index India was ranked 98 out of 132 countries, a slight improvement on the 2015 index where India was ranked 104 out of 130 countries. China by comparison was ranked 60 in 2016. India ranked below countries such as Vietnam, Philippines, Laos and Sri Lanka. India's relatively low positioning results from the blend of relative good numbers on the measures of intensity of competition, and process and product innovation, but weaker scores on measures of technology absorption, opportunity start-up, networking, and high growth. How does one reconcile this picture of India as a relatively poorly developed entrepreneurial ecosystem with the growing perception, very firmly confirmed by my own interviews and experience, of India as a land of entrepreneurs in which, as Drucker put it, 'a profound shift' is occurring?

A more familiar picture of India's new up-swell of entrepreneurship is painted by NASSCOM in its report 'Start-up India: Momentous Rise of the Indian Start-up Ecosystem'.[36] This ranked India as the third most vibrant technology start-up ecosystem after the US and UK and ahead of Israel and China. It identified 4,200 technology start-ups in India, compared with 48,000 in the US, which employ 80–85,000 people. Two thirds of these start-ups were concentrated in three cities, Bangalore (26 per cent), Delhi/National Capital Region (23 per cent) and Bombay (17 per cent). Seventy-two per cent of the founders of these companies were younger than 35 years old. They were nurtured by an increasingly rich ecosystem of role models and mentors; investors, both angels and funds; evolving technology, and improving institutional support. This included positive government policy, 110 incubators and accelerators, and plenty of networking events, conferences and seminars.

---

[36] 'Start-up India: Momentous Rise of the Indian Start-up Ecosystem', NASSCOM, 2015.

The key to reconciling the GEI's picture of an India of floundering entrepreneurs of necessity, lacking skills, ambition, technology and finance, and NASSCOM's vision of a rapid path to 10,000 tech start-ups, lies in what Rama Bijapurkar calls 'the great Indian rope trick',[37] in other words the magic of very large numbers averaging out new spikes. There are many Indias in which contradictory things can co-exist and be equally true at the same time. In the modern, youthful, educated, connected India of Bangalore, Gurgaon and Powai, there is clearly a tsunami of ambitious, often technology-based start-up activity. At the same time, in more traditional and rural India, referred to as Bharat, the old thinking, challenges and constraints persist. Bharat remains much larger, geographically and in terms of population, than modern India. The GEI is averaging out NASSCOM's spike in tech start-ups by the sheer weight of numbers still in the old economy.

In the new India, among the educated young in particular, there is a boom happening in entrepreneurship of aspiration. As Vani Kola, Managing Director of Kalaari Capital, a successful VC fund, put it, the kindling has always been there in the land of entrepreneurs, the sparks have caught and now the flame is developing. Or to use a different analogy, the virus is quickly spreading within but also away from the main clusters, most notably Bangalore, to secondary centres and to small towns, from India to Bharat.

Ratan Tata noted how he had been surprised by the speed with which the people of India have adopted the smartphone, enabling them to become customers of new-era ventures like Bharti, MakeMyTrip, ShopClues or Paytm. The same connectivity is spreading a new ambition among young people, just as Peter Drucker saw in the US 34 years ago. Anand Mahindra, Chairman and Managing Director of Mahindra & Mahindra, observed, 'There is a much larger, disproportionate hunger among young Indians to succeed because of the sheer number of educated people who are savvy about new technology.'

Before describing this New Generation of young entrepreneurs of aspiration and ambition, it will be interesting to get a glimpse of the earlier

---

[37] Bijapurkar, Rama, *We Are Like That Only: Understanding the Logic of Consumer India*, New Delhi: Penguin Books India, 2009.

generation, Manmohan's Children, some of whom started their business adventures before economic reforms began to change India's business landscape. Their narratives are more replete with the challenges of growing businesses in a hostile environment, though their success gathered pace along with the opportunities triggered by economic reform.

Manufacturing for Bharat

R. RAVINDRANATH

'I knew my own character and I cannot be someone who takes instruction, that's not my nature. I need to be my own boss even at home. My father used to instruct me to do this or that; I used to follow my own rule. He wanted me to do Civil Engineering but I chose Mechanical.' R. Ravindranath, co-founder and Managing Director of Milltec, always wanted to work for himself. He and Rajendran Joghee have built Milltec, established in 1998, into India's leading manufacturer of rice mills.

Ravindranath is clearly full of pride for his creation as he guides me around the state-of-the-art factory outside Bangalore. I struggle to grasp his rapid and enthusiastic technical briefing about the inner workings of a rice mill delivered in a strong Kannada accent above the noise of the assembly operations.

Coming from an agricultural background without family capital, Ravindranath was initially not in a position to set up on his own. After graduating from an engineering college in Bangalore he joined Bühler, the Swiss engineering firm specializing in food-processing equipment, which is where he met his business partner, Rajendran. The Bühler international design for rice mills was not well-suited to Indian par-boiled rice, which differs from the rice typically milled elsewhere in Asia. 'We used to get information that the machines were not working well, so we started giving our ideas. Being a multinational, Bühler were not receptive to these ideas; all ideas had to come from Switzerland and get approved in Germany. So then I discussed with my partner [if], during our free time, we could do something on our own.'

Their families initially opposed their leaving a good job to set up a company. 'None of our family members were businessmen so we are the first generation,' Ravindranath explained. 'From my wife's perspective, this was not the right time to [start] a business. [She said] if at all you want to [start] a business, do it after some time. My parents were dead against me starting a business as well. In fact, they advised me to get employed in a government job that is secure and [in which] you get a pension. That's what many people thought in India at that point of time.'

Another issue was capital. The two young engineers, without resources of their own, persuaded two brothers, V. Ramanaiah and V.G.N. Prakash, to join them and invest ₹8 lakh ($12,000) in return for 50 per cent of the new business. 'Because we didn't have a business background and nobody was available to guide us, we thought, we are four people and let us make the shareholding as 25 per cent each. All four people have to be working in the business. One person was experienced in a machine shop and we told him to outsource the machine components. The other person was not a technical person so we told him to take care of all administration and bank-related work.' This arrangement with no formal agreement was to cause problems later, when the four partners could not agree on key issues.

The key innovation that Ravindranath and Rajendran had recommended to Bühler was in the design of the grinding wheel in the rice mill. 'They were using smoother grinding wheels and the revolutions per minute were higher. We realized that in boiled rice, the rice being hard, it does not matter if you scrape out a little deeper. At the same time when the powder comes out, it comes out with a higher percentage of oil in the powder, which is called bran. So the bran gets sticky very fast and it used to stick all around the screen in the Bühler machines. We used a coarser grinding wheel so that we could remove the rough bran instead of smoother bran, and then we used higher pressure to suck the air out from the machine. These were the exact changes that we had recommended to Bühler as well.'

Having built a prototype, the partners needed to prove it worked better than other machines in the field. They visited 50 rice mills, but no one would let them test the machine as they had no references from anywhere where the machine was already working. Eventually, they found a better-educated mill owner who understood their design and decided to allow them to prove their promise to reduce broken rice by 1 per cent. Ravindranath recounted, 'We took the machine for testing in the rice mill, but we could only get broken rice out. That was a moment which could have changed the entire proposition for us.

We were about to lose all our confidence and close down everything because all the money, whatever we had, was invested in this machine. If you are not successful, you have to close it down; that was the situation.

'I discussed it with my partner and we made some changes to the machine. We went to the same rice mill to test again, but the person refused to test it this time, saying, [that we had] wasted a lot of rice last time. So I then went in search of a new rice mill where I could test this modified machine. When I was searching for a rice mill a thought crossed my mind: why not go to the place where the Bühler machine had failed? I am very proud to say that the first machine made in Milltec was sold [there], and 100 per cent payment was received even before the machine got shipped. That was the greatest cheque ever for us. Today if I get a cheque of ₹1 million, I am not that excited. The first machine was sold for ₹2.4 lakh, I still remember that.'

Ravindranath then went from mill to mill selling his newly designed machine, collecting payment from one sale to finance the manufacture of the next machine. The business grew organically until 2012, when the four partners fell out over future strategy. Ravindranath and Rajendran wanted to make some acquisitions to grow and gain technology, while their partners, the two brothers, wanted to enjoy the dividends of the now-profitable business. Eventually, the PE firm Multiples bought out the brothers for a handsome amount.

According to Ravindranath, Multiples has been a very good partner. They do not interfere excessively but have worked with Milltec to develop a plan both to expand its product range beyond rice mills into other cereals, as well as extend their sales coverage internationally.

CHAPTER 2

Manmohan's Children

'There was never a question that I would not go into business, because I was surrounded by a business environment and people talking about business. It is in my blood, I guess. And I didn't have a choice. When I graduated in 1976 I was 18 years old, I could have probably got a job for 1,000 bucks a month. I had no qualification, nobody was giving me a job and I wouldn't take any minor job as I was proud. So it had to be my own business.'

Sunil Bharti Mittal, Founder and Chairman, Bharti Enterprises

Ronnie Screwvala launched his career as a media mogul in 1981 when he was 19 years old. He started by stringing wires between buildings in south Bombay to offer cable television, then new to Indian consumers who were previously offered just two channels by the state broadcaster, Doordarshan. We were sitting in his book-lined office in Worli in Bombay looking out over the Arabian Sea. Dressed like an Indian Steve Jobs in black, sharp yet relaxed, Ronnie warmed to his theme. 'I didn't want to work for anybody,' he told me. 'I wanted to try and do something, to experiment and do things on my own. Once you have that sense, and if it is strong enough, then you can go out and do it.'

Ronnie started in business before India began its economic reforms in 1991 and had a hard struggle before the new opportunities in the 1990s brought initial success. Ronnie's journey echoes many of the common themes among the older and earlier group of entrepreneurs I interviewed, 21 in total. They were the early beneficiaries of the reforms introduced by the then prime minister, P.V. Narasimha Rao, and his finance minister, Manmohan Singh.

Most of the people in this group were young, like Ronnie, when they started out. A number of them spoke of the family issues they faced when they decided to set up on their own rather than joining the family business or following a safe career. Many of them took years to develop their business, often switching direction along the way, or pivoting, as we would now say. Many struggled early, even failing initially in four cases. Only two of this group of interviewees, from later in the period, raised institutional equity backing early in the life of their businesses. The majority bootstrapped their business, getting by with financial support of family and friends, raising debt and reinvesting income generated in the business. In many ways this group matched the profile sketched by Amar Bhidé based on research in the US, described earlier, of entrepreneurs who tend to feel their way forward intuitively, changing direction often, without formal planning or VC backing, until they achieve an inflection point and things become easier.

Ronnie Screwvala is known for his success in media businesses, culminating in his sale of UTV Group, his network broadcaster, to the Walt Disney Company (Disney) in 2012. He set up UTV in 1990 to take advantage of the production opportunities that the state broadcaster, Doordarshan, was beginning to give to the private sector. UTV grew over the years into a broadcaster in its own right and then a movie studio, partnering along the way first with Rupert Murdoch's News International and later with Disney. 'Grit and determination are the keys to success,' Ronnie said. He illustrated this by recalling the risks he took and the legal battles that resulted. 'Every time we made a controversial movie we had 17 FIRs[38] and four court cases against us.'

While the arts and communication have been Ronnie's love, rooted in his theatre interests as a boy, he was always flexible in his approach, believing that opportunity 'strikes like lightning.' One of his first ventures in the early 1980s was in toothbrush manufacturing. 'I recognized the growth potential for a simple product [toothbrushes] that offered to fill a vacuum

---

[38]   First Information Report, the first stage of a police investigation process in India.

in India's growing market,' he explains in his book, *Dream With Your Eyes Open*.[39] Lazer Brushes came out of a chance tour of a factory in the UK when he spotted two surplus machines and offered to buy them on the spot. He returned to Bombay with an option on the machines. He then set out to hustle for a purchase order from customers for an unproven product from a non-existent company, to find debt funding to buy and import the machines, and to sign up a partner to run the business. He also needed to overcome all the bureaucratic hurdles, then in place, related to importing equipment and establishing a factory.

Ronnie's family office, through which he now invests, is called Unilazer Ventures, echoing this early venture in oral hygiene. Unilazer has made a number of investments in early stage businesses in India but is now focused on Upgrad, an online higher- and vocational-education enterprise. His charitable activities are through the Swades Foundation named after the hit film he produced in 2004 starring the Bollywood mega-star Shah Rukh Khan. His other great love is kabaddi, a traditional Indian contact sport. Ronnie owns the U Mumba team franchise of the Pro Kabaddi League launched in 2014 and is heavily involved in developing the quintessentially Indian sport into a professional and televised league.

Given his vast experience, huge capacity for success and inherent drive, Ronnie has become a passionate advocate of the importance of entrepreneurship for India. His book is almost more a call to arms for aspiring, risk-taking entrepreneurship than a chronicle of his own journey from a small flat on Grant Road, Bombay. 'We need 10 million entrepreneurs in the next five years,' he said with conviction. 'But, also, we need entrepreneurs at scale. The core of what constitutes an entrepreneur is one word: aspiration. We should be ten times more ambitious than we are; we need to be ten times more aspirational than we are. We need to think 40 times bigger in terms of scale.'

Ronnie's parting thought surprised me. 'When I started up 20 or 25 years back, obviously the ecosystem was different from now in many ways, like not being able to raise funds and not looking at scale. What I found out in

---

[39] Screwvala, Ronnie, *Dream With Your Eyes Open: An Entreprenurial Journey*, New Delhi: Rupa Publications, 2015.

the last few years while interacting much more with other entrepreneurs is that I *thought* things have changed, but actually in some ways things have not changed so much.'

While Ronnie might not be satisfied with how much has changed in India, and how much more could change, it is clear that the world of Manmohan's Children was very different from that in which the New Generation operates today, and much more challenging.

Starting out

Ronnie's early passion for setting up his own business was unusual in Bombay's Parsi community of the 1980s. For others among the early entrepreneurs, like Sunil Mittal of Bharti who is quoted earlier, a business career was the only choice they could consider. This was especially true of those from India's traditional business communities, like Ajay Piramal, Chairman and Managing Director of the Piramal Group, a Marwari by background. He told me, 'At that time (the 1980s) you didn't really think too much. I was born and brought up thinking I was going to be in the family business. I didn't even think of any alternatives, which is very different from what it is today.' Ashok Wadhwa, founder of Ambit Capital, an investment bank, a Sindhi by background, did choose a different path initially, becoming a chartered accountant (CA) with Arthur Andersen. 'Nobody in my family had ever done a job,' he recalled. 'I was the first person to actually step into employment.'

For others, especially from backgrounds in what Indians call 'service', that is employment in government or large organizations, becoming an entrepreneur at a young age was a less obvious choice. Coming from a Bengali family that traditionally joined government service, and passionate about the creative arts, Sanjoy Roy, co-founder and Managing Director of Teamwork Arts, thinks of himself as a rather surprising entrepreneur. Teamwork is the organizer of many cultural festivals across the world, including the now world-roving Jaipur Literature Festival (JLF). He observed that, in the 1980s, 'The economy was largely controlled and much of it was legacy economy, so businesses were handed down from father to son. Everybody else had to become either an engineer or a doctor or an accountant; there wasn't the sense that you could become a businessman.

The legacy of Nehruvian India for us was that making money wasn't necessarily a cool thing.'

Ajay Sethi, founder of ASA & Associates LLP Chartered Accountants, an accounting and advisory firm, and Zia Mody, one of Indian's leading corporate lawyers and Managing Partner of AZB & Partners, created their own firms as they were dissatisfied with the opportunities that existed at the time in professional firms.

'The firms at that time were fairly Dickensian,' Zia explained. 'I had worked for a large firm in New York called Baker & McKenzie, but when I came back [to India] there was no corporate merger and acquisitions (M&A) which was cross-border and overseas, which is what my skill-sets were. So by default I had to end up doing litigation, which is a solo practice.' Ajay had wanted to be his own boss from an early age. 'I had these visions of starting a business of my own from when I was young, in school and college. Probably, it was because I saw a lot of businessmen who were around my father. I would see their lovely cars and all – and don't forget we're talking about the time [when] the economy was closed. To see these people with these cars fired my imagination.' Yet, he gave in to family pressure not to get into business right out of college and instead trained at Arthur Andersen before finally hanging up his own shingle in a temporary structure on a friend's terrace.

Kiran Mazumdar-Shaw, founder of Biocon, now India's leading biotech business, faced the additional challenge of being a woman trying to enter a traditionally male industry. She stumbled into creating her own business while trying to pursue job opportunities. She returned from studying brewing in Australia in 1975 and could not get a job in a brewery despite her father working in a senior capacity for United Breweries. 'The doors shut on me because they felt that this wasn't a job for a woman,' she recalled. 'I don't think any brewery in India was willing to risk having a woman in charge.'

Narayana Murthy, founder of Infosys and one of the international icons of a new India, had a different motivation for creating his first business, Softronics, in 1976. As a student, he says he was something of a leftist idealist. After graduating from IIT Kanpur in 1969 Murthy went to France to work. There, 'I was slowly convinced that the only way that societies can solve the question of poverty is through the creation of jobs, and that the only people who can lead the creation of jobs are entrepreneurs. So I said let me go back to my country [to become an entrepreneur].' Softronics, focused on offering software to Indian clients, failed. 'Computers were not available in India at that time. Indian companies had not realized the value of IT,' Murthy told me.

After closing Softronics, Murthy joined Patni Computer Systems as head of their software group. 'But the entrepreneurial fire was still burning in me,' Murthy recalled. He had learnt much from the failure of Softronics, and the new company he would found in 1981, Infosys, would focus on software exports rather than on the domestic market. He carefully selected a group of youngsters to work with from among his 200-strong team at Patni. 'I looked for a set of attributes: First, an enduring value system; second, how bright they were in learning new things; third, their ability to work in a team; and fourth, complementary skills and strengths. I came across six youngsters who were 7 to 8 levels below me, all of them with hardly a year of experience as software engineers.' All of this group of Infosys founders are today playing important roles in supporting entrepreneurship in India, recycling their wealth and providing their support as mentors and advocates.

A few others were similarly altruistic in their motivation to become entrepreneurs. In his biography of Dr Prathap Reddy, founder of Apollo Hospitals, titled *Healer*,[40] Pranay Gupte quotes Dr Reddy explaining his drive to create a private sector hospital in Madras (now Chennai), unprecedented in the India of the early 1980s. Dr Reddy recalled the stunned look on the face of the young wife of a patient at H.M. Hospital where he was working on his return to India from the US. The patient needed heart surgery which was not available in India then, and treatment at Texas Heart Institute which was on offer would cost $50,000. 'On that day,' Dr Reddy told Gupte, 'I resolved that I would create a healthcare infrastructure in India that would offer the best of what was available in the world and make it affordable to most. Apollo Hospitals is the result.'

---

[40] Gupte, Pranay, *Healer: Dr Prathap Chandra Reddy and the Transformation of India*, New Delhi: Penguin Books India, 2013.

Such entrepreneurship of purpose was clearly unusual. More typical was the motivation of the young Kishore Biyani, founder of Future Group, the pioneer of organized retail in the country. 'I chose to become an entrepreneur because I wanted to do things my way,' he wrote in his book, *It Happened in India*,[41] which he told me has been a bestseller in multiple languages across India. Kishore explained further when we met in his office in Vikhroli in north Bombay, his point interrupted by the azan, the call to prayer, from the mosque outside his large window. 'I like thinking big. I was the contrarian and rebel in the family system. Entrepreneurship is an act of creation because of a need or a want or a desire to do something. I always believed that whatever you do should impact a lot of people in life, otherwise there is no fun in what you create.'

Kishore's conflict with his family, who were 'small-town businessmen, very religious, very pious, a large family with no big aspirations', is a theme echoed frequently by the earlier entrepreneurs. Those from traditional business backgrounds usually faced concerted pressure to join the family firm. Those from professional backgrounds experienced family concerns over the risk they were taking.

Uday Kotak, founder of Kotak Mahindra Bank, was from a conservative Gujarati trading family and was brought up in a traditional joint family home. Sitting in his futuristic, glass office block in Bombay's Bandra Kurla Complex, Uday reflected that entrepreneurship 'is all about imagination, dreaming different dreams'. After graduating from Sydenham College in Bombay and getting an MBA degree at the Jamnalal Bajaj Institute of Management Studies, he might have gone abroad for more education like many of his friends. However, there was family opposition to Uday going to the US arising from the fear that he might not return to the country and the family business. 'A lot of my friends haven't come back. India was a different place in the 1970s and 1980s, so going overseas was escaping to freedom. For me the option of going overseas was not there.' A cricket accident when he was in college put an end to his hopes of a sporting career and forced him to take a year out of college, some of which he spent in the family business. He recalled family members saying, 'Thank God that head

---

41 Biyani, Kishore, *It Happened in India*, New Delhi: Rupa Publications, 2007.

injury has cleared up his brain.' But he still found it hard to conform, as he wanted 'to have control over my own destiny' and the months spent working with his father heightened his concerns over what it would mean to join the firm full-time. Uday told me, 'I needed space for myself and my area of interest was finance, which was not what the family was in.' Eventually, his father agreed to support him in his ambition to set up a business in financial services. 'My father said, I'll talk to the family and maybe they may agree to give you a little bit of office space and allow you to do what you want.'

By contrast, Ajay Sethi's father, a banker, opposed his desire to create a business. 'As I was finishing my graduation, I told my father, I want to set up a business. But my father discouraged me because he and his generation believed in good jobs. Don't forget that from colonial times onwards the expectation was that you had to learn English, and then you had to get a secure job, and if you were intelligent then you would go for the Indian Administrative Service (IAS). My father's horizon was very controlled: Become a doctor, engineer, chartered accountant, architect or lawyer. Anything beyond that was for fools and idiots as far as he was concerned.' Later, when Ajay left Arthur Andersen to set up his own accounting practice, his father was horrified. 'My father thought I had cracked the code of life by becoming a CA, a merit lister. In the eyes of his peers he was *the* man, as his son had got into Andersen. When I left everything to start up my own practice he wouldn't even meet me.'

Family concerns could persist even into mid-career. When Pramod Bhasin, founder of the outsourcer Genpact, was spinning the company out of GE, and hence leaving a leadership role in one of the most respected companies in the world, his mother asked him, 'Are you okay? Are you getting fired? Is everything all right? Why would you ever think of such a move, why would you leave a company?'

Some like Kishore Biyani and Ronnie Screwvala knew their own minds from early on, but a number of those I interviewed credited the importance of older mentors in catalysing their step into the uncertainties of entrepreneurship. For Uday Kotak this stimulus came from a senior banker, Sidney Pinto, formerly of Grindlays Bank but then working in his own firm. Uday told me, 'One day we did not get a taxi so I was walking back to Fountain from Nariman Point with Sidney Pinto when he said, you must start something on your own. He encouraged me, saying, instead of staying as a division of the family business, Uday, move into a separate company.'

After failing to get a job in India in a brewery, Kiran Mazumdar-Shaw had decided that she would go back overseas and had accepted a job with Moray Firth Maltings in Scotland. Out of the blue, just before she was due to leave the country, she was contacted by Leslie Auchincloss, a Scot who had created an enzymes business in Ireland called Biocon. 'He tracked me down in Baroda the day I was leaving for Delhi by the Rajdhani Express,' Kiran remembered. 'The train was [to leave] in the evening and at 10 o'clock in the morning I got a call [from him] saying, I am Leslie Auchincloss and I'd like to meet you. I met him in Delhi and he just wouldn't give up.' Auchincloss proposed that Kiran should decline the job in Scotland and become the Indian joint venture partner for Biocon. Kiran tried to dissuade him, even introducing him to other, more qualified potential partners. She recounted Auchincloss telling her, 'I am actually looking for someone like you because I need someone who is fired up and who would not treat it just as a side business. Why are you so diffident about yourself and why are you running yourself down so much? When I set up my company I didn't have great business experience and I didn't have the kind of money that you think you need to set up a business. You basically need a good idea and you need to be passionate about it.'

Early struggles

Once launched as newly minted entrepreneurs, few of this earlier group of entrepreneurs found it easy or quick to gain traction.

Sunil Mittal is known for creating Bharti Airtel, India's leading mobile telecom network, but he started a number of other businesses before entering telecom. '[From] 1976 to 1996, those 20 years were tough,' he recounted, now ensconced in the calm opulence of the executive floor of one of Delhi's plushest office buildings in Vasant Kunj. 'In the first five years I used to complain to my Lord that you say hard work pays, I am working hard and smart, but nothing is coming through. Those first five years were very frustrating. But things began to move after that, and the next five years and then the next were better and better.'

Sunil's first business, after leaving school in his native Ludhiana at 18, was as a supplier of bicycle parts. 'In my first year I had very little capital, so I could have either done something for the hosiery industry or for the bicycle industry because these are the two dominant businesses in Ludhiana.' Through family connections, he knew of some of the people making bicycles, like the Munjals. 'In fact, Brijmohan Munjal was my first customer,' he says. Brijmohan Munjal founded the Hero Group, originally in bicycles but now the largest producer of motorcycles in India and, in terms of units, in the world.

Sunil told me a story that captures the business ethos in the Punjab of the 1970s and the juggling he constantly had to resort to in order to survive. Without electronic payment systems, cheques took time to clear through the banking system, so he often faced acute cash flow challenges, having to secure cleared payments from customers before he was able to place his next supply order. One time, he had completely run out of funds. 'I went to Mr Munjal and I said, "Uncle, I need some money". There was no concept of appointments, we just walked in. He said, "Today it's not Friday [when invoices were cleared]". I said, "Uncle, I am desperate, I really need it". He was not happy, but finally he said, "Okay, how much do you need?" He cleared two or three of my bills and, as I turned back to the door of his shabby cabin, he said, "Beta," which means son, "don't make this a habit." That is a moment I'll never forget. That incident changed my life because from that day on I've never let my finances get the better of me. Never.'

Kiran Mazumdar-Shaw finally agreed to Leslie Auchincloss's persuasion and became Biocon's partner for India. Due to the then regulations requiring majority Indian ownership in foreign joint ventures she found herself as a 70 per cent owner of the company, capitalized at the princely sum of ₹100 (then about $10). 'We had no capital in the business,' she recalled. 'I had ₹10,000 in my bank account in Bangalore which was my life's savings.' Her first challenge was to get permission from the Government of India for the new venture. 'This was all completely new to me. You can imagine, from nothing, I had to suddenly go to DGTD [the Directorate General of Trade and Development] and wander through the corridors of bureaucracy in Delhi and all the red tape that went with it. It was so funny because I used sit in those corridors until the peon came to usher me into the room [to meet the concerned official]. And very often touts would be hanging around saying, if you want us to help you with your project, you pay us so much and then we'll get it done. I said I have no money, there's no question of paying you anything. I said, I just have to get it done properly.'

Fortunately for Kiran, the officer in charge, a Mr Biswas, took pity on her. 'I said, first and foremost I don't know who to bribe, how to bribe, how much to bribe. I don't know whether it's worth starting at all. The man was horrified. He said, don't give up, I will help you. Now you don't sit in the corridors any more, you understand. He told his peon, "Every time this madam comes, you'll allow her to come straight into my office."' Biswas offered to help her as she wrote the required project report, advising her that approval would be based on either import substitution or the generation of exports, both of which her project achieved. 'Sometimes he used to say, no this is not the way to write the project report and he would tell me what was right. So, thanks to him, I wrote this so-called project report and I gave it to him. I got approval in one month's time, which was quite amazing.'

Kiran's challenges were, however, just beginning. 'I got the approval and started the company in my garage. I was 25 years old, and no bank would extend a credit line to me. In those days there was no question of venture funding so it was all about debt financing.' She persuaded Biocon Ireland to commit to buying her output of papain enzyme, to be produced from papaya in Bangalore. Armed with this contract she toured the banks, seeking the funds to fit out her shed. 'I needed at least ₹3 lakh to buy the equipment and to start up a semblance of a factory. Of course, no bank would lend me the money. Again I was told the same things: You're too young, you're 25 years old. You're trying to start some strange business which we don't understand. On top of that you have no money and you have no experience. It's a big risk for us. The woman thing came up a lot; they'd say to me, "You're a young girl."' Fortuitously, at a wedding reception she met a banker with Canara Bank who heard her story, asked her to come to the bank the following day and sanctioned the loan.

With the shed fitted out, Kiran now needed people to operate the equipment. 'I couldn't get anyone to work for me because, again, working for a chit of a girl was tough. Finally, I got some retired tractor mechanics to come and work for me.' Kiran smiled, remembering the first enzymes produced and shipped. 'Can you imagine? Exporting to Ireland, what a proud moment that was. I keep telling young entrepreneurs today, the start-ups, don't wait for the perfect product because your first milestone has to be a commercial transaction. I say, don't get carried away by trying to refine the product and getting it to be absolutely spot-on. A lot of these tech guys want the best technology and the best product and the best whatever.'

She started making money quite quickly by exporting enzymes to her Irish partner. He was encouraging her to think ahead as the shed would soon be too small. She saw an advertisement for 20 acres of land available in a distress sale, 6 acres of which had industrial classification and the rest was still zoned as agricultural. Her thought was to build the factory on part of the land and to use the agricultural land to grow papaya as raw material. She persuaded Biocon Ireland to advance money against supply, borrowed from the Karnataka State Finance Corporation, bought the land and started construction. 'And, of course, again I had a huge challenge because that was bang in the middle of preparations for the Asian Games [held in Delhi], so all the steel and cement was being diverted to the Asian Games. We used to get rations of cement and steel, that's why I took so long to build my factory. I started construction in January 1980 and I finished the project in 1983. If I built it today, it would take me less than a year for sure. I had to keep waiting every week for my quota of cement and steel, and then build the next bit.'

Rehan Yar Khan, founder and now Managing Partner of Orios Venture Partners, returned to India from Dubai to attend college in Bombay and set out on his own in 1992, after graduating. He went into the import and distribution of seeds for floriculture, and struggled. He explained, 'The way the industry works is that you have District Commissioners (DCs) everywhere, and they subsidize and organize a lot of the produce. So you have to go to DCs and say we have this new offering which is, for instance, a more pest-resistant variety. And therein lies the problem, because you collect your money through them. Collecting money from local government back then was like squeezing water out of a stone and you could have one year of receivables. And we are talking about early 1990s when there were no mobile phones and only poor air connectivity, so it was a tough business.

I did that until 1998 but it was a tough business to scale. However, I cut my teeth as an entrepreneur.'

I asked if it was an issue of corruption. 'The whole thing was massively corrupt,' Rehan answered. 'I remember working with one DC who was an amazing guy and would release payments proactively. So if he could do it I suppose the others could too, but they didn't.' Rehan pivoted in 1998 and went into a very different business, providing a service to reverse-route expensive outgoing phone calls from India into cheaper incoming calls, especially serving Bombay's international banks. This proved to be a huge money spinner for the few years while this regulatory arbitrage persisted.

Ajay Piramal made his money in pharmaceuticals, which he sold to Abbott in 2010 for $3.8 billion. Ajay argues that sometimes adversity gives you opportunity. He started his business career in the family textile business, but his father suddenly died when Ajay was just 24, followed five years later by his elder brother. Ajay found himself coping first with a crippling politically motivated strike across Bombay's mills led by Datta Samant. Then, on 1 January 1982, there was a division of the family businesses between brothers and cousins. 'We had two large mills and we employed almost 7,500 people. It was a problem and therefore I was forced to look at other business opportunities. I think if ours had been an average business, not doing too well, not doing too badly, we would probably have continued with it. Sometimes when you are pushed against the wall, it's an advantage.' Ajay decided to start afresh in pharmaceuticals and agreed to purchase Nicholas Laboratories, the Indian business of Astro Nicholas, for ₹6 crore. 'The deal was through the acquisition of shares of an overseas company to be paid in foreign currency. It was very hard to consummate the transaction. In those days, you needed the price to be approved by the Controller of Capital Issues (CCI). The FERA[42] regulations meant that the Reserve Bank of India needed to sanction the deal and would not approve any price higher than what was set by the CCI.'

Niranjan Hiranandani, founder and Managing Director of Hiranandani Group, was also propelled out of textiles and into the real estate industry,

---

[42] Foreign Exchange Regulation Act 1973 (FERA), a notoriously draconian legislation, which was replaced in 1998 by the more benign Foreign Exchange Management Act (FEMA).

in which he would make his name, by the industrial unrest in Bombay's textile mills in 1981–82. Although of Sindhi origin, his family was not traditionally in business. His father was a doctor who had come to Bombay from Karachi for his medical training. Niranjan recounts, 'I am a chartered accountant by qualification, I stood second in the University of Mumbai in commerce. Actually, though I was not really keen, my father persuaded me to do chartered accountancy because he said you should become a professional, and after that I lectured for two years in the Institute of Chartered Accountants for final-year students. While I was doing that, I also started in business. The first business I got into was a textile weaving unit in Mumbai. I had done internships in two companies and they happened to be textile mills and I had some contacts because of my father. So, based on that, we started weaving cloth which was then sold to mills to be converted into their clothing brands.'

In parallel, Niranjan started to make some investments in property development. 'In my late twenties we made some small investments in real estate, very small, and started learning that line. After a couple of years I found that I was doing badly in both. Also, I had debts to both the bank and to private people, and it was very difficult to make ends meet. So, on one great day, which was 8 January 1981, I had to take a view as to whether to do textiles or real estate. I was agnostic about both these lines. It so happened that on that particular day I received a letter from the union of my textile unit asking for a 100 per cent increase in wages. They never expected 100 per cent but that was what their demand was. Obviously the letter gave me an answer and I decided that I would sell off the textile weaving unit.'

Funding

One of the real challenges for this early group of entrepreneurs was raising capital, as Kiran Mazumdar-Shaw described earlier.

Niranjan Hiranandani is clear how much things have changed from his early days. 'It's a billion times easier now compared to what it used to be,' he said. 'Now both equity capital and debt funds are easily available. So, if you have an idea, you will be able to get funds. When I started out there were no easy funds.'

Challenges in securing funding, both debt and equity, clearly limited the level of ambition, the speed of growth and the choice of industry at that time. It tilted entrepreneurs towards sectors where capital was less critical. The funding sources for these earlier entrepreneurs included family and friends, scrimping debt finance and partnering with foreign entities. The first VC funds were only launched towards the later part of this period.

When Uday Kotak needed ₹30 lakh (then about $300,000) for his new business in 1985, his family agreed to put in ₹5 lakh, representing the profits he had made while working in the family firm. Other friends of the family lent a further ₹13–₹14 lakh and a number of other prominent people put in some money, including the father of Uday's friend, Cyril Shroff, now a leading lawyer. Uday had been discounting bills on behalf of Mahindra Ugine Steel, then run by Anand Mahindra who had recently returned from Harvard. 'I was meeting him regularly as a client and Anand came with a very open mind and an international perspective. It's difficult to say now whether I asked him to invest or he offered to invest, but the bottom line was that he put in ₹4.5 lakh. I then requested Anand to put the Mahindra name on the company. The original name was Kotak Capital and I suggested we should make it Kotak Mahindra instead. If you go back to the US firms like Goldman Sachs and J.P. Morgan, it's all family names. I thought we should be ready to put our reputation on the line. Anand has been on the board all the way and between us there is no piece of paper, it's just friendship and trust.'

I asked how well Anand had done on his angel investment. Uday paused, grinned, then said, 'Let me put it in the reverse; any original investor who put in ₹1 lakh and assuming they did nothing that ₹1 lakh is today worth ₹1,100 crore… So that's about 40-plus per cent compound return over 30 years.'

By the late 1990s it had become somewhat easier to fund a good business at an early stage in India, if much less common than now. Kiran Mazumdar-Shaw succeeded in raising private equity from ICICI[43] as early as 1989. The PE industry began to develop through the mid-1990s and by

---

[43] The Industrial Credit and Investment Corporation of India (ICICI) was set up as a development bank with the help of World Bank in 1955. ICICI is now one of India's leading banks.

the time I moved to Bombay in 1998 there were a number of foreign funds operating in India, including Warburg Pincus, who backed Bharti, CDC and Schroders. Jerry Rao left Citibank after many years there in 1998 to set up Mphasis to offer software and then processing services to financial institutions and quickly raised PE investment from Barings.

Ashok Wadhwa left Arthur Andersen in 1997 to create Ambit. He had been encouraged to do so by the activist investor P.C. Chatterjee, who had started investing in the US from 1989, initially working with George Soros, the hedge fund investor, but went on to create his own firm mainly focused on India. PC, as he is known, offered to invest in Ashok's idea for a new advisory firm in return for 51 per cent of the equity. Ashok asked the advice of Deepak Parekh, Chairman of HDFC and one of the most respected figures in Indian finance even then. Deepak asked Ashok why he wanted to give away control of his new firm and instead sanctioned a ₹2 crore loan for the new business which financed their new office and initial costs. Ashok quickly signed up a number of old clients, most importantly Warburg Pincus which he had earlier advised on its investment in Ronnie Screwvala's UTV. Warburg offered a ₹1 crore annual retainership plus success fees on deals, and Ashok rapidly helped them make a number of investments including in Rediff, Piramal and Marico.

By the later 1990s, therefore, equity finance for new businesses in India was becoming somewhat easier to raise as PE firms felt out the market, especially in favoured industries like finance, software and the emerging Business Processing Outsourcing (BPO) sector.

Creating a new industry

GE Capital International Services (GECIS), later renamed Genpact, was one of the first captive outsourcers in India. The idea for the company came to Pramod Bhasin in 1997. As Pramod told me, 'I was sitting in Chennai in a car park talking with my boss, saying that we have to do something more with the calibre of people we have. GE Capital had built a cheque-processing centre in Chennai, where we collected 36 post-dated cheques from every [finance] customer, that is, three years of repayments, in advance. Can you imagine managing all those cheques? The filing systems and processes you would need? Based on this experience, I said, why can't I do this for the rest of the world? My boss was an English guy, Nigel Andrews, a really lovely guy, and he told me to try it.'

Pramod had a different trajectory from most of the other earlier entrepreneurs as he was mid-career and created his business initially within a large corporate. After graduating from Shri Ram College in Delhi in 1971, Pramod went to London to train as a chartered accountant with Thomas McLintock. After a period in the Gulf with Blue Cross and Arthur Andersen, Pramod returned to London to join RCA Corporation which was acquired by GE in 1986. Pramod was transferred to GE Capital, then the fastest growing part of the GE group, and led leveraged acquisitions for a number of years in the US. Pramod says he learnt a huge amount working for GE for so many years. 'GE was entrepreneurial and I loved working there. If you had a good idea nobody would stop you and that's one of the reasons why I was successful when I came to India. I don't think this idea [for GECIS/ Genpact] would have worked in most other companies.' Pramod moved to India in 1993 to create and head GE Capital in the country and crafted joint ventures with SBI in credit cards and Maruti in car finance.

Even in the GE system, though, Pramod faced a fight to implement his idea, not least because at that time the perception of India as a place where quality work was done was so poor. 'Everybody I spoke with said it wouldn't work, including Jack Welch, who said I was committing suicide. We had to fight an internal battle for resources. Garry Wendt [the then CEO of GE Capital] sanctioned $2 million to roll out the idea. We had to figure out the business model from first fundamentals: what would work and who would pay for it, how to train people, how to transition complex processes.' Pramod later led a management buy-out of GECIS from GE in 2005 with PE backing in order to expand the customer base away from captive GE business. Genpact listed on the New York Stock Exchange (NYSE) in 2007 at a market capitalization of $2.3 billion.

In 1999, I visited GECIS in Gurgaon, then sprouting in what was still largely fields beyond Delhi airport, to try to understand this new outsourcing business. I had proposed to Jardines that we should create a group outsourcing centre in India, based on the processing needs of Jardine Fleming's fund management business and Jardine Lloyd Thompson's insurance policy administration. I met Raman Roy, often dubbed the father of the BPO business in India, first from 1984 with American Express and then on Pramod's team at GECIS. Raman explained the business for some time over repeated cups of tea. Then he asked if he could ask my advice on something. He told me that earlier that day he had met a team from Chrysalis Capital, one of the first India-based PE firms which had recently been created by Ashish Dhawan and Raj Kondur. They had urged him to leave GECIS and set up his own outsourcing business, which they would back. Raman asked if I thought it was a good idea. I left the meeting with an option to invest in what became Spectramind, on the condition that I could guarantee a certain number of 'seats' from Jardines business. My pitch to the Jardines board to make this investment was turned down as I was told 'we can't kiss all of the girls.' Two years later, Wipro bought 90 per cent of Spectramind for $93 million and Raman went on to create a second outsourcing business, Quatrro.

Pramod and Raman might have been the godfathers of the BPO business in India, but others quickly saw the potential of this new sector. Another early entrant into the BPO sector was Rizwan Koita, who set up Transworks along with Jagdish Moorjani in 1999. Rizwan graduated from IIT Bombay in 1992 and, like the majority of his class, went to the US for a Masters, choosing to go to the Massachusets Institute of Technology (MIT) on a scholarship. Rizwan estimates that 60–70 per cent of his IIT class went overseas and over 90 per cent of them stayed abroad after their studies, a situation very different from today. Rizwan decided to come back to India in 1995, partly for family reasons, and sought a good engineering job. He got offers from two excellent firms, L&T and Siemens, but could not face accepting either. First, the salaries offered were very low, about ₹15,000 per month (then about $500), and, second, the work environment was deeply unappealing. Rizwan remembers how at the end of his interview at one leading firm, the lunch bell rang at 12.30 p.m. and all of the engineering staff began to walk towards the canteen, carrying their tiffin boxes. 'I said, dude I can't do it. Somehow it seemed so rigid.'

Rizwan joined McKinsey instead, which had a much more attractive culture, salary structure and work environment, based out of the Oberoi Towers Hotel in Bombay. He was with McKinsey for about five years. 'That last year of the McKinsey stint, in 1998, we were doing stuff on what in those days was called remote services, now BPO or call centres. McKinsey wrote a report on IT services and I was one of the co-authors. One of the good things was that I could visit many of these captive facilities that were being set up for leading international companies like GE, American Express and British Airways, and I realized that none of these were offering services to third party clients.'

Jagdish Moorjani's family owned an old textile mill in Powai, and Rizwan and he launched Transworks as a third-party BPO provider from there. Like Raman, they raised VC backing from Chrysalis Capital. By 2003 they had understood that the basic BPO business was getting more competitive and commoditized so they sold their company to the Aditya Birla Group. The two of them remain in the same building today, now with a healthcare-focused IT business called Citius Technologies (CitiusTech), backed by General Atlantic. CitiusTech today has 2,700 healthcare technology professionals and is one of the global leaders in its field. Unlike Transworks, which was a cost-arbitration proposition, CitiusTech has significant domain expertise in healthcare.

The BPO industry emerged in India suddenly in the late 1990s and witnessed a number of pioneering examples of how ambitious entrepreneurs would increasingly be able to enter a new growth business with equity backing from VC funds. Often these entrepreneurs were more experienced and mid-career, like Rizwan or Raman. Rizwan's entrepreneurial journey from Transworks to CitiusTech also reflects the evolution and development of IT services in India over this period; a business model based on cost-arbitrage alone proved short-lived as Indian costs rose and the big American IT companies moved to India, so Indian IT companies have sought to develop other sources of competitive edge.

Gathering pace

By the late 1990s, the time that I moved to India, there was a gathering sense of change in the country. Growth was faster, foreign investors were increasingly interested and capital was becoming more readily available. The businesses of the early entrepreneurs were gaining scale.

In 1995, Zia Mody gave up court work as a barrister and created her own firm, Chambers of Zia Mody, with 12 young associates. When I first met her in 1998 she was a single partner sitting in a cramped walk-up office in a lane near Kala Ghoda in Bombay. Her client base was almost entirely foreign companies investing in India. By the time Zia created AZB & Partners by merger in 2004, she had built one of India's leading law firms. Kishore Biyani set up the first outlet of his first retail chain, Pantaloons, in Gariahat, Calcutta, in 1997, which in many ways was the start of organized retail in India. IT companies were ballooning, fuelled by the impending Year 2000, or 'Y2K', bug, including Narayana Murthy's Infosys and Saurabh Srivastava's IIS Infotech, which later became Xansa. The BPO business was just getting started.

Niranjan Hiranandani's story graphically illustrates the pace of change at this time. In 1984, he had the courage and vision to purchase 250 acres in the distant Bombay suburb of Powai. It was then, he said, 'Wasteland, quarries and stuff like that. Nobody wanted to come here. There was no way anybody could have thought that they could make a building or an apartment here and sell it.' What attracted Niranjan to the site was the potential to shape a whole development, including the infrastructure, the green spaces, the schools and amenities. 'One of the objectives of picking up a large piece of land was that everything in view, to the left and right, was ours and we were able to create one integrated complex. I really felt that it was like an empty canvas, even if it was a horrible and dirty canvas. It was far away from the madding crowd, [in] no way close to humanity. But we said that if we make something nice, people will come here.' The development took years, but slowly he began to make progress. 'First we made seven-storey buildings then we made 14-storey buildings and slowly we went on. Each time, we improved the quality of the building. Obviously, we didn't make a lot of money in the beginning; in fact, we may have lost some money. Over a period of time we built a school, a hospital, a go-karting track, the first supermarket company in Mumbai, set up a good hotel, and so we created a holistic township. You didn't really need to move out; you could walk to work, you could have all kinds of facilities. And, in the meantime, the city grew towards me, so it was not really me going to the city, it was the city coming to me.'

Changes in government policy, too, created new opportunities for the early entrepreneurs. Sunil Mittal seized the new liberalization of telecom to set up Airtel to bid for the Delhi circle license in 1995. This was a huge undertaking and beyond Sunil's financial capacity. He set about the task with his accustomed energy, determination and persuasiveness. He told me, 'Helicopter surveys, satellite imagery...I went to the best in the world. I needed about $50 million to kick off the business and that's one reason I wanted foreign partners. SFR from France [later on acquired by Vivendi] was the main partner along with Emtel from Mauritius and Mobile Systems International (MSI) from the UK. I always felt that when we had a big balance sheet as a partner, as a shareholder, getting money was easier.'

Sunil managed to leverage the equity from foreign partners not just with bank debt but also supplier credit. He told me, 'I needed to buy equipment for Delhi to start off at a cost of $27 million, which was a princely amount in those days. We finally went for Ericsson because I liked them, they seemed to be a serious, good company and we signed the agreement. I had lunch with Kurt Hellström of Ericsson and I told him that I had a problem. I said, "Mr Hellström, I don't have the money to pay you but I promise I'll pay 15 per cent advance and the rest will be paid on happiness." He laughed and asked what I meant by happiness. I told him that happiness is when my customers are making a call on the streets and they're happy, that's the happiness. I don't know what came over him, he looked at me, and said, "Okay, done." Later, when I asked him about that incident, he said that he had seen so much passion in me that he had agreed. He gave me a credit of $24 million.'

Uday Kotak also seized the opportunities of the new liberalization. Kotak Mahindra had grown in the late 1980s as a Non-Banking Financial Company (NBFC), first discounting bills, then offering asset finance. The growth of sales of Maruti cars gave Uday a new opportunity to scale up. He began booking blocks of a thousand or more vehicles at a time which he could then sell to eager buyers once the cars were with the dealers, with a loan package of course. In 1991, Kotak picked up a stockbroking license and then the easing of capital controls enabled him to enter investment banking.

He decided he would need to partner with a foreign bank and set about courting Goldman Sachs. In March 1992, he attended a Euromoney conference in Delhi and ensured he met the delegates from Goldman Sachs.

That led to a visit to New York in May 1992 to meet Goldman at their 85 Broad Street headquarters and he persuaded them that his fledging firm should be their Indian agents for Global Depository Receipt (GDR) issues. Mark Evans of Goldman then invited Uday Kotak and Anand Mahindra to fly to Hong Kong in December 1993 to have dinner with two senior Goldman partners from New York who did not know India well. After the dinner, Evans later told Uday, the two visitors had asked if Goldman could hire Uday and Anand. One of those partners was Hank Paulson, later US Treasury Secretary, who then visited India in 1994. This led to a full joint venture with Goldman in 1995, with Kotak as the 75 per cent majority partner. Further joint ventures followed with Ford in car finance and with Old Mutual in life insurance.

By 2000, India had begun to change in dramatic ways, notwithstanding the inconsistent pace in reforms set by the government. 'Manmohan's Children' were gaining in both scale and confidence. In Bangalore, Kiran Mazumdar-Shaw made a dramatic change in direction in the late 1990s by exiting the enzyme business that had made Biocon and focusing instead on the much more challenging biopharmaceuticals. She explained, 'For 20 years I developed enzymes; I was very successful, but my business was less than $100 million. I wanted to build a billion-dollar company and I realized that enzymes were not going to get me there.'

Liberalization was allowing private investment in previously restricted sectors like telecom and television. Kishore Biyani had triggered the development of modern retailing. India had quickly developed a globally recognized IT industry and the BPO industry was scaling up. Ratan Tata was contemplating a drive to create India's first multinational. New business opportunities were developing and there was an increasing availability of capital. Most importantly, the culture was changing in ways positive to business enterprise, especially among the young but also among mid-career professionals. A new generation of entrepreneurs were being incubated, and in much larger numbers than previously, as the following chapter will chronicle. The year 2000 not only launched a new millennium, but in India there began a transition to a new era of entrepreneurship.

Making Money from the Creative Arts
SANJOY ROY

I first met Sanjoy Roy at the Jaipur Literature Festival in January 2008. William Dalrymple, the writer and co-founder of the festival along with Sanjoy, had appealed to us at Tata for emergency funding as the sponsorship required for the festival had not come through. Sanjoy, co-founder of Teamwork Arts, was everywhere at the festival, distinctive in his colourful designer clothes and aviator shades, long white hair pulled back in a ponytail.

Since 2006, Sanjoy, William and Namita Gokhale have built Jaipur into the world's most-attended literary festival. In 2016, according to Sanjoy, 330,000 people visited the festival. Over a simple Indian lunch of dal, rice and chapatti in his office in Delhi, Sanjoy explained Jaipur's success: 'It was really a combination of accidents. First, we were very clear that what we wanted to do at this festival had to have democratic access, and we would not do any of the normal reservation of seats for government, and the good and great. Two, we wanted it to be seen as a city festival and a festival for India. Three, it was at Diggi Palace, which had a charm that we wanted to preserve. And, last, was that interest in India had been sparked by then, and people wanted to come to India.' Publicity for the festival has also been helped, year after year, by controversies, including the cancellation of Salman Rushdie's planned attendance in 2012 after the intelligence services said assassins were en route to kill him.

Sanjoy looks like a trendy hipster, a 'lovey' as we would say in the UK, branded by his flamboyant sartorial sense, long white hair held off his forehead by shades. Indeed, he started his career after graduating from St Stephen's in Delhi as an actor, turning down a place at Berkeley, and then quickly took over the management of the Theatre Action Group (TAG) in Delhi at the grand salary of ₹1,000 a month. His prospective father-in-law was so unimpressed by his financial prospects that he tried to block his marriage to his wife, Puneeta.

Underneath the creativity and apparent chaos surrounding Sanjoy lies a shrewd business person and activist who passionately believes that the arts create development. 'I am an entrepreneur, absolutely,' he told me. 'We are a for-profit company and our idea, right from the beginning, was to show that the arts can create tangible wealth. I was very clear that what we needed to prove was that the arts could create wealth and we could create wealth for the artists as well. Because of the Salaam Baalak trust [set up in 1988 based on the proceeds from Mira Nair's film, *Salaam Bombay*], we knew what the effect [of the arts] was on kids. In countries like India, or any country that has history and built heritage, the marriage of built heritage, arts, culture and entertainment can and does contribute to local economies. And it can and does create equitable platforms of expression for young people who otherwise have no such platforms. Most importantly, it creates jobs.'

In order to generate income for TAG's actors, Sanjoy, along with his business partner Mohit Satyanand, who later became a seed and angel investor, set up Teamwork Films and by 1995 he was producing 15 soaps and gameshows for television. After a while, however, Sanjoy and his colleagues grew weary of making light television entertainment. 'Every Saturday we used to have an afternoon meeting with all the producers and directors of the mini-shows. We used to talk about who had to shoot what, and which actor had created mischief and would have to be boycotted. Several staff members came to me and complained that they were brain dead and could not do this any more. I said, okay, we will shut it down...let's go back to the arts.'

Teamwork's first international exposure came from attendance at the Edinburgh Festival in 1999 and 2000 which resulted in a UK office, followed by an office in Singapore. They now have 25 performing arts, visual and literary festivals in 11 countries which showcase Indian arts to the world, including India by the Bay in my adopted home, Hong Kong. Sanjoy designed the closing ceremony for the Commonwealth Games in Melbourne in 2006, which led to an invitation to tender for events at the 2010 Delhi Commonwealth Games. Sanjoy refused on the grounds that he had advised Ernst & Young on the design of the tender documents. 'Someone called my colleague in finance, Rahul, and said, what is your boss's problem? We are not asking you for money. You give us your budget, we will add it to that budget, we will send it back to you to put into that tender and you just give us the difference. We are not asking you to give us money. So I said, this is not what we do and I am not interested.'

A unique feature of Teamwork Arts is that it is now PE backed by Ambit Pragma who invested $10 million in 2013. As usual, Sanjoy is self-deprecating in describing how this came about. 'I get a call, somebody whom I knew, who said these people are trying to get through to you, can you please take the call? I said, I have an hour – I was flying to Australia or somewhere, but I've got an hour, meet me at the Taj. I thought they wanted to understand the industry so I gave them an overview. At the end of the hour I had to leave for the airport, and they said, the reason we have come to see you is because we want to invest in Teamwork. So I laughed and I said, you must be crazy because we are an arts company and we do not do weddings and events, and there is no exit nor any money!

'They came back after a month and said, we would really like to present our vision of what you have created. They showed it to us, a comparison with some big event management companies and similar companies in terms of IP [intellectual property]. My colleagues said we should not be interested because had we wanted to make money we would have joined a bank. Then they just came and sat at the office and worked with us and translated everything that was in my head into a proper business plan. It was a huge learning, and I love learning. It excites me a lot to learn. It taught me how to create a plan and what a plan means, how it gave you goals. After one board presentation, Rajeev [Aggarwal of Ambit Pragma] stopped and started laughing and said, we are in the most bizarre situation. He said, every week we get proposals from people for investment, and we keep rejecting them. We have been running after you for nine months and you have this commitment phobia and you are refusing to take our money. I am not able to explain to our IC [Investment Committee] what kind of human being you are, walking away from this deal that we are offering to you.'

Sanjoy finally decided to take the offered investment. He recalled, 'One night I woke up and asked myself, what are you frightened of? Somebody is giving you an opportunity.'

Teamwork's revenue has grown five times since the Ambit investment. Sanjoy wants to turn Teamwork into a ₹100 crore ($15 million) company in the next few years, and is just beginning to think about how his festival platforms and library of content could be offered and monetized digitally. His other passion is promoting the importance of the arts for Indian society and the economy. As many as 350 million people across India are involved in the arts professionally, part time or socially. 'We know that the Indian DNA has the arts [woven into] it, and from birth to death everybody is engaged at some point with the arts. Everybody can tell us stories and sing a song.' Sanjoy's mission is to support, promote and showcase these traditions, whether temple dance, folk music, textile crafts or vernacular literature, and to prove that money can be made from high-quality creative arts.

CHAPTER 3

The New Generation

'I had not lived in India by then for close to 22 years. I saw a completely different country and I was fascinated. It was not the country I had left.'

Vani Kola, Founder and Managing Director, Kalaari Capital

'Infosys, of course, was called the original start-up company and was a phenomenal success, and I was there for 29 years. Then I went to the government and I was not really paying attention to the entrepreneurship side of things because I was busy navigating politicians and bureaucrats, and I didn't have time for anything else. So, when I came back, I suddenly found that right here, down the road in Koramangala, I was at the epicentre of a revolution. That was an "aah!" moment for me, that within walking distance of my house, there were 100 start-ups… That was quite outstanding.'

Nandan Nilekani, Co-founder, Infosys, and former Chairman, Unique Identification Authority of India (UIDAI)

Deep Kalra was one of the first-wave Internet entrepreneurs in India, setting up MakeMyTrip in 2000. 'The Internet was my trigger to do my own thing,' he told me, pouring green tea for me in a hotel lobby in Gurgaon. 'I suddenly realized, you don't need a big plot of land, you don't need a lot of capital. My view of entrepreneurship changed because entrepreneurship itself had changed. Entrepreneurship could now be done very differently.'

By 2000, the pace of entrepreneurship was perceptively speeding up and it would continue to strengthen into the new millennium, with periodic wobbles. Things slowed after the 'dot-com' bubble burst in the US in 2000, again after the full implications of the Lehman Brothers' collapse in 2008 exposed a world in financial crisis, and once more during the paralysis of government policy-making and lower business confidence that marked the last years of Manmohan Singh's second term as prime minister leading the United Progressive Alliance (UPA) government (2009–14). From 2012, after the scandal concerning the allegedly corrupt allocation of telecom licenses, referred to as the 2G scandal, the workings of the government and reform intent were bogged down. Officials were reluctant to make decisions for fear of being accused of taking money from any of the beneficiaries. Then, in 2014, the election of the government led by Narendra Modi restored business confidence and contributed to the start-up boom of 2015. Even though these events impacted the pace of change, throughout the years from 2000 onwards, an entrepreneurial revolution was strengthening and spreading through India.

The development of the entrepreneurial scene from the year 2000 is illustrated by the contrasting experiences of four companies founded in the same year and four 'unicorn' successes founded later in the period. The stories that emerge are increasingly different from those typical of the earlier entrepreneurs from the 1970s, 1980s and 1990s. Moreover, the launch experience of the later four companies was markedly easier and more rapid even than the four from 2000, illustrating the exponential acceleration of new venture activity. The four later companies that started in 2000 and analysed here are MakeMyTrip, SLK Software, Micromax Informatics and Fractal Analytics. The four unicorns are Flipkart, Ola Cabs, InMobi and ShopClues.

Origins

The backgrounds of the founders of these eight companies are more diverse overall than those of the earlier entrepreneurs, having become broader and marking the beginnings of a democratization of entrepreneurship that has still further to run. Parth Amin, founder, Chairman and Chief Operating Officer (COO) of SLK Software, and Sachin Bansal, co-founder and Executive Chairman of Flipkart, are the only ones among them to have come from business-oriented families. All of the other founders of these eight companies come from families with roots in corporate employment ('service'), government or academia.

Parth Amin is the grandson of two prominent industrialists, S.L. Kirloskar, founder of the Kirloskar Group, and Bhailal Amin, founder of Alembic Chemicals. Despite being a highly successful software services business focused on a limited number of US financial service customers, SLK Software maintains a low profile. Over a simple home-cooked lunch in his office in Bangalore, Parth told me that he had never talked publicly about his entrepreneurial journey. He graduated in 1985 from the Illinois Institute of Technology, Chicago, and returned to India to join the Kirloskar Group, initially in Pune with Kirloskar Oil Engines. Parth described how he used to read international business magazines which, during the 1980s, increasingly covered software as the next growth industry. In 1991, he persuaded the family to move him to Bangalore to take over the running of Kirloskar Computers which was then making significant losses. Despite succeeding in growing the business and turning it profitable, Parth was increasingly dissatisfied with his role due to the complexity of being in a family business. He saw software as 'the next big sexy thing' and wanted to seize the opportunity as an entrepreneur. So in 2000 he left the Kirloskar Group and, together with his brother Gopal, launched SLK Software, named after his grandfather (S.L. Kirloskar).

None of this group of eight reported an early intention to become an entrepreneur. Deep Kalra of MakeMyTrip explained that, although his father was a senior executive with the DCM Group, his entrepreneurial adventure was 'accidental and not really planned'. He followed a conventional track from St Stephen's, Delhi, to IIM Ahmedabad, which in turn led to a good job in a bank, ABN Amro. Srikanth Velamakanni, co-founder and CEO of Fractal Analytics, remembered, 'When I was growing up I had this notion that entrepreneurs have to be corrupt, and that it was the only way to be a successful businessman. My father used to work for the materials management division of Oil India Ltd and I remember seeing people come in and offer him cash. I asked him why he was being offered money and was refusing it. I was a really young kid at that time so it had a deep impact on me and I told myself that there was no way I would ever start a business.'

From among the later group of founders of unicorns, Sachin Bansal of Flipkart was clear that he had no intention early on to become an entrepreneur. He intended to follow his interest in science rather than create a business. Bhavish Aggarwal, co-founder and CEO of Ola Cabs, recalled that his father had been shocked by his decision to set up Ola. 'My grandfather was an engineer and my grandfather from my mother's side was also in professional life. Both my parents have seven siblings and all of them are either doctors or engineers. When I started off, my dad thought that I was crazy and asked me why [I was] becoming a travel agent.' Naveen Tewari, co-founder and CEO of InMobi, was brought up on the campus of IIT Kanpur where both his parents taught and his father became the Dean. While business was not looked down upon, the focus was on getting a good education and 'the dinner-table conversations were very deeply intellectual'. Neither Radhika Aggarwal nor Sanjay Sethi, co-founders of ShopClues, expected to be entrepreneurs. Both are from similar family backgrounds in government service in north India. Sanjay's father was in the irrigation department and Radhika's in the army. Sanjay told me, 'We are both accidental entrepreneurs. I had never imagined myself as an entrepreneur because my dad worked for the government all of his working life of 33 years.'

The triggers that changed their views, and opened up entrepreneurship as an avenue to risk and to pursue, were education, exposure to role models and influencers, time spent overseas, especially in the US, and a realization of the burgeoning new opportunities made available in a growing India by technological change.

The impact of attending one of the leading universities in India or the US was a repeated theme of my interviews. Bhavish from Ola credits his years at IIT Bombay until 2008 with widening his views of the possiblities. He told me, 'At IIT Bombay, I was exposed to such a broad spectrum of people. Also, as part of the programme, the institute runs different initiatives on aspects of life, including a particular focus on entrepreneurship.'

Naveen Tewari's years at IIT Kanpur, his family comfort zone, had still left his perspectives quite limited. Encouraged by his father he stumbled into a job at McKinsey. He told me, 'They called me for an interview and had me stay at the Taj [in Bombay]. I remember, I reached the door to my room and I had this swipe key, but I had no idea what it was. There was a guy who was carrying my bag, which was really funny because nobody carries your bag when you are aged 20–21 years, and he was stunned that I didn't know what to do with the swipe key.' Three years at McKinsey in Bombay introduced him to the business world. His outlook on life – shaped by 'my middle-class upbringing in a small town, in a society where education was valued most and something of a government environment which disliked risk [prevailed]' – was expanded at McKinsey. But the projects he worked on at McKinsey, though intellectually challenging, did not inspire him as he didn't 'have ownership' – 'that was for the likes of the Tatas, Birlas and Ambanis,' he said.

What really changed Naveen's views was his time at HBS, where he learnt from classmates, and those who came to talk to the students, that 'Great things are achievable, and that such things are not done by people who are extraordinary, but by ordinary people.' His first contact with the world of entrepreneurship came in a summer internship at Charles River Ventures. 'It allowed me to work with entrepreneurs who respected me because I had access to money. But I really wanted to be on their side of the table because they were solving the things that I always wanted to solve. These were entrepreneurs of my age, maybe a little older than me… I could relate to them.'

An exposure to the US, through study or work, is another uniting and growing theme among these entrepreneurs. Of the first group, from 2000, Parth studied in the US and Deep worked for two US companies, AMF Bowling and then GE Capital. Among the later group, the unicorn founders, all have a US connection. Sachin and Bhavish worked for US companies after graduating from IIT, Sachin at Amazon and Bhavish at Microsoft. Naveen, as described above, went to HBS and then, rejecting an offer to rejoin McKinsey, spent two years in Silicon Valley doing project work for a number of start-ups. The founding team of ShopClues were all based in the US for many years and the company was conceived and founded in California. Radhika and her husband, Sandeep, went to the US to go to business school at Washington University in St Louis, while Sanjay moved to the US after graduating from IIT Banaras Hindu University and IIT Delhi to work in IT roles, eventually joining eBay.

Another common influence on many of these founders, helping to shape their decision to become entrepreneurs, was the impact of role models, mentors and friends. Srikanth of Fractal described how his negative view of entrepreneurs was reshaped while at IIT Delhi and then at IIM Ahmedabad, especially during an internship at ICICI Securities (I-Sec). Infosys had then recently completed its IPO and the company was followed with great interest by I-Sec analysts. Srikanth told me, 'We were discussing whether to invest in Infosys because it seemed like it was going to do well. Later that year, I met Narayana Murthy when he came to the campus to speak as part of a course on Business Ethics. I found him inspirational and could see that he was creating a clean, values-driven company. Then when I saw the dot-com excitement in 1998–2000 and that a couple of my friends had started businesses and got VC funding, I felt that maybe there was a possibility of starting a business in India without being corrupt...and still being successful.'

After graduating from IIM, Srikanth joined ANZ Investment Bank. But he began to see college friends set up companies and secure venture backing, including Ashish Goyal, founder of e-Gurucool, and Manish Gupta, co-founder of Indegene. This led to frequent long evenings in a house in Bandra, a leafy Bombay suburb, with a group of friends talking about what business they could create. Srikanth recalled that 'people used to come in every evening and we spent time on weekends brainstorming about business ideas'. From these 'jamming' sessions emerged the group of six founders of Fractal and the idea of a comparison-shopping website.

Deep Kalra of MakeMyTrip left ABN Amro in 1995 and spent the next four years trying to build AMF Bowling's business in India. Deep was sold on the idea that India was ready for bowling and that the malls sprouting across the country would follow the US and then Chinese model of installing bowling alleys alongside their cinemas and food halls. It did not succeed principally due to the high cost of real estate in India, but the experience introduced Deep to many entrepreneurial business contacts and taught him much. 'The biggest thing it taught me was to hustle. As a banker, I didn't know how to hustle. It gave me the confidence to be an entrepreneur, which I only realized later. I wasn't planning anything then, and I fled back to the safety of work in a big company.'

Thinking he needed to carry on learning, Deep joined GE Capital, though, as it turned out, only for a short period of a year. It was at GE that he began to understand the possibilities of the Internet and to realize that he could set up a business himself. His boss at GE, Nitin Gupta, then President of GE Countrywide, offered Deep the choice of working either on Customer Relationship Management (CRM) as a development opportunity or on the Internet. He chose the Internet and soon, as he told me, his wife pointed out that 'the only thing you talk about is the Internet'. He began to research two options for a business of his own, an online travel company or online stockbroking. It was while booking a holiday in Thailand, the last before his first daughter was born, that he decided that the travel business provided the right opportunity. After lots of frustrating back and forth with a traditional travel agent, Deep took the plunge and booked the holiday online. 'We were going there for six nights and I said, what the hell, we should just book it. I was scared but we finally dropped the credit card and I said let's see what's going to happen. And it lived up to the promise. I was afraid because Amrita was pregnant. I [told myself], God, if we don't get this hotel, with an overnight flight and a connecting flight to get there [it will] be terrible. But everything worked like a charm and I was convinced of the potential of online travel.'

For the ShopClues founders the catalyst was Sandeep, Radhika's husband. She explained, 'Sandeep came up with the idea. We were based in San Francisco and he was covering Internet and e-commerce for a series of banks. He has been a closet entrepreneur pretty much since he was six years old; he has always wanted to be an entrepreneur. He had a few small entrepreneurial gigs when he was in college and then, after he finished his MBA, he got to set up a small start-up while doing his internship. Then he joined Charles Schwab and worked with Microsoft, before he got into Wall Street, but he always wanted something of his own. He says that his own success was the biggest barrier to entry into the entrepreneurial world.' Sandeep roped in Sanjay Sethi whom he'd met through their children's school, though it turned out they had spoken before as Sandeep used to cover eBay as a bank analyst (Sanjay joked that he had not made the connection as there are hundreds of Sandeep Aggarwals on LinkedIn). Radhika joined them, bringing her expertise in retailing, soon followed by Mrinal Chatterjee as Chief Technology Officer (CTO).

Whether entrepreneurs from six years old or accidental entrepreneurs later in life, what unites all of these eight founding groups was the realization of a huge, emerging opportunity in India. This is markedly different from the earlier entrepreneurs, Manmohan's Children, most of whom became entrepreneurs more because they temperamentally needed to work for themselves or because they stumbled into it. The 'New Generation', from 2000 onwards, had many other opportunities they could have pursued in India or the US. All were well-educated and all but one were in good jobs before they took the plunge. Only Naveen Tewari, who returned to India from Silicon Valley in 2006 without a job, had not been in good employment before creating his own business. All of them saw an exciting opening created by India's growth and by emerging technologies, particularly around the Internet, and took the risk to venture out for themselves. As Deep Kalra put it, 'The more I got into the Internet, the more I was convinced that it was going to change everything.'

The story of Sachin and Binny Bansal's start-up, Flipkart, is probably India e-commerce's seminal creation myth to date. Friends from school and college, both were employed in Bangalore for US IT majors after graduating from IIT Delhi. Sachin explained, 'What excited us was the opportunity. Till 2006 or 2007, most people thought that e-commerce in India had already been done because there were ten e-commerce companies by that time. Binny and I first started thinking about building a comparison-shopping website. To build the website we needed to know what features to build in, so we went to talk to a few customers of these existing websites to know their thought process and what they thought the sites still lacked. But we could not find a single guy who bought anything from these ten websites. What we found was that there were a lot of people trying to do e-commerce but it was yet to really happen. We concluded that everybody so far was wrong and that we had found something new, which was essentially that technology could create a better customer experience. We believed that by bringing a combination of customer focus and a deep application of technology to the business we could make a big difference. That's what excited us.'

Getting going

One of the strong strands from the earlier entrepreneurial stories was the long struggle and slow build-up that many of the earlier entrepreneurs endured, very often changing course at least once along the way. For the later entrepreneurs, the New Generation, success was also not immediate or easy. However the pace is progressively picking up, and the cycle from launch to success, or from launch to pivot, is shortening. India is becoming an easier place to start and scale a business.

Parth Amin of SLK Software was convinced by the 1990s that 'software was the future of the world', and he knew this was the opportunity that he wanted to pursue. But up against the major Indian IT services companies, who were then seeking to broaden themselves after the Y2K spurt of activity, SLK Software found it tough, initially, to win business as its credentials were limited. At first they took sub-contracting work from a friend who ran a software business. More than a year after creating the company, on 11 September 2001, an otherwise bleak day for the US and the world, they were awarded their first contract from Emerson Electric, which they delivered well. However, it was the decision to focus on serving US-based banks that has underpinned their growth and competitive positioning. Like CitiusTech in healthcare, SLK Software has built deep expertise, a strong reputation and long-term relationships in a single specific sector: Financial services.

Micromax Informatics, now India's leading mobile handset maker and ranked tenth globally, was set up by four young friends in 2000, also as a software services company. The inflection opportunity, as co-founder Vikas Jain explained it to me, came in 2005. They secured the opportunity to work on machine-to-machine applications for Nokia for fixed wireless terminals, used mainly in India's then huge public call office (PCO) business. PCOs, essentially manned public phone booths, were on every street and in every village before the majority of the population got mobiles of its own. Initially, it proved to be a great business for Micromax and in the first year they did principally ₹10 crore (then $2.2 million) of business with Nokia. But Nokia suddenly decided to exit the business. The four founders reasoned that they had the competence to launch their own fixed wireless product under the Micromax brand, and achieved traction selling it to Indian telecom operators like Airtel, Vodafone and Idea. This business enabled them to develop a nationwide distribution and service business, including in smaller cities.

By 2008, however, the business was beginning to decline with the rise of wider mobile phone ownership and the consequent decline in PCO usage. Vikas credits his co-founder Rahul Sharma with pushing the idea that they could enter handset manufacturing against international majors like Nokia and the emerging Chinese players whose products were imported for the lower end of the market by telecom operators. At that time, at Tata, we had developed a huge supply chain from Chinese manufacturers like Huawei and ZTE Corporation in order to offer affordable handsets to subscribers. Other operators, most importantly Reliance, were doing the same. The key to Micromax's initial success was a simple market insight that had not been adequately addressed by the foreign phone designs. In much of India, electricity supply was unreliable, so longer battery life was a critical criteria for many users. By using a larger battery, 1,800 mAh rather than the standard 1,000 mAh, and reducing power usage by simplifying the phone's functionality, co-founder and CTO Sumeet Arora was able to design a phone that offered a 30-day standby battery life. Initially, Micromax phones were contract-manufactured in China and imported, though subsequently they have invested in manufacturing in India.

Like the Bansals of Flipkart, the founders of Fractal Analytics started with a business idea around comparison shopping. With ₹2 lakh from each founder and cheques from two friends in the US of about $10,000 each, they launched the business in early 2000. The exuberance of the dot-com bubble had infected India too. By March that year they had a term sheet from two of the senior people at HCL, one of the large IT services companies, who proposed to invest ₹3 crore ($660,000) in Fractal at a ₹9 crore ($2 million) pre-money valuation, good going for a pre-revenue start-up. However, negotiations broke down over the terms of the investment, in particular over the prospective investors' demand for board control. Shortly thereafter, the dot-com crash in the US soured the investment mood in India as well. Srikanth recalled, '[By] the next month everything collapsed, and six months later we realized that we had a product but we didn't have any money, and we'd already spent nine months without any salaries. We needed to figure out what else we could do.'

The team of five agreed to focus on analytics to support business decision-making. 'By January 2001 we had the business plan and we went to a few investors but, given the collapse in the market, nobody would listen to a new concept. Investors like predictability, they want to know that somebody has done this before and has been successful. We had great difficulty in explaining this idea of data analytics to anybody, even though we were looking for less than half a million dollars.' They pitched the value they could offer through data analytics to Onida, the television manufacturing business owned by the Mirchandani family, as a prospective customer. As often happens, the conversation went in an unexpected direction and, instead of a sales discussion, Onida became interested in making an investment, which was eventually agreed at $600,000. This was the first venture investment overseen by Sasha Mirchandani who went on to co-found Mumbai Angels and Kae Capital, one of India's first seed-stage funds.

At the urging of its new investors, Fractal focused on Indian clients over the next four years, a decision Srikanth now regrets as it led to a slower, if cheaper, growth path. Soon, they had Citibank India and then ICICI signed up as clients, followed by Hindustan Unilever. 'We had this notion that we should sell in India, be successful, and then go abroad. We wasted four years of our lives, which greyed my hair, trying to sell to Indian clients.' He contrasts this strategy with that of Mu Sigma, a competitor in data analytics, which started years later, but had a US focus from the beginning and scaled much more successfully.

Deep Kalra's MakeMyTrip also experienced only modest success in its early years. Deep told me, 'I was more focused on travel into India because I knew India itself wasn't quite ready. So I went to the NRI market in the US, guys who were already online, with the brand "India Ahoy". For the first five years, till 2005, we had no real B2C [that is, consumer] presence in India. We did launch in India in October 2000 but shut down within three months because we had lot of lookers and very few bookers.' Two things triggered the Indian B2C market from 2005, and made MakeMyTrip the travel major it is now. The first was the huge impact of Indian Railways's introduction of e-booking of trains on their IRCTC website. And the second was the launch of low-cost airlines, starting with Air Deccan in 2003, followed by SpiceJet and then finally the enormously successful IndiGo. The Indian consumer had been introduced to booking and paying online, not just looking. Deep went on, 'My proposition to the budget carriers was that I will be your lowest cost distribution channel, but in return I need your content.' Online travel agenting in India had finally arrived on a huge scale.

All four of the companies founded in 2000, therefore, experienced relatively slow growth early on and began to gain scale after some years of effort. The unicorn group also struggled to some degree initially, but their take-off was faster than that of the earlier group. Market opportunity, customer behaviour, technology and, as we shall see, financing, had all developed further during the decade from 2000, making it much easier and swifter to start-up a good business concept.

The smoothest launch was that of ShopClues, the youngest company in the group, founded in 2011. Sandeep Aggarwal's insights into the market and customer dynamics, as well as his ability to raise funds, combined with Sanjay Sethi's operational and technical expertise from eBay and Radhika Aggarwal's marketing skills, led to a very rapid ramp up. Sanjay and Radhika explained that their differentiation in a crowded market of websites was to be one of the first to offer a marketplace model, rather than an inventory-led e-commerce site. Furthermore, they focused on Tier 2 and Tier 3 cities rather than the metros and targeted the emerging lower middle class, especially the young. They enabled thousands of small suppliers to extend their market reach across the country. 'Rather than the mall-like experience of branded shirts and smartphones then offered by most of the other e-commerce sites, we wanted to sell the stuff that is available in Indian bazaars,' explained Radhika.

After rejecting their initial comparison-shopping concept, the Bansal duo launched Flipkart in 2007, initially selling books online. Sachin Bansal explained that the choice of books as a category was not to imitate Amazon, his former employer, but because books were easier to sell online in India in a number of practical ways. Once they received an order they could pick up a title from the wholesaler or another shop, so they did not have to hold inventory. India Post, at the time, could handle books but could not deliver other items reliably. Moreover, books could be shipped nationally without inter-state tax complications, and could also be imported duty-free. Business was slow to begin with. Sachin recalled, 'I wrote a piece of code to send me an SMS every time we received an order and sometimes we would just keep staring at the phone. We passed the time in a coffee shop waiting for the phone to buzz, but it didn't. The first three months, from October to December, were very tough. We used to celebrate when we got at least one order in a day.' The two men would stand outside bookshops handing out bookmarks with their logo and website address, and deliver books themselves in Bangalore. By early 2008 sales began to grow as word of mouth spread about the superior customer service offered by Flipkart. 'Whoever ordered from us was super-excited and would tell lots of people. Suddenly, I found there was a huge need, there are so many office-going people for whom it was a waste of time to go to a store to buy their books.' The launch of imported books in late 2008 added to the momentum.

InMobi's founder Naveen Tiwari's story is somewhat similar. On his return to India at the end of 2006, Naveen Tewari was not sure what to do. Staying with his sister in Delhi, helpful relatives tried to find him a job as, clearly, 'he had lost his way'. He declined an offer to work in a factory at a salary of ₹25,000 a month. With time on his hands, he began working on a business plan for a search engine for mobile phones. He showed the idea to a friend of his father, someone he respected, but this man told him it would not work. While driving back after the meeting, the same man called and said that he would introduce Naveen to a possible investor from Bombay. This turned out to be Sasha Mirchandani, the early backer of Fractal, who had just set up Mumbai Angels. Naveen was surprised when he met Sasha because Sasha did not fit his idea of an investor; he was a young man, casually dressed, and had long hair.

Sasha invited Naveen to come to Bombay to present his ideas to an early gathering of the newly formed angel group. 'So I went to Mumbai and in came ten people, old-economy people, and I talked about this whole mobile idea. They were laughing because they had no idea what this kid was talking about. They understood it was something to do with clicks, and clicks generate money, but they didn't know how clicks generate money. They knew there was a company called Google which made a lot of money by clicking.' Despite this generational chasm, InMobi became the Mumbai Angel's first investment and the group agreed to put in $500,000.

Within weeks, however, it was clear that the original business idea for InMobi, a search engine for mobiles, was not going to work. 'Six months in, we had spent half the money and it was clear that this was not going anywhere. We sat and discussed it for 18 hours one day, thrashing out the issues, and finally we agreed to shut it down. But then we said, do you think there is a possibility for an advertising play on mobile Internet?' InMobi was truly born in its second avatar.

Bhavish Aggarwal of Ola was under pressure from his parents to give up working for Microsoft and travel to the US for a Masters or a PhD. From his days at IIT Bombay, he knew that he wanted to be an entrepreneur but thought that he first needed work experience. After two years he decided he was done and it was time for him to try working for himself. He launched his entrepreneurial career in August 2010 with a business called Olatrip.com which aimed to sell short-duration holidays online. When I asked him about the origin of the name, Ola, Bhavish laughed. 'It's just an abbreviation, but that's private,' he said. 'You'd need to get me drunk for that story to be told.'

He continued, 'I started Olatrip.com in Delhi because the Commonwealth Games were happening there and the idea was to sell weekend breaks. But the Commonwealth Games were screwed up and nobody came, so I didn't sell a single trip. But I learnt a lot through trial and error, and shifted to Olacabs.com. The idea came to me because when I used to try to sell people these trips they said that they could figure out the hotel stays but they needed help booking a cab to get to Shimla or Mussoorie. And I said, okay let me put up a website for booking you a cab.'

Bhavish shifted from Delhi to Bombay and was joined as co-founder by Ankit Bhati, his friend from college, who focused on the technology back end. From a cheap flat in Powai they tried to match customers with rides – Ankit back in the flat, building the website, and Bhavish travelling the city by bus, local train and auto-rickshaw, signing up taxi operators. 'E-commerce was hot but our sector was not hot, so we started off very organically. In the first month we had one customer and in the second month we had four. Yes, one customer – and we were so excited! And the next month we had 10 or 15 customers, and things started looking up after that. But for six months we struggled to get the word out.' At the same time Bhavish was trying to raise equity, approaching everyone he knew. By mid-2011 he had managed to raise ₹30 lakh ($55,000) of angel funding, but only after being turned down frequently. 'Sasha [Mirchandani] – I pitched [the idea to him], but he didn't give me money. Kashyap [Deorah, another college friend and serial entrepreneur] turned me down. It was a bunch of individual angels, like the founder of Shaadi.com [who finally funded the business]. I met people in conferences and I pitched to them and some said, okay, I will give you ₹5 lakh, I will give ₹10 lakh.'

Founding teams

Listening to these stories of struggle and success, I became fascinated by the role that the dynamics within a founding group played. As a co-founder myself, I was sensitive to the potential complexities within a founding team. In each interview, I tried to probe the dynamics with which each founding team had developed. In some cases, one of the co-founders was clearly dominant. Parth Amin appeared to be the prime mover in SLK Software, as did Deep Kalra in MakeMyTrip. The default response, in most cases, was that the team worked well together and had their own clear areas of responsibility, but as in even the most successful marriage, the truth about intense partnerships is usually more nuanced.

Vikas Jain told me that at Micromax, 'There is a tremendous amount of comfort [with] and confidence in each other's capabilities. We define our work areas and there is no overlap'. Unusually, the founders of Micromax have swapped roles at various times. Sumeet Arora has always focused on technology and Rajesh Agarwal on manufacturing, but Rahul Sharma has recently taken over marketing from Vikas, who is now focused on the supply chain. The four founders share an office and have lunch together every day. They know enough about each other's areas to cover for each other if required, which must have proved critical after Rajesh Agarwal was forced to step back from the company for a while after being accused of involvement in a corruption case in 2013. They have tried several times to induct more experienced industry talent into the leadership team, but so far without success. Vikas observed, 'When you bring seasoned professionals into the company, they see what the founders have done and they create a personal target of bettering that.'

The ShopClues team also lost a critical member in 2013 when Sandeep Aggarwal was accused of insider trading by the FBI in the US. Sandeep decided that he had to step back from ShopClues to focus on his legal defence. Radhika explained, 'Sandeep got stuck in the judicial case and he stepped down from the company. The investors did not ask him to step out, he wanted time to focus on the case and it was a decision that was taken by the team together. Sandeep had the original vision, but the plan was set and each one of us owned our domains completely. One of the compliments that we got from the VC folks was that it was a very well-organized company. We were growing phenomenally fast. Now, having said that, for something like this to happen is a very big stumbling block and terrible in personal terms.' Sandeep clearly remains engaged with ShopClues to some degree, as Radhika put it 'around the dining room table', but after resolving his legal case he has now applied his extraordinary funding and start-up talent to the creation of a new business, Droom, an online marketplace for second-hand cars and bikes.

In January 2016, Flipkart announced a change of roles between Sachin Bansal and Binny Bansal, with Binny taking over the CEO role from Sachin, who in turn became Executive Chairman. The press speculated on the reasons for this change, pointing out Flipkart's mounting losses and that its legendary customer service had slipped somewhat. Sachin told me that he and Binny worked very well together. They had occasional disagreements but these were resolved quickly and rationally. Despite their similarities in background, including sharing the same home town, the same education, and the same family name, Sachin told me that he and Binny were different from each other in important ways. 'There are two kinds of leaders, right; two kinds of people who make decisions. There are people who start with a sense of what the decision should be and then they find data to validate or invalidate the hypothesis. The other kind of people are those who will assimilate massive amounts of data, just keep looking at it, and derive deep insights from the data. I do the first and he does the second.'

I asked if they shared an office, but the question revealed my old-economy background. 'We don't have the concept of an office. We attend meetings together. And we have this age-old thing that we call Wednesday dinners, when we meet. Sometimes other people are also there, but mostly it's just the two of us.'

Sachin went on to describe how they agreed that Binny would take over from him as CEO. 'I don't know why, but these super-critical decisions can be made after just an hour's discussion. I said that we perhaps needed to think about bringing in a different CEO. He said, how do you think I would do? I said, give me five minutes, and I just walked around. I came back and said, yes, that's a good idea. Why don't we discuss how it will work?'

There was a further change to Flipkart's management structure in January 2017 when Kalyan Krishnamurthy became the CEO of Flipkart, while Binny moved up to be Group CEO. The change was explained as permitting the two co-founders to dedicate more time to strategy and growth, by cutting down on the time they spent on operations. Given that Krishnamurthy came from Flipkart's biggest investor, Tiger Global, there was inevitable speculation about investor dissatisfaction with Flipkart's continuing losses. But more on that as we go along.

The most dramatic, and I thought the most honest, description of the issues that can arise between founders came from Srikanth at Fractal. Originally there had been as many as six co-founders, but one fell away early on in 2001. By 2005, Fractal was growing well and reached some $2.6 million of sales in 2006. The five founders had not clearly divided up responsibilities, so the shareholders (the Mirchandanis) suggested they should formalize things and appoint a CEO. Srikanth and Pranay Agrawal had recently moved to the US to build that market after years of ignoring it. So the five remaining co-founders met in London to agree on who should be CEO, and Srikanth found himself elected to the role, contested only by his close friend and current CEO of the services business, Pranay.

As Srikanth began to perform the role of a CEO, it resulted in conflict between him and some of his co-founders who, it turned out, preferred a 'coordinator' to someone acting as a real CEO. The eventual outcome was a proposal to split the business between two founder groups, an idea that Srikanth says he opposed strongly at first as 'if you cut a baby in two, you don't get two babies; rather, you get a dead baby.' Eventually he was persuaded – reluctantly – to acquiesce to the division. However, the details of the separation could not be agreed upon as the departing group were unable to settle terms with the investors, including on valuation. Two of the five left in 2007, resulting in acrimony and lawsuits, a mess that was eventually resolved only in 2009 when the remaining three founders reached a deal to buy out the two who had departed. Srikanth reflected, 'I think the biggest reason we are not ten times the size today is because we lost three years trying to get the situation back to square one. We were much bigger than Mu Sigma back then and we became smaller than Mu Sigma in those three years.'

Funding

None of these entrepreneurs has had an easy ride, but the tide of opportunity is clearly rising and starting a business has become progressively easier. The cycle of birth, struggle and rebirth, then success, is getting quicker over time. Other than market opportunity, one of the really critical things that has changed is the availability of venture capital and angel funding. The experience of the later unicorn companies in raising equity, despite many bumps and challenges, is clearly faster and easier than it was for the companies founded in 2000.

Among the group from 2000, Srikanth at Fractal was an early beneficiary of venture investing from the Mirchandanis of Onida. SLK Software never raised external funding and Parth is clear he never wants to, valuing the freedom and flexibility that results from pure family ownership. Micromax was launched based on ₹6 lakh invested from each of four sets of parents, and only inducted PE investment later as a secondary sale. But Deep Kalra needed external capital to build out and market his online travel idea.

Deep told me, 'The easy part was starting because I had a business plan. But I had no money, I probably had ₹50 lakh ($100,000), including my own savings and my wife's and what I could borrow. But I got e-ventures to put in $2 million. They were hungry for business ideas. Neeraj Bhargava found me, we met at Crossroads Mall in Bombay and signed our agreement on a napkin. I just trusted him.' However, in 2011, the Limited Partners (LPs) who had invested in e-ventures decided to liquidate the fund and Deep was forced to raise new money to buy them out. 'So I finally bought them out. We got back control of the company, this time the majority stayed with me, and the minority with two angels. They were great guys who stood with me through all of this crap. At no point at that time, between 2001 and 2003, did we have more than three or four months of cash, and at one point we had less than two months of expenses.'

MakeMyTrip subsequently raised a further $51 million in five rounds from 2003 onwards with SAIF Partners as the first investor who participated in all later rounds. Deep continued, 'Series A was SAIF Partners. I turned down Sequoia, or WestBridge, as they were then. The lesson I learnt [from the e-ventures experience] was to go with someone who was in control of the fund. Between SAIF and Sequoia, the only question I kept asking was who was the General Partner (GP), who is the guy that will call the shots? Ravi [Adusumalli][44] at SAIF is an awesome guy who clearly calls the shots.' MakeMyTrip did an IPO in 2010 on the NYSE at a valuation of $478 million.

Among the unicorn group of four, Bhavish and Naveen got angel support early on, as described above. Flipkart secured angel funding in two rounds in 2009 but was rejected by 20 VCs before Accel agreed to invest $1 million later in 2009. ShopClues raised a seed round of $1.8 million – 'Sandeep has money-raising charm,' as Radhika put it. Sanjay elaborated, 'Capital was very important and we would not have taken off without it. When we started, we had a term sheet for Kleiner Perkins for $5 million but they withdrew it when Amazon made an announcement that they would launch in India [Kleiner Perkins was an early investor in Amazon]. We had quit our jobs and were ready to go back to India. [At this time] Sandeep managed to raise about $1.8 million from former clients and friends. He hustled his way through the fundraise, doing four meetings a day. He would not walk out of there without a cheque in hand.'

The pace and scale of VC funding in India heated up dramatically from 2010. Based on data from CrunchBase,[45] to date Flipkart has raised $3.2 billion in 12 rounds (most importantly from Tiger Global, Naspers and Steadview), Ola has raised $1.2 billion from eight rounds (including Tiger Global, Softbank and DST Global), InMobi has raised $321 million from six rounds (Kleiner Perkins and Softbank) and ShopClues has raised $131 million from seven rounds (Nexus, Helion and Tiger Global).

---

44 See p. 1, 'A Long Struggle Rewarded: Vijay Shekhar Sharma'.
45 https://www.crunchbase.com/#/home/index

Naveen Tewari's tales of fundraising capture something of the quirks of the process – the importance of a good story, persistence and hard work on the one hand, and the role of timing and serendipity on the other. By 2008, InMobi's seed funding was running out and the business was kept running only through the use of the founders' personal credit cards. Twenty-one VC funds in India had turned down InMobi and the team was contemplating giving up, once again. A friend suggested that Naveen try to get funding in Silicon Valley instead. Naveen told me, 'One of my co-founders called this travel agency which takes care of senior executives and pretended to be my assistant. He said, my CEO wants to travel, we are looking for a very sophisticated agency who can take care of everything including the food and the car. We asked for the proposal by the end of the day but the only thing we were looking for was the payment terms. We took a first-class ticket because as a senior executive you can't travel economy. We were going bankrupt and I was travelling in first-class!'

Naveen continued, 'In the US I got more rejections, though the reason was no longer that we don't understand this space, as it was in India; it was that we [in the US] don't know you.' After a while Naveen was put in touch with Kleiner Perkins through an HBS contact. 'I was keen to go to their office as they had invested in Google, Intel and Amazon. We were pretty sure that we would get rejected there too.' The partner he met quickly agreed to invest, but said that he wanted to co-invest with Ram Shriram, the legendary early investor in Google. Naveen found himself presenting to Ram that same day, and he too quickly agreed to invest. 'Ram said, let's figure out the operating plan. I had no plan as it had been just about surviving for the past six months. Obviously I didn't tell him that, and I went through an hour's discussion of an execution plan for which I was completely unprepared.' Naveen walked out with a verbal agreement from Kleiner Perkins and Ram Shriram that they would invest $6–$7 million. That evening he sat in his rental car looking at the California sky, too stunned with this turn of fortune even to call his partners or his wife back in India.

InMobi's big funding round happened in 2011 from Softbank. They were looking to raise some $40 million, but had not thought to approach Softbank. A chance encounter caused by a delayed flight led Naveen to meet someone from Softbank who set up a meeting for him with Masayoshi Son, the founder and CEO of Softbank. Naveen explained, possibly disingenuously, 'I didn't know who Masa-san was. At that time he was better known in China and Japan. I made my pitch. He was listening. I told him that mobile advertising would be a $250 billion market by 2020. There would be Google and Facebook and globally there was space for five players in total. We certainly would be in that top five. He asked how much money we wanted. I said around $250 million. He said, that's a lot of money and for the next 30 seconds we negotiated. He brought it down to $200 million and I agreed.'

Ambition for scale

By the current decade, opportunities in India had developed massively and, unlike earlier, large amounts of capital were available for a good team with a convincing idea. The other critical change was in the level of ambition exhibited by Indian entrepreneurs. Young people were finally beginning to aspire to 'make a dent in the universe'.[46]

I met Vikas Jain of Micromax in the bar of a five-star hotel in Hong Kong, where he had just finished a talk at a *Wall Street Journal* conference. Other than India, Micromax was already selling in 12 countries and had just announced its intention to launch sales of handsets in China. I was staggered by the ambition and confidence this showed, an Indian phone maker intending to sell in China, the home of phone manufacturing. Vikas told me, 'If I am to get into the top five, there is no way I can't be in China. We have a vision that over the next four years we should be in the top-five club in mobiles. We are number 10 right now. It's a stiff climb from here.' This would mean displacing one of the market leaders – Samsung, Apple, Huawei, Xiaomi or Lenovo – from the current list by 2020.

Sachin Bansal of Flipkart is also not thinking small. He told me,

---

[46] 'We're here to put a dent in the universe. Otherwise why else even be here?' is a quote widely attributed to Steve Jobs, but it almost certainly is not a direct quotation. The words are spoken by the actor playing Jobs in the television film *The Pirates of Silicon Valley*.

'E-commerce is going to be massive in the country. The total market size last year was $10 billion and I think it will be $100 billion by 2020. We want to be the company that creates this market and makes it happen in India. And then we believe that what we create here will be relevant for the next 3 billion people [in comparable emerging markets] outside India.'

I challenged him by asking whether Flipkart really could lead the market over the long term given the competition from US and Chinese e-commerce majors, not to mention from other Indian players. Sachin argued that simply importing business models designed for the US or China would not work in India. 'China is like the Galapagos Islands and you'll find very different kinds of animals over there,' he argued, so e-commerce models developed for the Chinese market behind its Great Firewall would not transfer readily to India. This view differed sharply from that of Vijay Shekhar Sharma of Paytm, quoted earlier, who believes that China leads in the thinking on e-commerce systems. Sachin explained that India has its own peculiarities, including distribution challenges and unique consumer needs. He also suggested that India lacks some of the public goods on which an eBay in the US or a Taobao in China rely, such as the efficient parcel distribution of the US Postal Service or Chinese excellence in logistics. 'I think we have found creative solutions to some of these problems. For instance, cash-on-delivery is an example of an innovation we made to address the broken payment system in India. UPI[47] will be the next big innovation; it's a very Indian way of solving the payment problem.' He did not address my point that Amazon has redesigned its imported business model for the Indian market, including adopting Indian practices like cash-on-delivery, while Alibaba has invested heavily in both Paytm and Snapdeal, one of which could become its vehicle for entering India if its reported thinking of launching direct was to be abandoned.

Bhavish Aggarwal at Ola is similarly bullish about the future. He sees Ola as much more than a taxi aggregation company. 'We want to build mobility for the entire country. Mobility is a fundamental paradigm of any society because it enables freedom and choice. We look at mobility in a very

---

47   Unified Payments Interface (UPI) is an architecture and a set of standard app APIs introduced by the Reserve Bank of India to facilitate immediate online payments.

broad sense.' He explained that Ola was already offering auto-rickshaw and bus services. He illustrated the deep impact Ola was having on the country by the example of his own mother. When Ola was launched in Ludhiana, his mother was clear that she would not use it. Bhavish urged her to at least try it. 'I called her after a month and asked her, "Mom, what's going on? How do you do your grocery shopping these days?" She said, "Your Ola has changed my life. Now I can just press a button and the car comes in five minutes. I don't have to wait for your father to come home from [the] hospital and take me if the driver is not there. I don't have to deal with the driver's tantrums any more. I feel free. I can get around the city much better." I asked her, "What does the driver do now?" She said, "The driver has bought a car and is driving for Ola!" So we are giving people the freedom to move around cities easily, while at the same time creating gainful employment for thousands of micro-entrepreneurs.'

I pressed him on how he could remain competitive against Uber, given their global scale and enormous resources. Like Sachin of Flipkart, Bhavish argued that India was different, giving scope for a company like Ola to craft an offer more appropriate for the quirks of the Indian market. 'I respect what Uber has done globally, especially in the US,' he said. 'They have truly innovated, but innovation is always contextual. I think we are much more innovative when it comes to Indian grass-roots needs. Innovation needs to be broader than just a data science team.'

In December 2016, both Sachin Bansal and Bhavish Aggarwal made statements in public suggesting that Indian companies need more protection from foreign rivals. Sachin was reported as saying, 'What we need to do is what China did, and tell the world we need your capital, but not your companies.' Bhavish added, 'What's happening in both our industries [is that] there is a narrative of innovation that non-Indian companies espouse but the real fight is on capital, not innovation.' He went on to complain about 'capital dumping' while Sachin called for a 'more India-centric approach'.[48]

---

[48] http://economictimes.indiatimes.com/small-biz/startups/flipkarts-sachin-bansal-olas-bhavish-aggarwal-seek-governments-help-in-battle-against-foreign-rivals/articleshow/55862027.cms

The contrast between Manmohan's Children and the New Generation, and indeed within the New Generation between the earlier and later entrepreneurs, illustrates how much has changed in the Indian entrepreneurial ecosystem. From 2000, the velocity of change has accelerated, and the ease of creating and scaling a new business has sharply improved. That does not mean, of course, that entrepreneurs will not struggle, and it is in the nature of early-stage business that a large proportion will continue to fail. Taking the risk to do something new often does not work out. Yet, thousands of talented and driven people now seek to create their own businesses in India to offer better products and services, improve the lives of others and make money for themselves. Several factors have converged to trigger this change, the first of which – technological change – we will examine in greater detail in the following chapter.

Disrupting Decision-making

DHIRAJ RAJARAM

I was late for my meeting with Dhiraj Rajaram, founder of Mu Sigma, because the road from the Kampegowda International Airport in Bangalore was blocked by taxi drivers protesting against the damage Uber and Ola were inflicting on the traditional taxi business in 2016. For an hour I sat in a stationary queue of thousands of cars, held up by hundreds of drivers sitting on the road and shouting slogans. When the police finally arrived, a deal was reached with the union leaders to allow all except Uber and Ola cars through. A mob decided which vehicles would be allowed to pass. My car was hired from a taxi company, not Uber or Ola, but when it got to the front of the queue the leaders of the protest determined that we should not be allowed through. When I argued, I was threatened by a bandana-wearing man yelling in my face. An appeal to the police yielded nothing as they appeared unwilling to get involved. It looked like I would stay stuck on the highway all day. Suddenly, for no clear reason, the mood of the protesters shifted; someone pointed out I was a foreigner, tempers cooled and I was allowed through with handshakes, courteous smiles and good wishes. The kindness and courtesy of ordinary Indians, even in a heated situation like this political protest, continues to amaze me.

A while later, I watched Dhiraj, a short bundle of energy, bouncing around his huge office as thoughts tumbled out of him. He was very understanding of my lateness, saying that both the chaos and the humanity I recounted were examples of the complexity of India. 'It is full of dualities and paradoxes,' he said. 'The Indian ability to hold two opposing thoughts in mind at the same time [is remarkable].' He pointed to the image of Shiva hanging above his desk. 'Shiva is both creator and destroyer. But [he is] destroyer first, and that allows space for creation. He represents the fact that everything is in transience and will have to move away to create space for new things to come.' Most of the other pictures on Dhiraj's walls were of scientists and statisticians whose work underpinned the algorithms that have made Mu Sigma such a huge success in a few short years, the company growing much more rapidly than Fractal Analytics, as described earlier. Only the photograph of Einstein was recognizable to me, though there was also a large poster from one of the Iron Man movies and a quotation from Socrates.

Mu Sigma, with sales for the financial year 2015 reported at about $250 million, is one of India's unicorn start-ups. Its business is the analysis of 'big data' in order to support better corporate decision-making. Deepinder Dhingra, Head of Strategy and Products, told me that it is the largest pure-play data analytics company in the world with 140 of the Fortune 500 as clients and a staff of 3,500. Deepinder explained that the company's mission is to change the way corporates make decisions by combining the art of business analytics with the science of data manipulation and the scale of information technology. The contrast struck me forcibly between the chaos of India that I had experienced that morning in the taxi protest and Deepinder's explanation of the brilliant analytics that had taken Mu Sigma into so many leading American corporations.

'I never wanted to be an entrepreneur,' Dhiraj told me. 'I never felt the need to start my own company. I was more excited about solving a problem. I was obsessive-compulsive about an idea.' The inspiration which came to Dhiraj in 2004 when he was working at Booz Allen Hamilton Inc., a management consulting firm in Chicago, was that there must be a better way of making business decisions. He thought that management consulting thinking was too bespoke and expensive, while information technology was insufficiently flexible and agile. Instead, Dhiraj thought that he could 'change the world with a combination of math, business and technology coming together and doing it at a cost structure which would be one-fifth of the cost of management consulting and one half the cost of internal talent.' This he describes as his 'Iron Man model', nodding towards the movie poster on his wall, combining human thinking with machine scalability. The work for US clients would be carried out in India at a lower cost to achieve 'innovation arbitrage'.

'Our thinking has evolved from the realization that most so-called business intelligence is facile,' Dhiraj argued, waxing metaphysical in his rapid explanation. 'We like the phrase "organizational consciousness". Business intelligence is a form of seeking answers; consciousness is about asking better questions. Consciousness is never satisfied with itself, but is always seeking better questions and answers. Today, the West is crying out for consciousness because it is stuck in its own outdated intelligence. The West to my mind is extremely linear in its thinking, it is logical. India, by the very nature of its thinking, is Bayesian. This could be right, but that could also be right. This could be true, but that could also be true.' He waved towards a picture on the wall of a rather severe-looking Presbyterian divine whom I took to be Bayes.

The day we met had not been an easy one for Dhiraj. On the flight from Chennai I had read on the front page of the *Economic Times* that he and his wife, Ambiga Subramanian, were to get divorced. This difficult private family issue was further complicated by the fact that Ambiga was CEO of Mu Sigma and owned a significant share of the company. Dhiraj had held a town hall meeting that morning of senior employees to explain what was happening. He was clearly concerned about its implications for the business. His first decision was that he would need to return as CEO. 'The company is still at an early stage. I would say [that] for most organizations the founder CEOs are very hard to replace. In my case I was able to do that [step down in favour of Ambiga] but if a new CEO is somebody from outside, I will be sceptical about giving it up so easily. So I think that for the next 4–5 years I see myself being the CEO once again.'

For a while it appeared that Dhiraj's family issues were threatening the stability of the company. Dhiraj acknowledged that growth had been impacted to some degree while the leadership issues were resolved. There were press reports about concerns among the investors. Four months later, matters appear to have been resolved amicably with Dhiraj agreeing to buy Ambiga's stake, supported by external financing, taking him back to majority ownership. Both Sequoia Capital and General Atlantic confirmed their continued support of the company. In order to recharge the pace of growth, Dhiraj pressed through a corporate reorganization to split Mu Sigma into ten 'fulfilment units' led by a new generation of managers.

Born in 1975 in Mangalore, Dhiraj was brought up largely by his grandparents in Bombay. His grandfather was a stenographer at the *Times of India*, while his father worked for the RBI. He studied engineering at Anna University, in then Madras, before heading to the US for graduate studies at Wayne State

University. After a stint with PricewaterhouseCoopers (PwC) in IT consulting, he went to Booth School of Business in Chicago, graduating in 2003. He joined Booz Allen as a consultant, where his thinking about business decision-making coalesced into the idea that became Mu Sigma.

Dhiraj mortgaged the family home in Chicago to finance the creation of Mu Sigma. The first customer Dhiraj converted was Microsoft and the company started to grow as he was able to demonstrate that analytics could add value to clients.

The year 2008 was a time of crisis for the company as the US reeled from the financial turmoil that followed the collapse of Lehman Brothers. A pharmaceutical customer that represented 35 per cent of sales demanded that Mu Sigma should become exclusive to it, and that business was therefore lost. Dhiraj had raised money from a few angels and from Walworth, the investment company of the Ryan family, whose wealth came from founding the leading insurance broker, Aon plc. Walworth sought an exit at this time and it took Dhiraj some time to raise new money, first from FTV Capital and Sequoia, and later from General Atlantic. In 2016, Walworth was reported to have filed a suit regarding the price it recieved at exit in 2010, even though that was at a profit, alleging that the prospects of the company had been downplayed before it sold out and it had consequently lost 'hundreds of millions' in value. Reportedly, the suit attributed Dhiraj's 'perverse mindset' to his 'devotion to the Hindu deity Shiva the Destroyer, whose core philosophy called for destroying or selectively abandoning the past'.[49]

Dhiraj believes that people, or, in his words, 'differently wired people', underpin Mu Sigma's success. He seeks people with different backgrounds, people who can combine business analytics and applied mathematics, as he believes innovation occurs at the meeting point of different disciplines. Such people are not developed by even the best universities in India so he has created Mu Sigma University to train people in the skills he needs. Mu Sigma has just started recruiting in the US, and in the year 2016 had plans to hire 500 people there under its 'Columbus Programme' designed to attract, train and integrate young American graduates into an India-centric team.

---

[49] http://www.law360.com/articles/770022/aon-founder-says-he-was-cheated-out-of-mu-sigma-shares

'We are not building an Amazon of India, or an Uber of India, or an Expedia of India,' Dhiraj told me. 'We are building an original company. I think originality matters. To be original, you have to think about your narrative and your problem better.' Mu Sigma teams co-create with client teams to address specific business issues, a method he terms 'out-collaborating' rather than 'outsourcing', and at the end of a successful exchange the intellectual property rights to the solution are for the client to own and keep. Mu Sigma keeps ownership of the analytical tools and techniques that are created to solve specific problems and these can be applied across industries with pertinent adjustments.

Dhiraj is cautious about some of what he sees in India around start-ups. 'I would even say it can be negative to have people who just want to be entrepreneurs and start companies because, if they start a lot of bad companies, then the whole ecosystem goes for a toss. There's something of a bubble right now and some very simplistic thinking that the Internet will solve all of the country's problems. We have a whole generation of entrepreneurs who have been taught that valuation is far more important than value.'

His dream is to change the paradigm of corporate decision-making by lowering the cost of experimentation, and hence change the world. He clearly takes pleasure from being seen as a different sort of entrepreneur, a philosopher-king. 'You need the dreamer to be a little bipolar, and you need him to operate within the inter-temporal zone, and then suddenly move to the present zone, and then again move to the inter-temporal zone.'

While I was there, he suddenly changed direction, jumping up from his chair. 'Would you like to join my town hall meeting?' he asked as he rushed to the door. And so I found myself facing a different crowd from the taxi drivers who had almost made me miss my meeting with Dhiraj. I was in a room with about 400 Mu Sigma managers, and being webcast to the whole company. These super-smart analysts were not shy in shooting questions at their guest, as would have been the case in most traditional Indian companies. 'What do you think is the biggest challenge for us in India and why do you think we might fail in solving it?' 'What sort of apps are being created in China?' 'What feedback do you have about our company?' I escaped, as quickly as was polite, back to the Bayesian chaos of the India outside, leaving Dhiraj to face similarly probing questions on his personal life and what it meant for the future of Mu Sigma.

CHAPTER 4

Silicon Solutions to the Chaos of India

'The genesis of it was a crazy lunch with my ex-boss Jack Welch, when I went to his home in Boston and spent a couple of hours with him brainstorming about the world, technology and leadership. I told him that this is the challenge I see in this country where 300 million people live with no electricity, hundreds of millions with no water and a lack of healthcare. At the end of lunch, he says, why aren't you just doing it?'

Tejpreet Chopra, Founder, Bharat Light & Power

'There's a complete explosion of entrepreneurship. In the last 10 years, suddenly the barrier to enterprise has dropped, especially the technology barrier to enter has gone. Mobile phones and smartphones have become ubiquitous. And finally the dam broke because the social barriers have been broken.'

Nandan Nilekani, Co-founder, Infosys, and Chairman, Unique Identification Authority of India (UIDAI)

One of the many things I like about Saroja Yeramilli, founder and CEO of Melorra, is that she, along with other colleagues at Titan Company Limited, proved me wrong.

Like most people, I like being right about things. But it is also good to occasionally be proved wrong in a judgement, especially when you were sceptical about a new idea. As mentioned earlier, in 1999 I was doubtful about Titan's strategy to enter the branded jewellery market with the Tanishq brand. I saw the jewellery and gold trade as one of those typically complex traditional Indian businesses to which it would be hard to apply the ethos of modern design and manufacturing, and the concepts of branding and retailing. Indian consumers tend to have, I thought, an entrenched and conservative taste in jewellery and appreciate the highly individualized services of the traditional trade. Many Indian families have favoured particular jewellers over generations, partly out of fear of being cheated over the count of the gold offered. Moreover, a family jeweller would offer wealthier clients the convenience of being shown a selection of designs in their homes and much of the business would be transacted in cash. Despite all of this, Saroja was part of the team that made Tanishq one of the early successes on India's high streets.

Sixteen years later, Saroja and her recently launched Melorra jewellery brand embody many of the threads that have merged to create the entrepreneurial opportunity now emerging in India. Above all, she is demonstrating how the application of digital technology can address complex, fragmented consumer needs in entirely new ways. Technology offers many solutions to conquer the chaos that is India.[50]

Melorra, meaning 'forever young and beautiful', is a website offering affordable but fashionable jewellery. It is aimed at modern-minded women in India and abroad, a positioning Saroja calls 'the Zara of jewellery'. Rooted in a global sense of fashion, the website offers a great deal of insight and comment on the latest trends in New York, Paris and Milan. The company launches a new selection of pieces every week, although older designs can also be found in the archives of the website. None of the featured products physically exist when a customer browses the site; the images are all computer generated. A customer purchase online triggers the manufacture of the ordered design using a 3D printer and its rapid delivery through a courier. The business model combines a sharp focus on addressing the growing aspirations of a rising, international-minded middle-class consumer, interested in design and branding, together with the smart use of technology. Low inventory, prepayment and flexible manufacturing to order make for sound financials. The contrast with the traditional jewellery trade could hardly be starker.

---

[50] In many ways, the best book available that describes how to navigate India's complex business landscape without compromise is *Conquering the Chaos: Win in India, Win Everywhere* by Ravi Venkatesan, Harvard Business Review Press, 2013.

Saroja does not fit the stereotype of the New Generation Indian entrepreneur. She is a woman, she comes from eastern India, she did not attend an IIT, and was mid-career when she started Melorra. With her strong record of success in corporate life, with Titan, Marico and Dell, she could have secured a senior position in a large consumer-facing business after she had taken time out to work on Nandan Nilekani's unsuccessful election campaign in 2014. (Nandan stood for election on a Congress ticket in Bangalore, and despite his celebrity status as a co-founder of Infosys, he failed to be elected in the pro-Modi wave.) Saroja was encouraged to consider entrepreneurship by her husband, Shantaram Jonnalagadda, who has launched several ventures himself.

A chance introduction to Siddharth (Sid) Talwar of the VC firm Lightbox made her start putting her ideas on paper, and Sid coached and supported her for some nine months as the business idea developed. Saroja recalled, 'I asked them [Lightbox] for $2 million and they told me I was underestimating what it would take to build an e-commerce company, especially a brand, and that I should ask for $5 million, which they would give me.'

Technology and the chaos of India

'Opportunities for entrepreneurs abound in India, especially if you look for the pain points,' Pramod Bhasin, formerly of Genpact, told me. 'Suddenly people are realizing the opportunities in India, despite all of its issues. There are so many gaps, things that are available everywhere else in the world which you could bring here. E-commerce is just one of them but frankly it appears in every sector: Transportation, logistics, supply chain, healthcare, financial services…everywhere. It's incredible what's happening in financial services and healthcare delivery. I think it's very exciting because [there] were so many gaps and people are finding new solutions.'

At the core of so many of these new solutions lies the intelligent use of digital technology to overcome the challenges represented by what Narayana Murthy calls the 'frictions' of doing business in India, just as Saroja is doing at Melorra, Bhavish Aggarwal at Ola, or Sachin Bansal at Flipkart. India's success in the IT sector created its leading export industry and has attracted investment from the largest companies in the world. New ways of addressing some of the fundamental needs of the country are being born out of the skills honed by the IT sector and these offer huge opportunities for new entrepreneurs.

The focus on technology, especially digital technology, as a key booster of such opportunities, as well as a significant factor in reducing barriers to entry for new businesses, will inevitably impact digital entrepreneurs. Just over a third of the 92 entrepreneurs I interviewed were in the digital space, though, of course, almost all of them are applying digital technology in some form or the other to their businesses. My point is not that technology, digital and e-commerce, dominate Indian entrepreneurship. I believe that the new wave of entrepreneurship transcends sectors. Rather, the dramatic technological changes of recent years have been an important strand in the multiple changes that have freed entrepreneurial zeal. The discussion of solar entrepreneurship, another beneficiary of silicon-based technology, for instance, demonstrates how innovation in fields other than communications can have similar dramatic impact on the opportunities for new business.

In the West, identity is usually taken for granted, but it is not so simple in India. Years ago when we wanted our children's nanny, referred to in India as 'ayah', to travel abroad with us, she needed a passport. But without any record of her birth in rural Bengal this was not so straightforward and required much paperwork, including affidavits from relatives, a police certificate and a signature from a government officer to satisfy the passport office. Similarly, to take out a mobile phone subscription or open a bank account you need to prove your identity in increasingly complex ways. This has led to a whole industry of verification and background checks, including Footprints Collateral Services, whose founder, Director and COO Colonel Vijay Reddy, was one of my interviewees. This problem of identity, which is at the heart of much bureaucracy and fraud in India, is the issue that Nandan Nilekani, formerly of Infosys, sought to solve through the Aadhaar card scheme. Through this scheme, each applicant is issued a unique 12-digit number after his or her identity is established and biometric data collected. Starting in 2010, by the time of writing 1,120,112,468[51] Indians had been issued with a card, covering more than 90 per cent of the population.

---

[51]   https://portal.uidai.gov.in as of 24 February 2017

With identity established through the Aadhaar scheme, interactions with the government, banking, job applications and myriad other commercial contracts should become substantially easier and some of the frictions in India lessened.

Stimulated by administering the Aadhaar scheme, Nandan Nilekani now advocates the development of a series of comparable public goods, the so-called 'India stack' of IT platforms, enabling the private sector to offer solutions in a series of critical areas in which India lags. Nandan and Viral Shah, a serial entrepreneur and, for a time, a volunteer on the Aadhaar programme, explained their thinking in their book, *Rebooting India*.[52] As Nandan explained when I met him, 'The India stack allows you to completely change businesses and deliver everything through a phone, whether it's a bank account, a payment, an insurance policy or education.' Enabling such seamless transactions in multiple sectors would help streamline economic activity in much the same way as Uber and Ola have changed urban transport.

A retailing revolution, at last

When Jardines launched some of India's first organized retail chains in the 1990s, including Foodworld supermarkets, Health and Glow drugstores and Concorde Motors, we expected that well-run, large stores, supported by efficient supply chains, would rapidly revolutionize retailing in India. Today, modern organized retail, led by Kishore Biyani's Future Group, still only accounts for about 20 per cent of sales in India, compared to 90 per cent plus in most advanced countries. Yet, India is jumping with extraordinary speed to the online retailing of Flipkart and ShopClues, as well as more specialized e-commerce players. A recent McKinsey estimate valued the digital and technology industry in India at $110 billion today and suggested that the sector has created nearly half of the new formal jobs in India in the past 5 years.[53]

---

[52] Nilekani, Nandan, and Viral Shah, *Rebooting India: Realizing a Billion Aspirations*, New Delhi: Penguin Books India, 2015.

[53] 'India's Economy: Why the Time for Growth is Now', McKinsey Global Institute podcast, September 2016.

The persistence of traditional, apparently inefficient distribution and retail models, symbolized by small kirana stores or traditional jewellers, has many causes. International retailers tend to blame the protectionist policies of the government that still restrict foreign investment in retailing. However, India's physical geography and poor infrastructure have, almost certainly, played a more important role as, unlike in developed countries, it is difficult for consumers to travel any distance to shop given congestion in cities and poor roads in rural areas. The economics of retailing are further squeezed by the high cost of urban real estate and the hassle of a supply chain, further complicated by atrocious infrastructure and government impediments such as myriad regulations and multiple taxes. Mohandas Pai, co-founder of Aarin Capital, also formerly with Infosys, told me that logistics in India accounts for 14 per cent of GDP, compared to just 6 per cent in China and 5 per cent in the US, an indicator of how much India is disadvantaged by poor physical infrastructure. A truck can take five days to travel from Chennai to Calcutta (approximately 1,037 miles), given the state of the roads and repeated points of inspection and fee payment, compared to about two days in China or the US to travel the same distance. Most consumer businesses are forced by local taxation rules to maintain sub-scale distribution centres in each major state rather than consolidating into regional hubs, an inefficiency that the introduction of GST should help address.

Supply chain issues are particularly pernicious for fresh and perishable items. It is commonly estimated that up to 40 per cent of fresh fruit and vegetables are lost in the traditional supply chain made up of multiple middlemen, resulting in poor prices for farmers and poor quality and choice for consumers. Around 2000, Jardines's supermarket chain in southern India, Food World, developed a direct supply of fresh products from a number of villages with great benefit to consumers, farmers and the company itself as fresh food was delivered quicker and cheaper without the traditional tiers of middlemen. These structural issues persist today, but might now, at last, be addressed by new investment in cold chain and the application of technology. Kumar Ramachandran of GS Farm Taaza Produce, which was set up to modernize the fresh supply chain through technology, told me that, even now, the supply of fresh products remains the 'dirtiest business' with very weak controls over who is buying what and where it might end up. His platform is designed to address these issues, for the benefit of farmers at one end and retailers at the other.

Urban Ladder is another e-commerce business that solves problems for the new middle class through technology, as also through excellent design, affordability and convenience. It was Rajeev Mantri of Navam Capital who first told me about the company after he kitted out his new home in Delhi from the website that focuses on furniture and home furnishings. Inspiration for the site came when Ashish Goel, co-founder and CEO of Urban Ladder, and his wife were switching homes in Bangalore. Ashish recounted, 'We moved into our place in early 2011 and had a horrible experience trying to furnish the place through traditional furniture dealers. That was the trigger to realize the market opportunity and the consumer need in home furnishings.'

Ashish's background is more typical of a Bangalore tech entrepreneur than that of Saroja Yeramilli or Kumar Ramachandran – 'the classic IIT-IIM thing', as he termed it. Born and schooled in a small town in Uttar Pradesh, he was heavily influenced towards entrepreneurship by his years at IIT Bombay and the role models he was exposed to there. 'The biggest shift that happens at IIT is that your aspirations get reset. Suddenly, there are lots of people around you who are incredibly smart... I was just amazed with the world view of my classmates.' After IIM Bangalore, Ashish was 'clear that I wanted to be an entrepreneur, but very honestly I was a little under-confident'. So instead of taking the plunge into a venture immediately after college, he joined McKinsey and then did two general management jobs in the publishing business, first at Amar Chitra Katha and then India Book House.

Still wanting to be an entrepreneur, Ashish closely followed the clean energy business while still working, writing a blog on renewables – which also featured an entry covering our start at Kiran Energy – and toyed with the idea of starting an electric bike company. Then, in 2011, he left his job to start something, not knowing quite what, and persuaded his business-school friend Rajiv Srivatsa to leave Yahoo to join him. They worked first on an e-commerce idea around baby goods but found that the numbers did not work out. Then came insight into the market failures in furniture and the idea for Urban Ladder was born.

Unusually for a start-up, raising money turned out to be the easy part. Ashish knew Vani Kola at Kalaari Capital, a leading venture fund focused on India, and had shared the baby products idea with her. Once he and Rajiv had decided to focus on home furnishings, Vani invited them to present to the team at Kalaari. 'It sounds silly but it was 1 January [2012] when we decided to do the business; we did the presentation to Kalaari on 3 February, we had a verbal offer a week later and signed on maybe 20 February.' It was much more challenging to find product designs and suppliers. There was a furniture export fair in Delhi that Ashish went to in order to find suppliers. He had to sprint past the guard at the entrance to get in without a pass, but found that the exhibitors were not interested in a domestic start-up as a customer. He recalled that 'at least 120 of them refused'. Instead, at Vani's suggestion, Ashish went to Jodhpur, where he tried to contact 100 manufacturers, of whom only two responded. However, he achieved a breakthrough with one supplier and, even today, Jodhpur remains a major supply source for him.

Two things animated Ashish most during our conversation in his beautiful office filled with products from the website. The first was design, on which Ashish admitted to 'strong views'. He explained, 'I love working with designers. I mean I have a great time; that's the part I love the most, actually.' The second was when I asked him about innovation in the company, which he said was there 'by the bucketful'. The thing that brought out his enthusiasm in particular was a stair-climber they had developed, improving on a design from overseas. 'Imagine delivering a three-seater sofa in Indian building conditions in Bombay. The customer is staying on the thirtieth floor and the sofa doesn't fit in the lift. How is it going to go up? What we want is for one person to drive a truck to your apartment complex, open the truck door, press a button, the sofa comes down and the stair-climber machine takes it up the stairs.'

Urban Ladder is an example of a sectorally focused e-commerce company, of which there are multiple examples now in most sectors, from jewellery to pet supplies. At the other extreme are general e-commerce players like Flipkart and Snapdeal, and online marketplaces like ShopClues. Quikr is another e-commerce model. It started out as an online listing site, a combination of Craigslist and eBay, part media company, part online marketplace.

Pranay Chulet, co-founder and CEO of Quikr, sparked ideas and enthusiasm when we met in the boardroom of his new office campus, a converted textiles mill in Bangalore. Through the glass we could see the open-plan office, different levels linked with walkways, humming with activity like a healthy ant nest. Pranay's style is illustrated by his decision to move the company from Bombay to Bangalore in 2015 as 'the problems of Bombay as a city were getting in the way of our ambitions and we were not able to get enough engineers on the team'. About seventy people moved from Bombay to Bangalore and there are still 250 people left in Bombay, but essentially Pranay rebuilt his staffing in Bangalore, recruiting 1,200 new people.

He likened building Quikr to flying a fighter jet rather than a commercial plane, and said speed and innovation are critical. 'I am extremely bullish about the Indian Internet space in spite of the problems we are going through,' he told me. 'In the next four to five years our industry is going to go through a period of what I call violent growth; so there will be violence and there will be growth. There are no sacred cows and some companies that appear the coolest today may fail. Those that do succeed will be much, much bigger than they are today.' He reeled off a list of innovations he is proud of. These included enabling SMS chats in listings, introducing missed calls to book space and a mobile rather than website-based format.

After IIT Delhi and IIM Calcutta, and a short period in P&G in Bombay, Pranay moved to New York in 1996, and at first was in consulting. He quit his job in 1999, during the dot-com craze, and with three friends created a web-based company called Reference Check, focused on employment references, which was eventually taken over by Walker Digital. Pranay returned to consulting, joining PwC Consulting in 2002 and then Booz Allen Hamilton in 2005. In 2007, he took a sabbatical to make an interactive film, *Latent Lava*, which he describes as 'an amazing, incredibly ambitious, creative, crazy idea', and which he still carries on his laptop. While putting together a cast for the film, he found that he could readily recruit all of the actors for the US-based scenes on Craigslist, but in India there was no equivalent listings site. The gap led to an idea. In 2008, he and Jiby Thomas, who was previously with eBay, launched what was to become Quikr – originally branded Kijiji India – in collaboration with eBay.

From its start with online listings, which addressed the information failures of the old India traditionally exploited by brokers and middlemen, Quikr has now developed five verticals or sub-brands (QuikrCars, QuikrHomes, QuikrLearner, QuikrIntercity, QuikrJobs), offering marketplaces in cars, homes, jobs, services and eBay-like consumer-to-consumer transactions, with some 30 million unique users each month across these sectors. The verticals are marketed under the umbrella brand, Quikr, which Pranay said is 85 to 90 per cent of his cost.

Pranay has raised about $350 million in equity funding in seven rounds for Quikr. Clearly, he intends to be one of the winners in e-commerce in India and plans to return soon to the list of unicorns. The seriousness of his intent to build deep businesses in his five verticals has been demonstrated by the string of acquisitions Quikr has completed since we met. Under QuikrHomes they have acquired Commonfloor.com, Realty Exchange and realtycompass, under QuikrJobs they have bought Hiree, and under QuikrServices they have picked up Salosa.

E-commerce addresses through technology many of the issues that have held back the development of retailing in India, including the high cost of physical space and inefficient supply chains. Online commerce also blurs traditional business categories. Paytm, as we saw, started as a payment wallet, then developed into a marketplace, and may now become more like an online bank. Quikr, which began with advertising listings and was therefore in some respects a media company, encroached into InMobi's space as an online advertiser, and is now developing as a marketplace by enabling commercial transactions in sectors like real estate, cars and jobs that used to be handled by specialist brokers.

New technology, new media

Sharad Lunia's releaseMyAd uses technology to optimize a very old-fashioned business: classified advertisements in print media. Like retailing, the traditional media business is facing disruption as well as opportunity from the application of digital technology.

ReleaseMyAd is now one of India's largest advertising agencies, even though it offers little that a traditional agency would do. Based in a modest office building in Salt Lake, Calcutta, Sharad's was my only interview in the city – one of my favourite places in India, but well behind the other metros as a start-up hub. In most countries, print media is in decline due to the impact of electronic media, but not in India. The government estimated a daily average readership of newspapers and magazines of 450 million in 2013–14, which has grown at a compound rate of 13 per cent over 10 years, much of the growth coming from publications in Indian languages rather than in English.[54] With very low purchase prices of printed editions, most of this huge industry is financed by advertising. Classified ads remain the most important channel for many communication needs for both consumers and businesses.

Sharad is from a Marwari family in Calcutta, where his father ran a local advertising agency. He went to Wharton and, on graduating in 2006, worked in New York for Microsoft in their digital advertising group. His plan was to learn and then return to India to set up a digital advertising agency. He came home in 2008 to work on the digital agency idea with two friends from Microsoft. However, it soon became clear that India was not yet ready for a digital agency, particularly in Calcutta. Instead, Sharad spotted an opportunity to make it easier to place an advertisement in print newspapers through a website, starting with the volume categories of matrimonial, property and recruitment advertisements.

ReleaseMyAd offers convenience to individuals or small businesses in designing and placing an advertisement in any language and in any city in the country. It cuts out the traditional chore of visiting a newspaper office, standing in line and filling out a form. Sharad explained, 'Think about the hassle of going to book a ₹2,000 advertisement in the *Telegraph* [Calcutta's leading English daily], standing in line and not even knowing how the ad will look in print. Through releaseMyAd, the consumer gets convenience at the same price. And if you are in Delhi and you want to release an ad in Calcutta in *Anandabazar Patrika* in Bengali, how can you do that unless you use us?' He received his first booking for an ad on Valentine's Day in 2009; now releaseMyAd places 150,000 ads a year and is on track to achieve a revenue of ₹75 crore ($11.4 million) in the 2017 fiscal year.

---

54   https://data.gov.in/catalog/claimed-circulation-registered-newspapers-and-publications

This volume has now secured it media-buying power with the newspapers. Larger clients with big budgets and seeking display advertisements have also begun to use the site as releaseMyAd has become a major aggregator of offline advertising.

I was impressed by Sharad's hard-nosed, clear thinking. 'Strategy is choice,' he remarked. His decision to return to Calcutta rather than basing himself in Bombay or Bangalore, in part at least for family reasons, is a choice with implications for the business. He has a profitable, growing business yet has never contemplated raising external money and has no interest in selling part of his company despite various approaches from VCs. He is satisfied with the scale of his business but is also beginning to think about what to do next. I assumed he would be thinking about online advertising, but instead he observed that 'there is a lot of interesting inventory with media potential which has never been aggregated', such as restaurants, fleet vehicles, or elevators in buildings. Could a platform be developed to place media in these opportunities?

Digital technology has lowered the barrier to enter into media, as in other sectors, for people with ambition and new ideas. 'If Raghav Bahl[55] or Prannoy Roy[56] were to start again today, would they do it the same way with all that legacy of infrastructure, plant and machinery [of a traditional television network], or would they go digital?' asked Prashanto Das, co-founder of PING Digital Broadcast Network. He and his co-founder, Govindraj Ethiraj, were crammed into a small room with me at their studio in an old mill building in mid-town, Bombay. Both are long-time professionals in television: Prashanto works on the production side and Govindraj is one of India's better-known business journalists.

They met at Bloomberg UTV and in 2012 decided to launch their own multi-channel network, largely hosted by Google and YouTube. PING creates and aggregates digital video content and already puts out much more volume than any traditional network, offering 1,500 channels focused on knowledge and utility areas such as food and news, with 45 million hours a month of consumed content. Ninety per cent of their viewership is

---

55   Bahl founded TV18 in 2007, which he sold to Reliance Industries in 2014.
56   Roy founded NDTV in 1988.

outside India, particularly in countries like Turkey and Vietnam, and largely consists young people. Other than their ability to create and distribute niche content at a much lower cost, they stressed the importance of special-interest communities to their business. 'Television is just one-way communication, where you view only what is on. Content is now more democratized by digital. Today, we see traction because we have built huge communities with good two-way conversations,' Prashanto explained. Prashanto and Govindraj have raised ₹4.3 crore ($630,000) so far from angel investors to build PING into a business they expect to be about ₹45 crore ($6.8 million) in turnover in the fiscal year 2017. They are now seeking a bigger fundraise in order to expand further and faster.

Educating at scale

One of the greatest challenges faced by India is the quality of education offered outside elite schools and colleges. Although the key source of the competitive edge for India on a global platform is substantially based on its deep pool of educated, skilled, English-speaking people, and the tremendous impact of elite education in institutions like the IITs and IIMs is clear, there is another side to Indian education.

The Nobel laureate Amartya Sen has repeatedly exposed the failure of the state-run education system in India, which he and Jean Drèze described as 'horrifying' in their book *An Uncertain Glory*.[57] They relate how a survey of the state schools of one north Indian state found no teachers present in half the schools. Sen has remarked that India must be the only country with the absenteeism problem in schools being of teachers, not pupils. I recall an occasion some years ago when, visiting a friend in Delhi, now a minister in a state government, I found him without his driver. He told me that his driver had a menial yet secure and well-paying position in a school in his home state which he had sub-contracted out. Sometimes the driver had to rush home from Delhi if there was to be a school inspection and he was required to be present. It is no wonder that Indian parents from modest backgrounds scrimp to send their children to private schools.

---

[57] Sen, Amartya, and Jean Drèze, *An Uncertain Glory: India and its Contradictions*, New Delhi: Allen Lane, 2013.

Without a substantial uplift in the broad education system, India will not create the million jobs a month it needs to in order to employ its increasing young workforce. Digital technology has a key role to play in improving and supplementing education throughout India, but most especially in remote and rural areas.

Edutel is a Bangalore-based company that supplies teaching broadcasts via satellites operated by the Indian Space Research Organization (ISRO). In 2016, Edutel expected to reach 1 million children, mainly in the state schools of Karnataka. Edutel was set up by two brothers from a modest background in Hubli: Harsha Mahabala and Soorya K.N. While at M.S. Ramaiah Institute of Technology (MSRIT), Harsha developed an algorithm that compresses data in order to send it across a network more efficiently, using one-twentieth the bandwidth required by a normal television broadcast. Originally, the brothers tried to exploit this technology through a software company, Gumbi Software, but in 2010 they switched to offering educational content and launched Edutel.

By 2016, Edutel employed 680 people, including 150 academic staff, with a further 150 academic staff on contract. Each hour of broadcast required 240 man hours of course preparation. Harsha took me to see the content being developed on several floors of an old cold-storage unit in Bangalore. Through the heavy steel doors of the former refrigerated storage, in a meeting room, a group of teachers was developing a script for a fifth-standard math course, while in the studio next door a programme was being delivered to camera. In the open-plan office, scores of programmers were developing animations to complement the lessons. The company currently offers course material for fifth- to tenth-standards students in math, science and English, as well as for preparation for the exams in the twelfth standard, all delivered to state schools. They also offer vocational courses on a fully commercial, non-governmental basis.

The focus on education delivered through government schools has limited Edutel's ability to raise VC funding. Two funds that had expressed interest and proposed term sheets withdrew once they fully understood the overwhelming dependence on the government as a customer. This caution is not without reason as Harsha explained how long it takes to sell the content to state education departments. He has been trying for more than a year to extend from Karnataka into Andhra Pradesh, without making much headway so far. The programmes in state schools are free at the point of use, so revenue principally depends on payment under government contracts, supplemented by the commercial vocational courses and the limited number of private schools enrolled. The scale-up in recent years in Karnataka has been funded by an investment of $2 million from the Michael & Susan Dell Foundation in 2014 and loan support from the Emami Group. Harsha told me that the outcomes achieved have been independently monitored by a team from IIM Bangalore. They have reported a 53 per cent reduction in failures compared to the control score, that is, the percentage of students not getting qualified, and an 18 per cent increase in learning levels achieved.

Zishaan Hayath runs a very different, but equally impressive, education company out of an office in Powai near the Hiranandani development in the suburbs of Bombay. 'Education is huge in India and it's a super-critical need for most families; it's your only ticket to a better lifestyle or out of poverty,' he rightly pointed out. After IIT Bombay, Zishaan had, with Kashyap Deorah, co-founded Chaupaati Bazaar, a phone-based venture which they sold to Kishore Biyani as the basis of Future Group's online business. After leaving Future Group in 2012, he and an ex-colleague, Hemanth Goteti, conceived Toppr, a web-based coaching company. Toppr now has 1.1 million students on the platform. Ninety-five per cent of these users access the platform for free, while 5 per cent chose to upgrade to the paid subscription premium service at ₹400 per month. Remarkably, 55 per cent of its users are in rural India and more than half access it from a mobile phone rather than a computer.

Zishaan explained that there are two key features that mark Toppr out. First, they have developed half-a-million learning modules for standards eight to twelve. The industry benchmark would be a cost of $10–$12 per module, but by developing a technology platform the Toppr team has created a community capable of developing quality-controlled modules for less than $1 each. Second, they wrote algorithms which deliver an individualized experience for each student as the system adapts to their performance. If they get a problem wrong, or are too slow, the system presents them with another similar module – and, as they learn, the difficulty of the problem sets are progressively increased.

Toppr measures outcomes in real time, principally the speed and accuracy of completing the modules. On average, they have found that their students achieve an improvement of 33 per cent in speed and an increase in accuracy from 55 per cent to 71 per cent.

With a web-based model being easier to scale, and no government dependency, unlike Harsha's Edutel, Toppr has been well funded by VC investment. In the first year the founders carried the business supported by some angels. Then they raised a first round of about $1.5 million in early 2014 from SAIF Partners and Helion, and then a larger round in 2015 of about $10 million in which Fidelity Ventures joined. Zishaan has become a very active angel investor himself in recent years with a loose group of friends he calls Powai Lake Ventures. He has invested to date in 34 companies. His first cheque was ₹2 lakh for Ola, in a round sized at ₹35 lakh, just as Bhavish was starting. I suggested he should cash in and retire. 'Yeah,' he laughed. 'I think I should call him up today. That's decent money to retire. But think, what would I do if I retired?' Not all investments work out quite as well; his second cheque for ₹42 lakh on behalf of his investing group was to Housing.com, a company which has been troubled by issues widely covered in India's business press.

Digital technologies have offered new opportunities to entrepreneurs to solve challenges facing traditional services like retail or education, and to threaten disruption to established sectors like media. A different type of silicon technology, solar power, offers a ray of sunshine in the electricity sector in India.

New technologies in infrastructure

I recall a teacher in my prep school in the early 1970s rubbishing the long-lasting technical breakthroughs that had emerged out of the billions of dollars that were spent to put a man on the moon in 1969. 'The only things that came out of it were the non-stick frying pan and the hand-held calculator,' he fulminated. Yet the silicon chip developed for the space programme spawned the computing revolution that has transformed our lives and the digital technologies that are now helping to conquer the chaos of India across multiple sectors. One other spin-off of the space programme was the solar panel, also principally, like the computer chip, a silicon-based product.

Infrastructure weaknesses have long dogged India, adding to the cost of business. Principal among these infrastructure failings has been a shortage of electricity. India has failed for years to build enough generating capacity to meet the needs of its growing economy, to connect supply and demand through a robust grid and cement a sustainable business model to pay for it. Solar power, originally developed for space applications and for years considered entirely uneconomic for volume generation, has emerged recently as a major contributor to solving India's unmet hunger for power, and to do so in an environmentally friendly way.

My own entrepreneurial journey started in solar power when, together with Ardeshir Contractor, I co-founded Kiran Energy. For this book I also met with Sumant Sinha, founder, Chairman and CEO of ReNew Power, and Tejpreet (TP) Chopra, founder, President and CEO of Bharat Light & Power (BLP). Kiran, ReNew and BLP are all principally focused on large-scale, grid-connected projects, so to get a different perspective I also interviewed Abhinav Sharan, founder and now Director of Aura Renewable Energy, which offers solar solutions in off-grid, rural markets.

Since the economic reforms started in 1991, successive governments have identified investment in infrastructure, roads, ports, airports, railways and power as a critical driver of economic growth. In the annual Budget, finance ministers from all parties have claimed plans for greater investment in infrastructure. From the Rakesh Mohan Report (or India Infrastructure Report) of 1996[58] to Deepak Parekh's two reports of 2007 and 2014,[59] experts have urged the government to invest more in infrastructure and

---

[58] 'The Rakesh Mohan Committee Report on Transport Development' submitted by the Expert Group on Commercialisation of Infrastructure Projects 1996, chaired by Dr Rakesh Mohan, former deputy governor of the Reserve Bank of India.

[59] http://www.pppinindia.com/pdf/deepak_parekh_report.pdf and http://planningcommission.gov.in/sectors/ppp_report/3.Reportsper cent20ofper cent20Committieesper cent20&per cent20Taskper cent20force/1.Second-Report-High-Level-Committee.pdf

to permit the private sector to invest more. A $1 trillion investment deficit has been widely touted.

No doubt, some progress has been made. Liberalization and mobile technology has transformed telecom. Indian airports have improved, albeit slowly, and now both Delhi and Bombay have world-class terminals, even if runway capacity, air traffic control systems and ground connectivity remain challenges. Atal Bihari Vajpayee's 'Golden Quadrilateral' policy, launched in 2001, aimed to deliver modern multi-lane highways linking the major metro cities of Delhi, Bombay, Chennai and Calcutta with four or six lane highways. The current government claims the construction of 20 kilometres of new roads a day. Yet the pace has been too slow and patchy.

Power has been one of the more problematic infrastructure sectors in terms of reform and growth. Reliable and affordable electricity is clearly needed for economic growth and demand is sure to rise at least in line with GDP. In 1991, power generation, transmission and distribution were largely the preserve of the public sector, with a few private-sector hangovers from pre-Nehruvian days like Tata Power in Bombay and the Calcutta Electricity Supply Corporation. The distribution of electricity was a state, rather than central, question, so every one of India's states, 29 now, plus seven union territories, had their own policies, pricing and electricity supply systems. Political pressure to under-price power, particularly to favoured groups like farmers, high transmission losses, outright theft of power and non-payment of bills, all contributed to a parlous financial position of the state-owned power companies.

The result of these policy failings was a severe power deficit, particularly in certain states and during peak times and seasons, and widespread 'load-shedding'. Much of Indian industry and commercial activity was dependent on expensive, polluting diesel back-up generators. When I visited the world-class and world-scale JCB digger factory in Ballabhgarh, Haryana, in 2013, I was told that more than half of their power needs were fulfilled by their own diesel gensets, and the cost per unit of this polluting power was more than twice the price of grid power.

Things have changed considerably for the better since 1991. An independent system of regulation, led by the Central Electricity Regulatory Commission (CERC) but with regulators in each state, was created by the Electricity Act 2003. The regulators have introduced power markets and power trading. The state power utilities have been unbundled into generation, transmission and distribution companies. Private sector investment, including from overseas, has been encouraged, particularly in generation. However, problems have persisted and results have been slow, while the growth of the economy has only added to demand. In July 2012, most of northern India was subjected to a massive blackout over several days when the northern grid suffered multiple failures at the peak of summer, leaving more than 700 million people to swelter in the humidity and heat.

The Planning Commission, abolished by the Modi government in 2014, used to produce an *Annual Report on the State Power Utilities and Electricity Departments.* The 2014 Report recorded a generating capacity in the country of 228 GWs, 68 per cent of which consisted of thermal coal-based units. At peak demand, the generation deficit in the previous year was as much as 9 per cent. Key factors behind this included the financial health of the state electricity distributors, which had a combined revenue deficit of ₹67,956 crore ($10 billion) in 2013–14, unreliable coal supply, especially from the nationalized monolithic Coal India, and the challenges faced by the private sector in constructing and operating power plants.

Most international power companies, with the notable exception of Hong Kong-based China Light & Power (CLP), had given up on India as just too difficult and risky. Even local companies struggled. I recall working with Tata Power on a strategy review in 2005, which identified both the opportunities and the huge challenges in bidding for supply contracts, and then securing all the permissions and inputs to construct a power plant. Tata Power won the bid for the 4GW Mundra Ultra-Mega project which ended up as a major crisis for the company when the cost of imported coal spiralled after a minimum export price was imposed in Indonesia and this could not be passed through in the fixed tariff. CLP's 1,320MW Jhajjar coal-fired power station was commissioned in 2012 but suffered severe problems in enforcing coal supply contracts; in its first year of operation it achieved a Plant Load Factor of just 42 per cent as a result of the lack of coal. In the power sector, as in other areas, the national need for reform and investment was clear, the good intentions of policy-makers were explicit, but the complex interaction of vested interests and competing state actors resulted in maddening impediments, project delays and levels of risk to deter all but the boldest investors.

The development of the solar power industry from 2010 is an example of how technological change, the availability of capital and sound government policy-making can combine to offer entrepreneurs the opportunity to make a significant difference. By November 2016, India had an installed capacity of solar power in excess of 10GW, adding 3MW in the year to March 2016, and was emerging as one of the largest solar markets globally. Although only 3 per cent of India's installed generation capacity, and a much lower share of electricity output given the plant efficiency ('capacity factor') of about 20 per cent, solar has become the fastest growing generation source. India's excellent insolation, more than 200 days of sunshine in many regions, makes solar a perfect technology for India.

Government policy has been forward thinking and supportive of the emerging solar industry. Starting work in preparation for the Copenhagen Conference on Climate Change in 2009 (COP 15), the Manmohan Singh government announced the National Solar Mission (NSM) in 2010 with the target of achieving 20GW of solar generation by 2022. The incoming Modi government in 2014 raised the target to 100GW. Core to the NSM was the procurement by the central government – initially through the National Thermal Power Corporation (NTPC) and later the Solar Corporation of India (SECI) – of solar power through a series of competitive tenders. These auctions were administered with great efficiency and effectiveness by NTPC's subsidiary, NTPC Vidyut Vyapar Nigam (NVVN), and achieved costs per unit lower than expected and which fell rapidly from round to round. In 2011, CERC estimated the fair cost of solar power at ₹17.91 per kWh. The first round of NSM bidding that year produced winning bids at or below ₹9.44 per kWh. In the round of bidding in November 2015 winning bids had tumbled to ₹5.37 per kWh, and in a round in June 2016 winners were below ₹5, although on a different basis including a capital subsidy.

While the central government drove NSM as its prime policy initiative, the electricity regulators also played a critical role. In 2011, CERC announced that all utilities would need to fulfil Renewable Purchase Obligations (RPOs), with a specific target for solar which would progressively increase to 3 per cent by 2022. RPOs could either be achieved by the generation or purchase of green power or by acquiring tradeable Renewable Energy Certificates (RECs) on a power exchange.

Prompted by the central government, as well as the CERC and state regulators, state governments developed solar policies and state electricity utilities began to invite bids for solar power. Gujarat was the leading state in the race for solar until 2015. Then Rajasthan, with its advantages of better sunshine and plentiful desert land, pulled ahead. As chief minister of Gujarat, Narendra Modi had advocated action over climate change for some years, set up a state Department of Climate Change in 2009, and released a book on climate change in 2010 entitled *Convenient Action*.[60] Gujarat announced its solar policy in 2010, separate from and seemingly competitive with that of the central government, and proceeded rapidly to contract for nearly 1GW of solar power in two rounds of applications.

Ambitious and well-constructed policies alone would not have brought solar power into the mainstream of Indian electricity supply. What was needed was dramatic technological change. From Bell Lab's first photovoltaic (PV) cells for the space programme in the 1950s, solar PV has typically been seen as an expensive source of generation for specialized off-grid applications. As cell efficiency has improved and the scale of manufacturing has increased, the delivered cost of energy per kWh has fallen progressively, at an average per annum rate, or 'learning curve', of about 7 per cent. The introduction of feed-in tariffs, essentially a subsidy, in Germany from 2004 and the consequent massive expansion of supply in China transformed the market. The resulting boom in investment in capacity and consequent overcapacity among suppliers of solar modules has driven intense competition, causing the prices of solar panels to tumble.

In 2009, when Ardeshir Contractor and I co-founded Kiran Energy, we judged that, given the supportive trends in both solar economics and the policy environment, grid parity, at which solar power would become a competitive source of generation in India without government subsidy

---

[60]   Modi, Narendra, *Convenient Action: Gujarat's Response to Challenges of Climate Change*, New Delhi: Macmillan, 2010.

or incentive, could be expected to be achieved well within a decade. The potential opportunity for solar power in India was therefore enormous. Furthermore, solar plants can be constructed relatively rapidly, raise fewer environmental issues and require far fewer permissions and interconnects than do most infrastructure businesses. A plant can be designed, financed, permitted, constructed and commissioned within a year, compared to multiple years for a traditional power plant. Once we had closed our first equity raise in mid-2010, we were able to ramp up the business quite rapidly, winning projects under both the Gujarat state policy and then multiple successful bids under the central NSM scheme. We then turned our focus to selling power to corporate customers through the open-access regime, which permitted the transmission of power to a customer through the grid.

The growth of Kiran Energy was not without challenges, of course. Acquiring land, securing the right of way for our connection to the nearest substation and achieving the regulatory sanctions we required were often more challenging than they should have been. For our first plants, for instance, no one was entirely clear what permissions were required for a large solar plant. One regulator insisted that, as a power plant, we should secure a No Objection Certificate (NOC) from the superbly named Chief Controller of Explosives, an officer based in Nagpur, even though there is nothing explosive in a solar plant. The commissioning of our first unit was delayed by a day or so after our connector was severed by a back-hoe loader digging for a competitive facility. Another project encountered a challenge when an inspector insisted on a bespoke design at the point of connection at a substation. We worked hard at maintaining the goodwill of local communities around our plants through an active engagement effort and support of social projects.

Such challenges were overcome by the hard work of a strong team. India might have the reputation as being a tricky place in which to build new infrastructure, but our experience was that well-planned solar projects can be financed and implemented on budget and on schedule to the highest international standards of engineering and business ethics. Given our experience and credibility, we were able to develop a distinctive business based on a network of strong partnerships, a positive approach to interaction with policy-makers, an ability to execute projects and a competitive edge in financing. We were among the first to structure genuinely non-recourse project financing[61] of Indian infrastructure projects and succeeded in attracting project debt from leading Indian and international banks and institutions.

Kiran Energy is one of a number of start-ups that were launched to take advantage of the new opportunity in solar power created by the benign interaction of falling costs, evolving technology and supportive government policy. The stories of a number of our competitors parallel our experience.

Sumant Sinha's ReNew Power has now crossed 1GW of renewable capacity in wind and solar power. Son of Yashwant Sinha, a former minister of both finance (1990–91; 1998–2002) and external affairs (1998–2002) in India's central government, and brother of Jayant Sinha, currently a minister of state in Prime Minister Modi's government, Sumant studied at IIT Delhi and IIM Calcutta, followed by a Masters at Columbia. After a short stint at the Tata Group, most of Sumant's career has been spent as a banker in Citibank in the US. He returned to India in 2002 to join Aditya Birla as Group CFO. He got his first exposure to renewable power when Tulsi Tanti attracted him to join Suzlon, one of the largest manufacturers of wind generation equipment in the world, as CEO in 2008, where he quickly found himself trying to restructure a hugely overstretched business. He left Suzlon in 2010, initially to create Savant, his own advisory firm. By the end of that year, though, he had established ReNew Power, initially to focus on wind generation.

Sumant described execution as the most difficult challenge. 'Dealing with local elements across the country, I realized that a large part of India suffers from a significant law and order deficit. There is little local administration and you can't expect to get any help from the local political systems.' Sumant credited professionalism and persistence for the company's ability

---

[61] Non-recourse debt is extended by the lender based on an assessment of the projected cash flow and risks of a project rather than based on any sponsor support or other security. As such, it enables projects to secure financing with an acceptable balance sheet and without a backing entity.

to execute projects. 'From the beginning, I took the view that I wasn't going to pay money to anybody or accept money from anybody. Over a period of time it helps to build a reputation that this company does not do anything that is corrupt or morally inappropriate.' Where ReNew and Sumant have excelled has been in securing equity backing of both size and quality. Starting with support from Goldman Sachs of $200 million, ReNew has now raised $650 million in four rounds, including participation from marquee investors like Asia Development Bank (ADB) and Abu Dhabi Investment Authority (ADIA).

Tejpreet (TP) Chopra is another mid-career entrepreneur who created a solar power developer. TP had been the India head of GE and was encouraged by his interactions with Jack Welch and C.K. Prahalad to think about solving big problems at 'the bottom of the pyramid' in India. His first interest was clean water, but he was unable to develop a workable business model as people appeared to be reluctant to pay an economic price for water. So, given his experience from GE, he refocused on renewable energy, setting up Bharat Light & Power (BLP) in 2010. He now has more than 100MW of solar constructed and, he told me, a project pipeline of a further 400MW under development. His financing strategy has differed from that of Kiran or ReNew in that he has raised limited PE or VC backing in BLP itself, but instead has two joint ventures with overseas majors, with Enel for grid-connected projects and Statkraft for off-grid. A further twist to his strategy has been to develop a capability of remotely operating and optimizing renewable plants around the world as a service to other owners.

Abhinav Sharan, founder of Aura Renewable Energy, represents a younger generation of solar entrepreneurs. 'I switch frequently from India to Bharat. Delhi and Bombay are India, Patna and rest of Bihar are Bharat. The ability to talk [in] English with an Indian accent, talk [in] Hindi without any accent, and to understand the cultural nuances of people in every different state was a learning process for me,' he told me. Abhinav set up Aura Renewable Energy in 2011 on returning to India after graduating from Columbia University, New York. The idea for an off-grid solar business was sparked by a project on entrepreneurship while he was doing his undergraduate degree at Berkeley. He started by selling small-scale solar systems for rural use through resellers in select Indian states, and from there developed into an engineering, procurement and construction (EPC) contractor for rooftop solar and then went on to the manufacture of solar inverters. While Kiran Energy operates in the world of corporate customers, government off-takers and banks, Abhinav, with his youthful enthusiasm and American-accented English, needs to fit in with a more traditional India.

The new solar entrepreneurs have helped ease the power crunch through applying new technology at tumbling costs, just as the tech entrepreneurs of e-commerce offered new solutions to the inefficiencies of Indian retail and distribution through online innovations. While bootstrapping an e-commerce start-up might be possible, if slow and parlous, creating an asset-heavy infrastructure business as a start-up would not be possible without access to risk equity. New entrepreneurs in solar power would never have emerged without the ability to secure, as Niall Ferguson put it in *The Ascent of Money*,[62] 'bread, cash, dosh, dough, loot, lucre, moolah, readies, the wherewithal'.

The advent and growth of the venture equity business in India – the ascent of money – has been the second factor that has changed, enabling the entrepreneurial revolution, as the next chapter will discuss.

---

62 Ferguson, Niall, *The Ascent of Money: A Financial History of the World*, London: Allen Lane, 2008.

Changing the Way Healthcare Works
SHASHANK N.D.

'Do great. This is our philosophy. One day I found myself alone at the office at 3 a.m. on a Friday night. I was 25 years old and had been sleeping in the office for six days. I asked myself, what am I doing? Then I realized that it actually makes me happy. I am not doing this for appreciation, or for people to remember me, or to become wealthy. The only reason I am doing this is because I will create something great that I will be proud of. I think the joy you get from creating something great for yourself and for the rest of the world is far greater than any recognition or monetary benefit.' The tall, thin young man, unshaved and casually dressed in jeans and a T-shirt, stared at me intensely for some moments, lost in the memory of that moment of realization.

Shashank N.D. is the founder and CEO of Practo, a new-age healthcare company that helps doctors manage their practices and also offers a consumer-facing health app. Shashank and Abhinav Lal started the business while still in college. Their business model has in-built stickiness, more so than most other e-commerce platforms, derived from the interaction between the B2B [business-to-business] software business and the B2C [business-to-consumer] app. Practo sells software that helps healthcare providers manage their practices. Simultaneously, consumers use Practo's website and apps to find doctors, book appointments and order medicines. The healthcare professionals, principally doctors, pay a subscription fee for the software, so there is a recurring revenue, while there are multiple opportunities for additional income from consumers online, including web consultations and the e-pharmacy. For both doctors and consumers, once the health records of those seeking treatment are in the system, there is a real disincentive towards switching to a competitor.

Practo started with Practo Ray, a cloud-based software-as-a-service that provides practice management for doctors and other healthcare professionals.

Shashank told me that Practo is currently used to book and manage 40 million appointments a year, and has so far signed up 200,000 doctors, 10,000 hospitals, 84,000 laboratories and 4,000 fitness centres. They then went on to launch a consumer-facing app, which enables patients to access information on health issues and drugs, store medical records, find and compare doctors, book appointments and purchase medicines. The two avatars of Practo complement and strengthen each other in what Shashank called a hyper-loop. As he explained, 'Each of the hyper-loop pieces solves a different problem to start with. The software helps manage the doctor's practice, and hence it generates records. The marketplace solves the problem for consumers of finding and interacting with the providers, principally doctors. As more consumers use the platform, so more service providers are incentivized to use the software as it boosts their revenues and improves patient experience.'

Growing up in Bangalore, Shashank had no interest in business. Instead he discovered a love for computers. His mother was an IT professional and brought an old computer home, which captivated young Shashank. But it was his experience at college, at the National Institute of Technology (NIT) Surathkal, Karnataka, that opened his eyes to the excitement of entrepreneurship. He explained, 'I think there were two things in entrepreneurship that were fascinating to me; first, that you are doing something that has never been done before and, second, I found the personality type of the entrepreneur to be very attractive. I think there is a high level of clarity and purpose in an entrepreneur, and no bullshit in him at all. He is to the point and very clear and precise. He just doesn't have time. He is trying to get somewhere and brings a lot of energy and passion.'

As he neared the end of his time in college, Shashank's family urged him to get a job, and to satisfy them he attended one interview and received an offer. But he had already decided he wanted to be an entrepreneur. The trigger for the idea that became Practo was the experience he had when his father fell ill and he had to go through the hassle of finding the right doctor and arranging for the records and test results required for the treatment. His father's doctor was unable to send copies of the records he had by email to the specialist. 'I realized that the healthcare system had been built in a sub-optimal way that did not really work well for consumers,' Shashank remembered. Together with Abhinav, Shashank set out to build a software system for doctors that was based on patient needs as well as on what doctors required. They funded themselves by winning ₹50,000 as prize money from business plan competitions and borrowing ₹10 lakh from their parents.

Practo was launched in 2009, and by 2010 had about 400 doctors signed up, each paying ₹700 per month in subscription fees. Shashank recalled that many advised him that converting busy and conservative doctors to a paid software service would be impossible. 'That is the best part of entrepreneurship – the more you tell an entrepreneur that something is difficult, the more exciting it becomes for us to get it done. By that time some doctors had become friends and they said, Shashank don't do this, this business of selling software to doctors won't work. I am a doctor; I will never buy it. I know you, you are very good person...go to the US. I don't know why everyone wanted me to go to the US. Can you imagine your potential customers feeling sorry for you and discouraging you from doing what you are doing? They told us that this can never be done: How can you change healthcare?'

The key to converting doctors was to show them that their lives would be easier and their revenue greater by using Practo. For instance, Practo's team built in an automatic SMS-based reminder service for appointments, so doctors no longer had to call patients to remind them to attend appointments. No-shows fell by 70 per cent. Doctors were also brought on board with free trials, after which the team focused on those who started using the system, ignoring those who had not activated their trial subscription.

In 2011, Shashank received a wholly unexpected call from Shailendra Singh of Sequoia. Unlike in previous meetings with VC investors, Shailendra immediately understood the model and Shashank's vision of what could be done. Seed funding was agreed on, shortly followed by a Series A round of $4 million, despite the founders being only 23 years of age at the time. Shashank was clear he wanted to avoid working with investors who did not fully buy into the vision of what can be achieved. For instance, in later conversations, many potential investors questioned his ambition to internationalize quickly and wanted Practo to first scale in India. Despite such reservations, to date, Practo has completed three rounds of funding and raised $125 million from leading funds, including Sequoia, Tencent and Google Capital.

The initial funding from Sequoia allowed Practo to scale. They launched Project Blitz, to map and approach all doctors' practices in 35 cities in India. They have now reached a penetration of up to 50 per cent in larger Indian cities, although success is still much lower in small towns and rural areas. The key challenge remains getting more patient records on to the system as, once achieved, that will be their true competitive edge.

Practo has now launched in 15 other countries. Of these, the full 'hyper-loop' model has been introduced in Singapore, Philippines, Indonesia and Brazil, while in other countries the company sells only software. The system works best in countries in which doctors and patients are the decision-makers, rather than in nationalized healthcare models like the UK or insurance-led models like the US.

Shashank is a great advocate of the entrepreneur as a radical agent of change. 'I think what has happened in the last couple of years has been brilliant. Society used to look down upon entrepreneurship. They didn't understand the power of it and they didn't understand its significance and what it does for the country. In the last two years, big investments have happened, the media has highlighted start-ups, the government is looking into it more closely, and society has started accepting it.' Being based in India is advantageous in some ways, but challenging in others. 'I think the biggest thing India gave me was this fertile land in which we could build this thing out; there is no legacy system so we can create everything from scratch. It gave us the opportunity, but at the same time there are a lot of constraints. The [low] per capita income here prevents us from getting true recognition for our invention.'

Shashank's ambition and enthusiasm are infectious, and he has proved that he can execute well and build a business offering not just growth and scale but also positive cash flow. He explained, 'We are trying to help mankind to live longer and healthier. Data is how we think we can get there – personalized data which will help doctors treat you better. Data will also help us create better medicines [through constant monitoring of outcomes of medication]. This is what we aim to do, to help people live longer and healthier by simplifying ways to be healthy.'

CHAPTER 5

The Money Men

'Money should not stop you; it is not a massive precondition.'

Ronnie Screwvala, Founder, UTV

'There's a lot of angel and venture money available to support good and credible propositions. To begin with, a lot of this money came from overseas but now Indian family offices are quite happy to provide capital for start-up opportunities. Today, it's not difficult to raise money for any business that has credibility.'

Ashok Wadhwa, Group CEO, Ambit Holdings

'In India, I don't think the VC industry traditionally has attracted the best talent. Maybe they become arrogant and they stop learning, though a few people are very good. We almost walked away from our first VC investment [because of the behaviour of the investor] even though we had got rejected by a bunch of VCs before.'

Prominent founder, requesting anonymity

A critical change in India's entrepreneurial ecosystem in recent years, and an important boost to its development, has been the increasing availability of equity funding for early-stage companies. Difficulty accessing equity capital was among the leading challenges faced by the earlier entrepreneurs, Manmohan's Children. In contrast, progressively easier funding was a theme for the New Generation of entrepreneurs, especially those who started most recently. Securing equity might still not be simple for some entrepreneurs, depending on luck, timing, sector and the quality of their story. Not everyone can raise money in a few days as did Sandeep Aggarwal of ShopClues or Ashish Goel of Urban Ladder. Most take time to raise initial backing and experience multiple rejections, including unicorn successes like Flipkart and InMobi. But, overall, there has clearly been a dramatic improvement in the availability of risk capital in India. The money men – and, with a few exceptions like Vani Kola at Kalaari, they usually are men – have played a strong supportive role in enabling the rising tide of entrepreneurship in India.

In 2016, $15 billion of risk private capital was invested in India, according to data from VCCEdge, the data and analytics division of the VCCircle Network. This was 36 per cent lower than the $23.6 billion invested in 2015. Total private investment had trended upwards over many years, up 6 per cent on an annual compound basis over a decade, with spikes in 2007 and 2015, resulting in a step change in the market for direct investments into non-listed companies.

Investment in private companies, those not listed on a public stock exchange, is dominated by institutional funds that pool capital from sophisticated investors, which are termed Limited Partners (LPs). Such funds are typically managed by a fund manager, a General Partner (GP), which is remunerated both by a charge based on the quantum of funds invested and through a share of the returns made, a so-called 'carry'. Historically, most funds charged 2 per cent on the assets under management (AUM) and 20 per cent of the returns achieved over a hurdle rate, though these economics are now increasingly being challenged. Funds raise their capital from LPs based on an investment thesis which specifies how they will deploy the capital, by geography, sector, stage of company, and size and type of investment.

Progressing by stage of investment and typical ticket-size, for our purposes, we will distinguish between angel investors, who are usually wealthy individuals who invest small amounts in very early-stage companies, seed and venture funds (VCs) and Private Equity (PE).

PE investment, essentially growth capital and buyout for established businesses, was the first private investment class to develop in India and remains the largest element of the Indian market for direct investing: 53 per cent of the total in 2016. However, the fastest growing portion recently has been earlier-stage investment, angel and VC. Angel investing totalled $326 million in 765 deals in 2016, only 2 per cent of the total by value, but it had grown at 52 per cent compound over 10 years. VC investment was $2.8 billion in 384 deals in 2016, 19 per cent of the total by value, and had seen compound growth of 16 per cent over a decade. VC investment was the category most sharply down in 2016 from the previous year, by 49 per cent, as the over-exuberance of 2014–15 subsided.[63]

As Rajeev Mantri of Navam Capital told me, 'What's really changed in the last eight or so years is that there are investors now at every stage. You can find an angel investor who would invest ₹5 lakh and you can find a growth equity or a private equity investor who would invest ₹500 crore.' When Adi Godrej was President of the Confederation of Indian Industry (CII) in 2012–13, he repeatedly said that India was short of risk capital. When I met him for this book in 2016, he said that things had changed. 'I made those statements some years ago and now it's changing dramatically. Even in those days, private equity was not difficult to get but you had to be reasonably established before you attracted it. Venture capital has now become much easier to access but, most importantly now, start-up capital is also possible to access.'

The early-stage investing market, however much it has grown, nevertheless still shows signs of immaturity. The number of deals remains relatively low, with only 795 angel deals and, more surprisingly, 384 VC deals done in 2016. Exits remain relatively few, only 257 in 2016 across all categories of private risk capital. While total private investment is relatively well balanced across sectors, with each of finance, consumer and IT above 20 per cent of the mix and industrials at 15 per cent, VC and angel investment is much more skewed. IT and financial services have dominated the sectoral mix and, more worryingly, a small number of companies have accounted for the lion's share of the money. In 2015, four companies alone (Ola, Paytm,

---

[63] VCCEdge uses definitions of 'angel' to be investments of $1 million or less in companies less than one year old, and 'VC' as investments of $10 million or less in companies less than ten years old.

Flipkart and Snapdeal) accounted for 50 per cent of all VC funding for that year. It is clear that the venture investing industry needs to widen and deepen, as well as grow, as we will discuss. There is much truth to the complaints that, in recent years, investors have been overly enamoured of e-commerce propositions to the detriment of other sound business ideas. Well-conceived business ideas across different sectors can secure funding if well- and doggedly presented, as we proved with Kiran Energy, but sectoral fashion and herd behaviour have tended to play too large a role.

The year 2016 saw a correction in the market for private investment in India with total funds invested at $15 billion, down 36 per cent on 2015. The steepest fall was in VC activity, which was down 49 per cent in value terms from the previous year and 27 per cent in terms of the number of deals. Angel investing was down too, lower by 4 per cent in value terms, though actually increased in terms of the number of deals. The squeeze seemed to be particularly on the larger fundraises. Analysis by VCCircle of Tiger Global's activity illustrates this lower appetite for chunky Indian tech deals among international investors. Tiger Global has invested $2.5 billion in India from 2005 to mid-2016, $1.5 billion of which was in 2014–15. In 2015, Tiger Global made 38 investments in India; in the first half of 2016, it made only four, all follow-on investments, amounting to just $100 million.

The development of the private risk capital market in India has in one respect come full circle in 20 years, starting with informal angel investing and returning now to a new excitement about angel investing. The funding narrative of Manmohan's Children was typically limited to friends and family, essentially angels. In the 1980s and 1990s, access to institutional capital was very limited for early-stage companies. PE funds from overseas began to take an interest in India from the mid-1990s. By the late 1990s, a small number of international funds were investing in India, including Warburg Pincus, Schroders and CDC. At the same time a number of local firms were also setting up, including Chrysalis Capital, Infinity Ventures and ICICI Ventures. Typically, these PE investors sought growth opportunities with established companies, but the paucity of deals led some to try investing at an earlier stage. From 2000, there was a surge in the number of PE firms in the market, and by 2009 there were more than 400 registered with the RBI. From around 2005, a number of venture firms were established.

Some, like Sequoia Capital, were the Indian teams of international firms and others, like the teams that evolved into Saama or Kalaari, were entirely Indian, though typically their capital was raised offshore. More recently, the VC firms have been complemented by earlier-stage seed funds like Kae Capital or Blume Ventures.

India's rapid economic growth through the 1990s and after has resulted in a significant number of people having investible money. Many of these have sought to invest in the growing start-up scene in which, notwithstanding the higher risk, the potential reward from a good investment is much greater. Those with larger amounts of money, such as some of the Infosys founders or Ajay Piramal who sold his main business, have institutionalized their investment activity through family offices which might sponsor or be an LP in a venture fund. Many others have sought an exposure to early-stage companies through the sudden blossoming of angel investing.

As Nandan Nilekani, formerly of Infosys, noted, 'A lot of the older entrepreneurs have now become angels, and there is a whole class of people who made money in the previous generation who are now angels.' As noted earlier, prominent among these has been Ratan Tata, who has made early-stage investing his most high-profile activity post-retirement. In addition, there are angels from among Indians who left and went overseas, especially to the US, and there are now angels among the New Generation entrepreneurs. Of those I interviewed, Sachin Bansal, Vijay Sharma and Zishaan Hayath spoke about their angel investments. Promoted by media coverage, interest in angel investment has spread wider. Nitin Gupta, co-founder and CEO of Attero Recycling, told me, 'I was meeting an uncle of mine yesterday and he is not the angel kind, he is a consultant who has earned some money. He says, Nitin, I really want to put some money in some start-ups. I have ₹30 lakh, can you help me? Suddenly everybody and their mother is willing to take the risk of putting their money behind a young guy or girl [with a business idea].'

Nitin's uncle and his mother notwithstanding, the two leading networks of angel investors in India are the Mumbai Angels and the India Angel Network, both set up in 2007. I described earlier how Sasha Mirchandani of the family behind Onida televisions became a first investor in Fractal Analytics in 2000. In the years after that Sasha has made a few more personal investments. In 2006, he and his friend Prashant Choksi were chatting over coffee at the Oberoi Hotel, overlooking the sea in south Bombay, when they decided to join an angel network to invest small sums. Overnight, Sasha searched the Internet but could not find an existing angel network in India, so the next day he and Prashant agreed to set up Mumbai Angels. Sasha was working by then for a fund, Blue Run Ventures, so by day he was investing for the fund and in the evenings and weekends he was coordinating Mumbai Angels. InMobi was their first investment.

By 2011, encouraged by K.V. Dhillon of Guggenheim, Sasha decided to create his own seed fund, Kae Capital, to invest in early-stage companies. Until then VC funds viewed very early, seed investing as too small, risky and expensive and hence thought that fund economics would not work. Sasha proposed to make investments as low as $1,000, with a sweet spot of around $500,000, and a cap of $4 million for a full cycle with one company. He struggled to raise capital initially, getting commitments of just ₹8 crore ($1.2 million) in eight months of effort. Once Sasha won the active support of Sir Michael Moritz, the highly respected chairman of Sequoia Capital, the fund came together and closed at $25 million in early 2012. Kae Capital has made nearly 50 investments since then, and out of this large number of bets has had wins like InMobi, Myntra, Healthkart and 1mg. Sasha is now closing his second fund at about $40 million.

Saurabh Srivastava co-founded Indian Angel Network (IAN) at about the same time as Sasha was setting up Mumbai Angels. Saurabh had wound up Infinity Ventures by 2006 and had made a few angel investments on his own account. Through a friend, he visited an angel network in California and appreciated that this model could be brought to India. A dozen or so people coalesced around the idea and in the first year they saw about 200 deals and made two investments. By the end of 2016, IAN had become the largest angel network in the world with some 450 members. They now operate in six cities in India and also have a branch in London. So far they have made 130 investments, the majority of these have been in the past three years. In 2016 they saw proposals from over 7,000 entrepreneurs. Typical ticket sizes are about ₹3 crore ($450,000), with the majority going into tech or tech-enabled opportunities, but they also invest across multiple sectors. Saurabh claims that IAN has achieved an annual rate of return (IRR) of 40 per cent over the past eight years and a failure rate of barely 10 per cent because of the robust selection process and the deep involvement in each investee company of IAN members with genuine sectoral expertise. IAN is now planning to raise a fund of up to ₹400 crore ($60 million) to co-invest alongside its angels.

In addition to Kae Capital, the other seed fund I spent time with was Blume Ventures, founded by Sanjay Nath and Karthik Reddy in 2010, partly as a result of Sanjay's involvement with Mumbai Angels. The first fund was $20 million raised in 2011, and the second, just closed, is $60 million. They look to invest from $250,000 up to $2 million at a seed stage, earlier than the venture funds who typically participate in larger, later rounds, Series A and onwards. Sanjay and Karthik have observed a distinct improvement in the quality of entrepreneurs and business plans they have seen in recent years. They believe that the entrepreneurial system will continue to strengthen in India over time as more of the new founders spin out of the successful companies like Flipkart or Ola, and as entrepreneurs return for a second innings in a new venture. They are now seeing more distinctive and differentiated ideas proposed by more robust teams with true experience of working together. However, India still has got a long way to go to achieve the sophistication of Silicon Valley. 'We have just started a virtual cycle which will probably play out by 2025,' Karthik argued.

Kiranbir Nag, Partner at Saama Capital India Advisors, a venture fund, echoed many of these points. Kiranbir has also noticed a greater confidence and maturity in the entrepreneurs he sees now. 'The quality of entrepreneurs has changed and matured. We still see some "me-too" ideas, and solution-finding-a-problem type of business plans, of course we do. But even those are presented in a much more mature fashion. Entrepreneurs have just become better at selling their stories.' The team at Saama, led by Ash Lilani and Suresh Shanmugham, were together at Silicon Valley Bank (SVB) and ran SVB Capital in India from around 2005. They separated from SVB in 2012 to form Saama Capital. They look to invest $1 million to $3 million a pop, so they come in at a later stage than seed investors like Kae and Blume.

Kiranbir thinks that availability of capital is the biggest change in the Indian start-up scene in recent years. He dates the VC industry to around

2005. 'Sequoia clearly led the charge at that point, then came Matrix and Accel, followed by Indo–US, which is now Kalaari. I think all of them have made some really good investments.' In 2004 and some part of 2005, SVB Capital India was consulting to other funds and Kiranbir recalls the moment he realized that something different was emerging in India. 'There was a gentleman who used our offices regularly, a partner from Battery Ventures in the US. One time he came into my room and told me that they had just closed an investment in India, I think in Tejas Networks. Tejas was a pure Indian company without a US subsidiary or headquarters. So here was a US fund led by a six-foot-five-inch blond partner putting money in an Indian company, a pure Indian company. I just said, wow, if these guys can do it, so can others.'

Like Karthik Reddy of Blume, however, Kiranbir stressed how young the VC industry still is in India. 'We are just 10 years into this, which is not much compared to the US market. So I think all elements need further development. We saw the first wave [from 2005], then you had a trough in the middle and then you had that second wave [of 2015].' The wave of 2015 Kiranbir referred to was a bubble of over-hyped excitement focused on the e-commerce sector.

The e-commerce start-up bubble of 2015

Kashyap Deorah is someone who knows a bit about starting companies and is well networked in the world of Indian entrepreneurs and investors, as well as their counterparts in Silicon Valley. I met Kashyap on the day his book, *The Golden Tap*,[64] was being launched in Bombay in January 2016 and he has subsequently become a friend. He's now on to his fourth start-up, HyperTrack, which offers locational tracking as a service.

Kashyap started young as an entrepreneur, while still a student at IIT Bombay. Ashish Goel of Urban Ladder told me, 'He was one of the role models [at IIT]. He was incredibly smart, with awesome grades but also brilliant at dramatics and a fantastic debater. He started his own company at the end of the third year.' That on-campus start-up, RightHalf.com,

---

[64] Deorah, Kashyap, *The Golden Tap: The Inside Story of Hyper Funded Indian Start-ups*, New Delhi: Roli Books, 2015.

conceived as a marketplace for creative ideas where users could comment on and rate original ideas, secured angel backing in 1999 and then achieved a modest but successful exit.

After a period away working in Silicon Valley, Kashyap returned to India in 2008 and set up his second business, Chaupaati Bazaar, along with Zishaan Hayath, founder and CEO of Toppr. Chaupaati Bazaar was a marketplace for those who did not yet have Internet and allowed customers to phone a call centre which then matched demand with supply. They sold it to Kishore Biyani's Future Group in 2010. By 2012 Kashyap was onto his third start-up, Chalo, a restaurant payment product. He lucked out by selling it to OpenTable prior to a commercial launch, and then 'double-dipped' when Priceline's subsequent acquisition of OpenTable ramped up the value of the OpenTable stock he had received as payment for his shares in Chalo.

Other than a compelling personal narrative of his own entrepreneurial journey between India and California, Kashyap's argument in *The Golden Tap* is that the boom in funding start-ups in India, e-commerce in particular, had by 2015 become so over-heated that it was similar, in his words, to 'a Ponzi scheme'. Valuations, he says, became 'insane'. The huge wealth creation seen in Internet-related companies in China, culminating in Alibaba's 2015 IPO which raised $25 billion at a valuation of $231 billion, spurred global funds, many flush with cash, to seek the next boom. A number of leading funds, including Tiger Global, Softbank and DST Global, bet big that India would follow China, and other investors scrambled to join the party. They tended to back business models that resembled ones that had worked elsewhere – what Kashyap terms 'this-of-that investing', seeking the 'Amazon of India' or the 'Uber of India'.

The investment binge through 2015 funded unsustainable losses in the major e-commerce companies driven by aggressive marketing budgets and deep discounts on products offered online, as these companies strove to gain scale and market share. In his book, Kashyap argues that consolidation is now inevitable and an existential battle looms among the e-commerce majors in India: Amazon, which has pledged $5 billion of investment in India; Flipkart, backed by Tiger Global; and Snapdeal, backed by Softbank. Alibaba's huge investment in Paytm in 2015, reported to be $680 million, potentially added a fourth player.

A number of other voices expressed similar concerns over the bubble in Indian e-commerce start-ups, and the risk of a dot-com-like meltdown. Haresh Chawla, partner at True North, formerly India Value Fund, and earlier at Network 18, wrote a much-circulated article, 'The Fault in Our Start-ups', in *Founding Fuel*.[65] Chawla argued that, inevitably, 97 per cent of start-ups will fail and, of the balance, 1 per cent will get acquired, 1 per cent will become paper unicorns that eventually fail, and only 1 per cent will go on to survive as sustainable businesses in the long term.

Chawla's concern was not so much over the harsh Darwinian logic of start-ups, leading naturally to a high failure rate, but that the underlying business models chosen by many e-commerce companies never had a chance of working out. 'My problem is that you will die for the wrong reasons,' Chawla wrote. 'You will not die because your product sucked. Or your team fell apart. Or your competitor got funded beyond what is rational. You will die because you were supposed to. Your math never added up. You could never have made money, no matter how hard you tried.' He went on to describe a number of common mistakes made by e-commerce start-ups, and to suggest that the only successful long-term strategy is to out-innovate Western entrants in the Indian markets, to offer products and services that truly meet Indian needs and engender loyalty and stickiness among consumers.

A similar view is held by Sharad Sharma, a Silicon Valley entrepreneur who returned to India to become an angel investor and is now an active mover behind the India Software Product Industry Round Table (iSPIRT). He thinks that copy-cat, imported e-commerce models will fail in India. He sees two main fallacies in the investment theses of many fund investors. The first, Sharad thinks, is the belief in a substantial middle class in India with a spending profile comparable to the middle class of the West. Middle class in India means something very different, Sharad contends, and the size of the true, international-standard middle class is much smaller than the numbers of 300 million or so that is often quoted. He illustrated this by pointing to the very low sales in India of a brand like Levi's. Second, he refutes the argument, which I heard from Flipkart and Ola, that local

---

[65] http://www.foundingfuel.com/article/the-fault-in-our-startups/

competitors in the e-commerce sector will have indigenous advantages and be able to outcompete the foreign originals in the long term. Amazon and Uber would always have scale advantages from their global operations over their local, India-only lookalikes, Sharad argues. The real successes in India will emerge from companies that address not the international middle-class market of India but rather the much bigger local market, the 'other middle class' of Bharat. The international players would struggle to create business models and innovation for that huge but price-sensitive market.

It is hard to source reliable and comparable data on the financial performance of the major e-commerce companies in India. All are privately owned, and most have complex structures often involving offshore holding companies. The inventory-owning entities are usually separate from marketplace trading operations for regulatory reasons connected with India's restrictions on foreign investment in retailing. Nevertheless, even if the available information is not complete, consolidated, current or strictly comparable, it is clear that very substantial losses are being made by the e-commerce majors. The huge amount of equity raised in 2015 was deployed – invested, the companies would say – to buy growth both through price discounting and heavy promotional spending, with the intention of achieving scale and a leading competitive position.

According to data from VCCEdge, Flipkart India Pvt. Ltd (the main e-commerce entity) had net losses in the financial year to March 2016 of ₹545 crore ($80 million) on sales of ₹13,177 crore ($1.9 billion), while Jasper Infotech Pvt. Ltd (Snapdeal) had losses in the same year, 2016, of ₹3,316 crore ($488 million) on sales of ₹1,457 crore ($269 million). The sales of both companies have grown well in recent years; Flipkart's revenue was up 42 per cent in 2016 over the previous year while Snapdeal's was up 61 per cent. Flipkart's losses had reduced somewhat in 2016, but those of Snapdeal widened. Other companies in the space similarly reported significant losses. One97 Communications Ltd (the holding company owning Paytm, Paytm E-commerce and the payments bank) had been profitable up to 2014, but in 2016 reported losses of ₹1,535 crore ($226 million) on sales of ₹944 crore ($138 million).

Economics like this cannot be sustained for long. The year 2016 saw a correction in investment appetite, with VC funding harder to secure, lower valuations and the recognition of impairment in the carrying value of certain investments by a number of investors. Funds are driving harder bargains where they do invest. A string of e-commerce companies have restructured, been bought out or closed operations, and lay-offs have followed. Snapdeal, the third largest e-commerce player after Flipkart and Amazon, announced in February 2017 that it would be laying off an unspecified number of its staff in a drive to turn profitable within a two-year period. Kunal Bahl of Snapdeal was reported to have told staff by email, 'We started growing our business much before the right economic model and market fit was figured out…a large amount of capital with ambition can be a potent mix that drives a company to defocus from its core. We feel that happened to us. We started doing too many things, and all of us – starting with myself and Rohit [Bansal] – are to blame for it.'[66]

The most prominent reversal of fortune was probably the sale in July 2016 of Jabong by Rocket Internet to Myntra, itself owned by Flipkart, for $70 million. Jabong was once one of the stars of the e-commerce sector and at one time had a unicorn valuation ascribed to it. Rocket, which, unusually for a fund, had conceived the company, had reportedly invested $200 million in Jabong. Before the sale was announced, I interviewed Praveen Sinha, one of the two co-founders put into the company by Rocket. He had left in 2015 and was clearly still troubled by the way things had panned out with the investors. Praveen was careful not to say too much, claiming that his relationships with German shareholders had remained good and his decision to leave was because he wanted the greater freedom of working with his family business and other ventures. However, he pointed out that in India very few of the e-commerce entrepreneurs have ultimate control of their businesses in the way that Jeff Bezos, Mark Zuckerberg, Elon Musk or Bill Gates still do in the US. They are, therefore, at risk of meeting the same fate as Steve Jobs: Being asked to leave by the investor-controlled board.

An additional twist to our conversation was that it took place in the office of GoJavas, an e-commerce-focused delivery company which had originally been associated with Jabong. Praveen explained that Jabong had decided not

---

66 Chanchani, Madhav, and Payal Ganguly, 'Snapdeal layoff row: Will CEO Kunal Bahl's profitability gamble succeed', *Economic Times*, 24 February 2017.

to proceed to invest in the delivery business because it would have required approval from the Foreign Investment Promotion Board (FIPB). Funding for GoJavas had instead come from outside investors and later its key customer, Snapdeal. However, there were press reports in 2016 suggesting that the spinning of GoJavas out of Jabong was not as straightforward as Praveen suggested, at least from the viewpoint of Rocket, though the facts remain unclear – not least as some of the allegations were, Praveen told me, subsequently subject to a court-issued restraining order.

The most bizarre ruckus at an e-commerce business has been at Housing.com. Rahul Yadav, the co-founder, was fired by the company's board in 2015 after a series of extraordinary public attacks on other entrepreneurs and, in an email posted on a website, his own board and investors.[67] Rahul passed on the opportunity to speak with me. Nevertheless, it seems that the contortions on the board of Housing.com resulted from a combination of disappointing business performance with an inexperienced leadership team.

How much damage has the funding boom of 2015 and its correction in 2016, and the resulting conflicts between investors and founders, really caused the Indian entrepreneurial system? My own view is that frothy market exuberance and choppy waves of growth are to be expected and in the long term will be smoothed out by the secular swell of the incoming tide of entrepreneurial growth. Emerging growth markets experience spurts of enthusiasm and then periods of lower activity. In any start-up ecosystem, in the West or the emerging world, there will be prominent companies of promise that fail because they cannot secure additional funding or because insufficient numbers of customers adopt the technology or product. Some investors will overpay and lose money; some companies will go bust or be bought out. The very nature of starting a new business is to take risk, and not all risks work out as hoped. Boards and shareholders will sometimes

---

[67] https://www.quora.com/What-is-the-Housing-com-controversy-letter-from-the-founder-to-Sequoia, quoting Yadav as writing, 'Dear board members and investors, I don't think you guys are intellectually capable enough to have any sensible discussion any more. This is something which I not just believe but can prove on your faces also!'

fall out with, or lose confidence in, the founders. The skills required to create a business often differ from the competences needed to scale and institutionalize success in the long-term.

Neither I nor anyone else can predict with certainty as to which of the companies I have interviewed will succeed dramatically and which will fail. The nature of early-stage investing is that a few bets will be huge wins – 'ten baggers' or more, as VCs say – but most will not. I have, of course, developed personal views on which entrepreneurs and which businesses are more impressive and which, in my judgement, seem more likely to scale and create long-term value. I will be proved right in some cases, wrong in others. However, the point of this book is not to pick winners. Rather, the critical point is that India is now generating a rich population of credible start-ups from among which, despite many failures, will emerge a significant number of great businesses. And the cumulative effect of this rise in entrepreneurship, despite the booms and busts, the failures and disappointments, will be very positive for the country.

An immature industry

While VC, seed and angel investors have played a vital role in supporting the new wave of entrepreneurship in India, in some ways the venture industry remains strikingly immature. The over-enthusiasm that fed the bubble of 2015 was in the nature of market behaviour, and will no doubt be echoed at some point in the future. More profound, to my mind, are two glaring weaknesses of the VC market in India at this stage of its development. First, there are questions of judgement and concentration in capital allocation and deployment. Second, there are too many industry participants who lack the experience, finesse and surety of touch to fully support, shape and manage the entrepreneurs in whom they invest.

While some of the VCs I interviewed, and many of the entrepreneurs, endorsed these points, others strongly disagreed. Vani Kola of Kalaari, for instance, accepted that the VC industry was still young, but argued that what mattered ultimately to their investors, the LPs, was purely the delivery of results. 'I look at it like this. If you invest in a mutual fund, do you care whether the manager is getting results because he can crunch math, or because he builds deep relationships with management teams, or because he has an army that does market research and says that this is the next big technology?' While clearly this perspective – that VCs are there to make money, not primarily to support entrepreneurs or the country's development – is correct, from my view as a strategic manager I am struck by the shallowness of the investing industry in its current state. I would expect to see more differentiated investing strategies, more variety in the backgrounds and experience of investors, and greater insight into and support of the process of corporate growth.

The herd

Half of all the venture investments made in the boom year of 2015 went into four companies, all in e-commerce. One clear weakness in the VC market currently is not so much that there is inadequate money available in total for early-stage investment, but rather that too much capital has been allocated to similar business models in too few sectors. Of course, VCs seek to maximize returns while minimizing risk. Certain sectors, particularly e-commerce and comparable tech opportunities, appear to offer attractive economics, scalability and less exposure to the chaos of India and therefore appear to have lower execution or technical risk. However, as a result of VCs following similar investing strategies, too much of the available capital has been concentrated on a limited number of sectors with these perceived characteristics, and especially too few companies within those sectors. Valuations have been hiked as a result and some weaker businesses have secured funding because they were in the right sector when it was fashionable. The flip side, as Mohandas Pai of Aarin Capital pointed out, is that within the relative capital plenty, there are still 'large layers of entrepreneurs struggling to raise money'.

Stepping away from the herd and taking a different investment approach requires courage, hard work and the ability to judge different risks such as those implicit in technology, shifting regulation and uncertain market demand. Kiranbir Nag of Saama Capital accepted this when we spoke, noting that Saama is a generalist fund and lacks the expertise to judge certain sectors such as biotech. Even leaving aside complex technical areas, it is clear that however sound his investment proposal might be, an entrepreneur in a manufacturing business or a branded consumer goods business will find it more difficult to raise money than a plausible team with another e-commerce idea. K.R. Sundaresan, an entrepreneur focused on auto components, put it bluntly: 'VCs are not interested in manufacturing.' Srikumar Misra of Milk Mantra (see p. 150, 'A Fresh Brand with Rural Roots: Srikumar Misra'.), who has built a very impressive dairy brand in Odisha (formerly Orissa) for which he has secured venture backing from Fidelity Ventures, ruminated, 'I sometimes feel that all these investors talk about it, but really nobody pays value for an ethical business creating high impact. It would have been far easier for me to build an Internet tech company than to do all this hard work and not get value for it.'

Is this sectoral favouritism the logic of the market, reflecting that certain businesses are rightly more attractive to investors than others, or is it the result of market failure? The answer is, almost certainly, partly both. I know only too well how hard it still is to create and operate a manufacturing facility in India, even one as intuitively straightforward as a solar power plant. It remains much easier to run an IT-based operation staffed by motivated professionals with limited connectivity to the noise and chaos of India. I have experienced the complexities and economic challenges of running a traditional retailing business in India; how much more alluring to dispense with the physical investments and operate a virtual marketplace? And yet, with the skills and cost advantage available, it is more than possible to operate a fantastic and profitable manufacturing or service business in India, despite the complications. I have seen repeated examples of world-class manufacturing and service businesses in India that make superior shareholder returns. Without denigrating e-commerce and its opportunities, the point is that there are myriad opportunities in multiple sectors, including manufacturing. Milltec is one example of a successful manufacturer in a deeply unfashionable sector, rice milling machines (p. 35, 'Manufacturing for Bharat: R. Ravindranath'), which has succeeded in attracting PE investment. For many others of the businesses I researched, manufacturing constituted an important part of their strategic mix (including Micromax, Melorra and Attero Recycling, discussed later).

Some VCs have, of course, invested in sectors away from the currently favoured areas of e-commerce, financial services and consumer products.

Attero Recycling is a company with proprietary technology in the recovery and recycling of metals from electronic devices, especially mobile phones. It is a technology-driven business with hard-core operations, including a system of collecting old devices nationwide. Yet it succeeded in raising early-stage equity backing based only on a business plan; it was funded by Draper Fisher Jurvetson (DFJ) venture capital. Nitin Gupta, the co-founder of Attero, told me that 'there are not enough Kumars', referring to Kumar Shiralagi, the DFJ partner, now Managing Director, India, at Kalaari, who spotted the potential of his chemistry.

I sit on the board of Vyome Biosciences alongside Kumar, so I appreciate Nitin Gupta's point about him. Vyome is a relatively rare example of a VC-funded true biotech start-up in India. It is developing a range of molecules to better treat drug-resistant acne, and from similar science also has a portfolio of molecules that offer the potential to treat other drug-resistant microbes. The scientific innovation is driven by Professor Shiladitya Sengupta of Harvard Medical School, with a team of scientists doing the development work in Delhi. The initial seed funding, and indeed encouragement to do the science in India, came from Rajeev Mantri of Navam Capital. After graduating in the US, Rajeev spent some time working for Lux Capital, a firm which specializes in science-based early-stage investing. Rajeev returned to India determined to deploy a similar investment model. Navam Capital has made three investments to date: EnNatura, a natural ink company that did not work out, Vyome, and Invictus Oncology, focused on supramolecular therapeutics to treat cancer. Even though Vyome and Invictus are drug discovery businesses, after Navam seeded them they succeeded in securing Indian VC investment from Aarin, Kalaari and Sabre Fund Management. However, Vyome's latest round of funding of $14 million in August 2016, was raised in the US from Perceptive Advisors and Romulus Capital, funds specializing in biotech, as the appetite and confidence in India to invest this amount behind drugs in clinical trial is limited.

The Indian VC scene is still dominated by generalist funds for whom technology risk is hard to understand and hence indigestible. The market is yet to develop any significant number of specialist funds with differentiated approaches and the deep sectoral insight required to make technical judgements. For every Kumar Shiralagi who has the technical inquisitiveness to understand Nitin Gupta's chemistry or Shiladitya Sengupta's biology, there are a dozen firms staffed by generalists without the time, inclination or skills to explore something so different. There are, of course, exceptions. Dhananjaya Dendukuri is the co-founder and CEO of Achira Labs, which has developed a 'lab on a chip' for cheaper and faster blood tests. After expending considerable effort and various false starts, he was funded by Narayana Murthy's Catamaran Ventures, which prides itself on taking a long-term view. Dhananjaya told me, 'There is so much low-hanging fruit for investors. There has been a mad rush to the e-commerce and other sectors, so technically demanding things are really not on the radar. Some people are honest enough to say they don't understand the technology and don't have the tools to know if what we are saying is right.'

Sharad Sharma of iSPIRT argues that similar weaknesses also exist among angel investors. For the ecosystem around early investing in India in true technology companies to develop, it requires more time and a full cycle of investment, including profitable exits. Once a cohort of people has made money from a sector they will be much more confident in, and able to add value by, investing in the next generation of businesses in the same sector. He told me, 'If you made money in coal mines, then investing in tech start-ups is extremely risky; investing in coal mines in Indonesia may be less risky for you. You always tend to invest in things that you know.' He went on to suggest that India has lacked success in deep technology companies; most successes in the IT industry in India has been in IT services, companies like Infosys or TCS. These differ fundamentally in approach and skills from IT products. Sharad argues, 'People from the IT services industry will never become lead investors in the product industry. The investors for products will come only when we have had many exits from a first generation of product businesses. Eventually, say, Sachin Bansal might invest in more start-ups in products because he came from an R&D background.' Sharad went on to note that two US-based investors, Ram Shriram, the early investor in Google who backed InMobi, and Chamath Palihapitiya, who made his money working at Facebook, have invested more in Indian product start-ups than all of the prominent India-based angels put together.

The venture investing industry in India will no doubt continue to develop, in terms of amount of capital deployed, the number of firms and also more differentiated and specialized investment strategies. Sasha Mirchandani of Kae Capital argued, 'It will happen; this is still a 1.0 or 2.0 version of the ecosystem. As it gets more crowded, you will start seeing segmentation and focus on particular sectors. As the world gets more competitive, you will see new funds coming and saying we will only focus on one particular strand. For example, a friend of mine, Kanwaljit Singh, who was a partner and founder of Helion Ventures, a $600 million general fund, has now started his own family office called Fireside Ventures where all he does is focus on consumer (FMCG) brands.'

Adding value

The second point about the immaturity of the VC industry in India is in some ways related, and certainly more contentious. Given my experience in industry and then as a founder, my natural empathy tends to be with the entrepreneur. I enjoy supporting operating management and helping them, but I also love to challenge them. Having been on both sides, as an investor and an entrepreneur, I am conscious of the demarcation between the role of an investor or board member and that of the founding team and operating management. Some fund investors in India appear to lack the sensitivity and the surety of touch required to work well with founding and operating teams. Too few investors are able to adequately support the growth of the companies in which they have invested. And it is, consequently, all too easy for the interests of founders and investors to diverge and conflicts to develop.

Logically, this should not normally occur as everyone involved should have a shared interest in building value in the business. However, too often, in my experience, while the staff at investing firms have experience in consulting or financial services, they have limited personal experience of starting a business or operations. VC funds in India are yet to achieve the size to support operating partners – colleagues with deep industry backgrounds – as is common in the US or Europe. Hence their ability to sympathize with and support the founders and their business is constrained. Some investors misjudge the role of shareholder and director, and seek to meddle in matters that effective boards leave to management, or waste time with excessive requests for information. Worse, to my mind, some do not demonstrate adequate inquisitiveness and effort to learn the business. You cannot be an effective director if you are too busy to visit operations in far-flung areas, call on customers or take time to meet staff. The creation of value in a business is not driven by improving the assumptions in an Excel spreadsheet and consequently achieving higher valuation metrics. Businesses are about people who need to get things done in the messy real world. Entrepreneurs shape teams that make change happen and deliver results. As they do so they need support, advice, clear boundaries, encouragement and sympathy from their investors and board members.

Founders tend to feel emotional and protective about their businesses and, by their very nature, are often prickly, obsessive and driven characters. They often feel they want to be left alone to get on with the job and that they would not benefit from even well-intentioned interventions from their investors. The potential for the corrosion of mutual respect and even deepening mistrust is apparent. Investors need to strike a careful balance between imposing structure and laissez-faire, between supporting and challenging the entrepreneur. They do need to act to safeguard their funds' interests, particularly in India, where there is an unusual degree of risk of errant 'promoter' activity. One of the most pernicious side-effects of the years of excessive control in India has been the development of a culture among some businessmen, 'promoters' as they tend to be called, that views rules as obstacles that can be bent to suit them. Boundaries between personal and corporate interests, and cash, can become blurred. Out and out fraud has been all too common. A few years ago I was asked to look into the background of a businessman who had raised more than $100 million from a group of prominent PE investors. The investors had carried out due diligence using reputed professional firms before investing. Yet, a few months later, a fraud was uncovered, akin to that in Satyam Computer Services discovered in 2009, in which sham transactions between related companies had been used to boost reported numbers. In digging into the background of the promoter, we found something that the professional advisers had missed. Twenty years ago, the same businessman had been involved in a comparable fraudulent activity.

Even without mala fide intent, there are structural reasons why the interests of investors and founders can diverge. VC and PE funds typically have a defined fund life, so their prime motivation is to secure an exit in good time at the best possible multiple, which is not always in the best long-term interest of the company. Where the funds are international, the investor representatives onshore in India are not typically the ultimate decision-takers as they report to Investment Committees (ICs) in the US or elsewhere. These offshore decision-makers will often have a limited feel for and understanding of both India and the business, and their onshore colleagues are put in the position of negotiating two ways – with the company but also with their offshore principals. When the company is seeking additional capital in a further round, it is competing for funds against other opportunities that the fund sees, sometimes in sectors that are suddenly more fashionable. Where the business has not delivered its growth or profit targets, as often happens in early-stage companies, investors are faced with the decision either to inject more capital to protect their sunk capital or to leave the investee company to flounder without new money. If in such a situation a fund sees an opportunity to improve the terms of their investment, whatever the spirit, or indeed letter, of any prior agreement might have been, they can feel justified in seizing that advantage in the interests of their own LP investors, often causing great bitterness among the founders. Where the earlier investors decide not to fund any new capital need in full and, instead, to seek additional money from a new investor, the demands of price and terms that the incoming investor seeks need to be balanced against the entrenched position of the existing investors, not to mention those of the founders.

Divergence of economic interests in part explains the tension that can arise between investors and founders but inter-personal factors, too, have often played a part. Founders are very often complicated individuals and can react emotionally to perceived threats, insults or challenges. Too few, even among the mid-career entrepreneurs, have prior experience of taking and satisfying VC investment. Many lack self-awareness and do not welcome the suggestion that they need to develop stronger teams, delegate more or cede leadership to others with more relevant skillsets once a company has evolved beyond the start-up phase. Equally, investors can too often behave insensitively, arrogantly and without empathy. They appear to forget that it is in their interests to keep founders positive, motivated and engaged.

Such issues between founders and investors are certainly not universal. Some founders have learnt to manage investors with care and consequently secure help from them. Some fund principals have either developed an effective way to handle their talented but potentially difficult founders, or have the personal stature or operating expertise that readily commands respect.

During my interviews, some entrepreneurs were circumspect about being asked about their relationship with investors, for understandable reasons. Others were effusive about the positive support they have received from their investors, whether angels or VC funds. A few founders spoke freely about the issues they perceived, but then asked me to be diplomatic in what I recorded, given their need to work with their investors. Naturally, few of the investors I interviewed admitted much of an issue here, putting any conflicts down to the inexperience of young founders. However, reading between the lines during interview after interview, I saw the warning signs of sub-optimal relations between founders and investors, which I have experienced too often in businesses in which I have been personally involved.

While such faults in the relationship between founders and their investors can occur anywhere, my belief is that such tensions arise too often in India. The result is under-achievement of the business and, when tested by adversity, a fracturing of the shared goal of value creation.

I have witnessed this from the perspective of both a founder and an investor. It is striking how much difference board members with industry and operating experience can bring to the quality of discussion and in the level of support the entrepreneur feels he or she is receiving. On one board on which I serve, we inducted two new members with deep relevant experience to complement the members representing the VC investors. The improvement in board performance was rapid and marked. To add value, and fully support and challenge the founders, boards need a mix of experience, industry-specific and general, financial and technical, and such skills seem in short supply among board nominees of Indian VC investors at this point.

For founders, it is easy to see raising the money to start with as the most difficult challenge. Many entrepreneurs have experienced arrogance and rudeness from potential investors as they pitch their business plans, and repeated rejections before they secure funds. Making a pitch for money requires determination, persistence and the skin of a rhino in the grasslands of Kaziranga. I have sat in a waiting room in Delhi for an hour from the agreed appointment time, only to be informed eventually by a secretary that the investor I had come to meet was away in Dubai that day. On a different occasion, I was told by a young investor that the idea I described was a good one, and had I been a 24-year-old who had never owned a suit but instead was wearing a tee-shirt, shorts and chappals (slippers), they might have considered investing.

Many of the entrepreneurs I interviewed told stories of months, even years, of struggle to find investors. For example, Ajay Bijli, Chairman and Managing Director of PVR, told me how tough it was, after the joint venture he had with Village Roadshow ended, to raise external capital for the expansion of his cinema chain. Eventually, he secured some $10 million from Renuka Ramnath, then at ICICI Ventures (and now at Multiples). Ajay bounded over to the bookshelves in his office to find the framed letter from Renuka confirming the offer. 'That was a very nerve-racking period for me. My CFO and I went from pillar to post for nine months to raise funds. Renuka was the only one who got excited because she saw that we were the only brand in the sector. She did well out of it; she came at ₹47.5 per share and she exited during the IPO at an average of ₹225.'

Those setting up funds have to go through a similar experience raising money from LPs. Siddharth (Sid) Talwar, co-founder and Partner at Lightbox told me, 'Our journey for raising money began at maybe the worst time, between 2012 and 2013, for anything to do with India. We kept a count of it – I think we got rejected some 540 times. One guy walked out of his own conference room laughing. He never came back; 20 minutes later we were still sitting there when the receptionist came and said we should clear out of the room.' Going through this process, you have to believe there must be a better way of matching investment opportunities with interested investors than the current dance most entrepreneurs seemingly have to do, however carefully they plan and however well advised they may be. Luck, timing, personal connections and the chemistry of personalities play too big a role for the process of fundraising to be deemed entirely rational.

In reality, whatever the challenges and the time it takes, raising the money initially is often the easiest part of the entrepreneur's complex relationship with invested money. Once the courtship is over, and entrepreneur and investor are respectably married, economic logic should dictate that all parties work hard to make the business grow as fast and as profitably as possible. The trajectories of few early businesses are smooth; there are always bumps and issues to face, and founders and investors need to work well together to create and sustain a successful business.

Some of the entrepreneurs I interviewed gave full marks for the support they received from their investors. Neeraj Kakkar, co-founder and CEO of Hector Beverages, which owns the Paper Boat brand of soft drinks inspired by traditional flavours, told me, 'Catamaran is brilliant. I haven't faced any sort of problem with Sequoia either and Footprint has been great. They have all been very understanding about how we are building a business. It's not that we didn't go through any bad patches, like just before we launched Paper Boat. Tzinga [a health drink] was doing okay but we were missing targets by a distance.' Paper Boat has been a huge success, but it must have required great faith for the investors to back the team to launch a third brand after the first two had not achieved their promise (see p. 176, 'Creating New Consumer Brands: Neeraj Kakkar and Amuleek Singh Bijral').

Similarly, Nitin Gupta at Attero was full of praise for Kumar Shiralagi, now at Kalaari. Soon after Attero raised $6.3 million from Kumar's then fund, DFJ, Nitin and his brother, Rohan, altered the plan radically with a new emphasis on the development of proprietary technology. Nitin explained, 'Because Kumar has a technology background he understands that things can go wrong and you have to be patient. For the first five years, 80 per cent of board meetings were in Roorkee and we had board meetings every six weeks. I am yet to come across another venture capitalist who would spend two days every six weeks coming from Bangalore to Roorkee, by flight and then train, and spending the night in a local hotel as there were no business hotels then in Roorkee.' Perhaps more remarkable than the stamina and commitment required to visit Roorkee so frequently was DFJ's support of a business plan so radically changed from that on which the money had been raised. Most investors would probably have told the Gupta brothers to stick to the agreed plan.

Bhavish Aggarwal at Ola was diplomatic and balanced about the support he receives from his investors. 'I think every investor has his own unique value to the entrepreneur and it's important for both sides to understand the value proposition of that relationship and to set expectations [accordingly]. I think operating experience is not the only thing that is important and there are other things that matter. For example, Lee [Fixel of Tiger Global] helps me to understand the global macro context: What's happening in China or the US and how the financial markets are looking at things. Then I have somebody like Avnish Bajaj of Matrix on my board, and he has built and sold a company.'

Other founders, even of unicorn businesses that have grown dramatically, were not so positive about the contribution of their investors at board level. One founder, asking not to be identified, said some investors were useful, while others were not. 'I think some of them, yes...some of them not so much. There are people who know the business well and then naturally they can contribute fully. I really appreciate the relationship with investors who see themselves as partners in the business where they are bringing the capital and I am the one building the company.' Another founder explained that he had asked a VC investor to replace their nominee on his board, because the first person they nominated had tried to meddle excessively, to the level of suggesting what computers to buy for engineers. He went on, 'We do not think that investors should be dictating on purely operating matters. If you are able to create a relationship where they know they are only advisers, it becomes good.'

Dhiraj Rajaram at Mu Sigma was realistic about the potential contribution of investors. 'I don't think entrepreneurs should be looking for operating guidance from many investors. They can offer specific help, like best practices from other companies, but other than that I would not depend on them too much.' He quickly added, 'We have been very fortunate to have Sequoia Capital and General Atlantic, guys who put money into Google, Facebook, YouTube and Apple, and so have a fantastic pedigree. The institutional investors are a little easier to deal with, I would say, than individual investors, because they are professional and they know what they are getting into. But, again, they can also be difficult.'

Sanjoy Roy at Teamwork Arts went through a similar period of settling into a positive relationship with Ambit after they had invested. Sanjoy praises Ambit for how they helped him think through a business plan and add a degree of governance to a creative business. But he recalls more difficult conversations. 'I said, why do we need to change things? I don't get what you are trying to do. Ambit had a diverse portfolio of companies in cold storage, a big transport company and a hospital. I said, we are an arts company, this is what we do, this is how we do it. We cannot be the company that you want us to be and I have said that to you right from the beginning. I had to be cranky, off and on, to ensure that some lines were drawn.'

Jerry Rao, puffing on his cigar on the veranda of his office off Hughes Road, Bombay, was the most outspoken, no longer needing to mince his words. 'Yes, they [the investors] were very powerful after the merger [of Mphasis with BFL Software] and quite difficult. They added little value. They just asked questions, like, why is your growth rate not higher, why can't you improve margins? All inane MBA-type questions. I don't think that they damaged the business but they certainly took up a lot of management time and attention. Very painful fellows. We had to have three people just answering their questions and wasting time. I would say, get me introductions for new business but they couldn't do that; they didn't add anything that really helped.'

Nandan Nilekani summed it up well when he told me, 'I think there are many VC partners who have come from an operating background or who have run a business. But too many of their young guys are pure finance people armed with a spreadsheet and they think that makes them VCs. But I think the bigger problem is funding genuinely innovative ideas. There is a hesitation and the tendency [is] to prefer the next e-commerce company, the next furniture company.' Zishaan Hayath at Toppr made a similar point. 'There are lot of senior Indian VCs who have run businesses, like Ashish Gupta at Helion, Avnish Bajaj at Matrix and Sid Talwar at Lightbox. The thing is that while many partners at the top of the best VC firms have solid operating experience, too many of the analysts and associates are straight out of McKinsey and the business schools. What's more, all of the really good people are doing their own start-ups. You might have wanted me to be a junior guy in a VC firm after Chaupaati [Bazaar], but I was not available for hiring.'

Sasha Mirchandani warned that there is no single path to success in VC investing. 'There are some VCs who are awesome because they have been entrepreneurs, but I have also seen entrepreneurs who have been terrible VCs because they select very badly and try to influence the company too much. So I don't like to paint with one brush, one stroke. It depends on the individual.'

The most impressive VC investors, to me, judging on reputation, feedback of entrepreneurs and track record, are clearly those with a broader background that very often included a period as a general manager or entrepreneur. Just intellectual smarts, a stellar degree and a good pedigree at Goldman Sachs or McKinsey does not add the same feel, judgement and ability to support and shape an entrepreneur. Vani Kola at Kalaari had done two start-ups of her own in the US before becoming an investor. Kalaari's portfolio includes Snapdeal, Myntra and Germin8 (a social media intelligence platform), in addition to Urban Ladder and Vyome, discussed earlier. Rehan Yar Khan had struggled and then succeeded as an entrepreneur (Flora2000.com) and then was an early investor in Ola and Druva, a cloud-data protection and information management company, before founding Orios Ventures Partners.

The most glowing words I heard about a VC firm were from Saroja Yeramilli of Melorra concerning her investors at Lightbox. 'They are just amazing people. Sandeep Murthy is the founding partner along with Siddharth Talwar and Prashanth Mehta. Sandeep, of course, comes from deep VC background. He was with Kleiner Perkins India before he started Lightbox. Siddharth was an entrepreneur himself before he sold his company to NIIT.' What impressed Saroja, as a highly experienced manager, was how the Lightbox team challenged and supported her as she developed Melorra's innovative business model.

It's complicated...

Entrepreneurs and investors have a complicated relationship, one of love and hate, respect and conflict. Some entrepreneurs have consciously avoided raising external money because of the issues that can arise. Sharad Lunia has declined several offers of funds for releaseMyAd; Pankil Shah, co-partner at Neighbourhood Hospitality, which runs bars and restaurants in Bombay, including the very popular Woodside Inn, my favourite pub in town, has avoided talking to investors as he does not think they understand his sector. Gautam Ghai, CEO of SourceFuse Technologies, was equally sceptical about the value of raising capital for his software business, though he has taken angel money for his Happy Hakka restaurant chain. Parth Amin at SLK Software has refused external funding to preserve his flexibility to do what he wants with his business.

Despite such tensions and cribbing, disputes and sackings, there is little doubt that the rising tide of entrepreneurship has swelled in India very largely because of the easier availability of risk capital. Entrepreneurs may complain about their investors, but without external risk capital their success, if there was any, would have been a long drawn out affair and as tough to achieve as in earlier generations. The angel and VC industry in India is relatively young, immature and far from optimal, but it has developed phenomenally in a decade. It is sure to deepen and mature going forward, addressing its current shortcomings in resource allocation and deepening its ability to add value and give support to investee companies. The fact remains that India's unicorns have scaled as rapidly as they have because of the availability of venture funds on a scale not seen before.

The following chapter discusses another critical contributor to the new upsurge in entrepreneurship in India, the role of government.

A Fresh Brand with Rural Roots

SRIKUMAR MISRA

'Paneer is probably the most adulterated product in the entire food chain in India,' Srikumar (Sri) Misra told me. I have always detested paneer, so this played to my prejudices. 'The way you have paneer in India, you cook it with all that masala,' Sri continued, 'so you can't taste it. Most packaged paneer sold in India is frozen and the texture is not good. But taste a piece of our Milky Moo paneer, it is like cheese. You can make out the difference [from other local brands].'

Sri has chosen an entrepreneurial path significantly different from the beaten track, and miles away from Bangalore's e-commerce start-ups. First, his Milk Mantra company and its Milky Moo brand is based in Bhubaneswar in Odisha in eastern India, a poorer state according to central government's per capita data, where there is very little entrepreneurial activity compared to other parts of India. Second, he is building a consumer brand in a perishable product that relies on rapid distribution and thin margins. Finally, his business is based on a complex supply chain across rural Odisha, collecting a few litres of milk every day from 40,000 farmers.

'I just felt that it was my calling to be an entrepreneur,' Sri told me. Initially, family circumstances were against him following his instincts. His father had set up a manufacturing business for electrical transformers, but had died early in a car accident, leaving debt in the company secured against the family home. After college, Sri joined Tata as a fast-track graduate trainee (in the Tata Administrative Service, TAS) and worked to clear the debt and consequent litigation. After the initial training, he joined Tata Tea, first in Calcutta and then in South Africa and London with Tetley, the tea brand Tata had bought in 2000 in the group's first international acquisition. The brand marketing and business skills he learnt in those years were critical to his setting up Milk Mantra.

By 2009 Sri felt ready to return to India to start his own business. He decided to base his strategy around functional innovation in a category with real scale. Milk offered that – since, of the $40 billion market in India in 2008, only $5 billion was in the organized sector. Moreover, most fresh milk was adulterated either with added solids or water, while ultra-high temperature (UHT)-processed, packaged milk was too expensive for most consumers. He saw the opportunity to build a major brand based on trust. He chose the east partly because it was home and partly because there was much less branded competition in the region compared to western India where Amul and other brands were established.

He needed to raise ₹25 crore ($3.8 million), principally to construct a milk-processing factory and a chilled supply chain. It took 18 months and was hugely difficult, with most VCs expressing no interest in a milk brand in Odisha. At last, he was able to raise ₹11 crore of equity from 22 angel investors and one fund, Aavishkar Capital, making Milk Mantra one of the first agro-food start-ups to be VC funded. Based on this equity, the company was then able to take a loan of about the same amount from IDBI, a government-owned bank, secured on the factory assets and the personal guarantee of Sri and his wife, Rashima.

Construction of the factory was another challenge. He had started on that alongside the fundraising. No industrial land was available from the state industrial development agency, so he was forced to buy agricultural land from 10 owners and consolidate it. 'I put my own money in, bought the land and got the land converted [from agricultural to industrial usage], which took me a year. I needed to get 20 odd licenses in place, from pollution to factory and boilers, and sometimes I wondered if there were any more that I was supposed to get.' There were further challenges to face, not least of which was tackling local mafia goons. 'Here [in Odisha] the government has a hands-off approach and it's therefore more difficult than in other states. Only now, when people have seen all the good work we are doing, do we get police support, so people don't mess around too much with us. Otherwise this was damn difficult. Even getting the power supply needed some pole to come up somewhere, but the electricity department just washed their hands off it. They said, you sort out the pole locations and then 20 people emerged claiming that this was their land and they needed this much money to permit a pole to be put up.'

The supply system was the next nut to crack. Only 10 per cent of farmers were selling milk through an organized system. On the first day that Milk Mantra collected milk, only seven farmers showed up with 35 litres. Supply took time to build up but they persisted and found that progressive farmers who signed up influenced others to join. Now they collect 100,000 litres of milk a day at 400 collection points, where the milk is measured and tested before being moved to the factory to be pasteurized and packed, or converted into paneer and other products. Farmers are paid based on a combination of volume and fat content. Milk Mantra has a policy of ethical sourcing, ensuring that the farmers are paid within 10 days for their milk and offering other benefits like loans to buy more animals, insurance, feed and veterinary advice. They estimate they have put about ₹150 crore ($23 million) into the rural economy in the past three years, providing a small but important regular income to thousands of families.

To the consumer, the Milky Moo brand offers assurance of a fresh, pure and premium product at an affordable price. The milk is packed in a flexible sachet to save cost compared to a cardboard carton. Milk Mantra has introduced a distinctive 'tripack' which has three layers, the middle one black, in order to reduce temperature and light damage to the milk and therefore extend shelf-life. In addition to the regular milk, fresh paneer and probiotic curd, the company has now launched flavoured milk shakes containing curcumin, offering 'the goodness of haldi' but also the advantage of a longer shelf-life, enabling wider distribution compared to the fresh dairy products.

In 2014 the company raised $13 million from a mainstream investor, Fidelity Ventures, and plans to do a further round of fundraising soon. This year Sri expects sales to double and reach ₹180 crore ($26 million). The scope for scaling beyond that is enormous through geographic expansion beyond Odisha as well as product extensions.

CHAPTER 6

Netas and Babus

'Startup India and Stand-Up India should be our mantra[68]...I see start-ups, technology and innovation as exciting and effective instruments for India's transformation, and for creating jobs for our youth.'[69]

Narendra Modi, Prime Minister of India

'I am not sure how many understand the power of what is being done right now. The long-term impact will be transformative for India.'

Sunil K. Munjal, Joint Managing Director, Hero Motocorp

'Government does not create entrepreneurs. The only thing they need to do is to make it easy to do business in the country, because that is a genuine problem. Imagine our cruise speed if you didn't need to spend 40 per cent of your time on government issues.'

Ronnie Screwvala, Founder, UTV

Narendra Modi is the first Indian politician I have heard making the case for fundamental economic reform in India in simple words that make sense to ordinary people.

The first time I heard him speak live in public was in April 2012, when he was still the chief minister of Gujarat, at the inauguration of the Charanka

---

[68] From Prime Minister Narendra Modi's speech from the Red Fort on Independence Day, 15 August 2015.

[69] From Prime Minister Narendra Modi's speech at a start-up event in San Jose, California, on 27 September 2015.

Solar Park in the arid land abutting the Rann of Kutch. Typical of Modi's ambition, Charanka was the largest such facility in the world with millions of glinting, blue solar panels, soon to be 500MWs in capacity, on 5,000 acres of former wasteland. After arriving by helicopter at the Solar Park's new helipad, Modi gave a barnstorming speech in Gujarati and Hindi to a crowd of local residents and farmers who had come for the free lunch in a huge air-conditioned tent put up for the occasion. Modi explained in blunt colloquial terms to the *dhoti* and Gandhi-cap wearing crowd how economic progress, symbolized by the ranks of solar panels outside, would support jobs and a better life for their children.

Some days earlier, the private-sector developers with operating solar assets in Charanka had been summoned to the Chief Minister's residence in Gandhinagar to be told that we should contribute towards the cost of the launch event. When it came to my turn, the only foreigner around the table, I regretted that as a PE-investment company we could not make a monetary contribution to an event that might be construed as political. Instead, I offered to invite and host a group of foreign journalists to cover the launch. Modi paused momentarily, then switched to English to agree. Here was a man capable of understanding business, I thought.

Modi built his reputation as a strong and effective administrator in 13 years, starting from 2001, as the chief minister of Gujarat. The terrible anti-Muslim riots of 2002 in Gujarat tarnished his image for many in India and overseas. However, his effective rule in Gujarat dissipated the negativity as the years passed. The Hindutva[70] social agenda of the Bharatiya Janata Party (BJP) and its parent organization, the RSS, of which Modi had been an activist from childhood, was not overt and clearly took second place to good government and economic progress. In January 2007, Ratan Tata attended the huge Vibrant Gujarat convention and embraced Modi on stage, declaring that you would be stupid not to do business in Gujarat. Based on his track record as chief minister, Modi's campaign in the general election of 2014 was fluent, effective, high-tech and caught the mood of

---

[70] Hindutva, meaning 'Hinduness', is a complex set of the social beliefs and political policy associated with the Bharatiya Janata Party (BJP), which in turn is sponsored by the Hindu nationalist volunteer organization, the Rashtriya Swayamsevak Sangh (RSS).

the country.[71] He promised change after years of an ineffective Congress government; he promised development and jobs. I was surprised during the later months of 2013 and into 2014 by the number of encounters I had in all parts of the country with people who, not traditional BJP voters, said they would vote for Modi: an IT worker in Bangalore, a hotel receptionist in Darjeeling, a driver in Calcutta. He was swept to power and an unexpected Parliamentary majority on a wave of optimism.

Most Indians, especially those in business, have learnt to take a cynical view of the effectiveness of government. The well-meaning socialism of Nehru became increasingly anti-business through the 1950s and 60s. As has been discussed earlier, the noose tightened further on business after Indira Gandhi moved more towards a socialist model with the objective to eradicate poverty ('Garibi Hatao') but instead tightened the regulatory stranglehold on the economy, nationalizing many sectors and squeezing out foreign companies. The result was throttling red tape, widespread corruption, and multiple and high taxes. The unwinding of some of these constrictions in the reforms made from 1991 onwards, under another Congress government led by P.V. Narasimha Rao, spurred economic activity and gave new opportunities to entrepreneurs in newly liberalized sectors. Nevertheless, the government sought to balance growth in a new, confident India by talking of 'inclusive growth' which maintained a wider social agenda. The perception that poor policy and governance was at the root of India's ills persisted, and was only reinforced by the ineffectiveness and scandals that came to characterize Manmohan Singh's second term in office from 2009. Few, at least in business, saw government as a positive force for change.

In presenting India to foreigners, I have often contrasted India, with a competitive private sector held back by an ineffective and seemingly unhelpful government, with China, where the government is typically proactive and ambitious, and a true private sector is only now developing more fully. While that characterization has a strong factual basis, in reality

---

[71]   For an excellent portrayal of Modi's campaign of 2014, read Lance Price's *The Modi Effect: Inside Narendra Modi's Campaign to Transform India*, London: Hodder & Stoughton, 2015.

India's private sector, and now its explosion of new entrepreneurship, could not have developed without government policy. India has preserved many of the aspects of a market economy from colonial days, most importantly the rule of law. The excellent elite colleges, most notably the IITs and IIMs, are government institutions. I termed the first cohort of entrepreneurs I interviewed Manmohan's Children because much of their success was enabled by the reforms of 1991, not least by opening many sectors of the economy to the private sector. The growing pace of entrepreneurship in India pre-dated Narendra Modi and resulted from years of incremental government policy change.

Modi's arrival in government has resulted in new policy initiatives, including those encouraging entrepreneurship and resurgent business optimism. Modi changed the tone of India's central government after he swept into power in May 2014. He espoused a vision of the future that was confident and positive. He promised strong, clean and effective rule. He was avowedly pro-business. His pro-development agenda was noticeably different from the narrative of inclusive growth that preceded it. His policy priorities included investment in better infrastructure and passing the unified national GST to reduce complex and accretive state-level tax systems. His drive to improve the ease of doing business in the country was well judged, his focus on manufacturing welcome. Modi's language, positivism and apparent effectiveness altered the perception of India internationally. His 'gigs' overseas, in Wembley Stadium and Madison Square Gardens, were masterful in the way they enthused NRIs about the potential of the 'new India'.

Modi's next step was to issue a clarion call for new start-ups to play a major role in creating growth and employment. In his Independence Day speech from the ramparts of the Red Fort in Delhi on 15 August 2015, Modi promised an entrepreneurial India in which new jobs would be created by new businesses. He called on India to 'start-up' and 'stand up'.

The question was whether he could fulfil all of these promises.

The Minister

I have known Jayant Sinha for many years, from his days at McKinsey where he was the prime mover in the firm's thinking on globalization and the creation of new multinationals from emerging markets. He interacted with us at Tata extensively and we remained in contact after he moved on from McKinsey and became an investor, first with a hedge fund in the US, Courage Capital, and then the VC fund Omidyar Network. He and his wife, Punita, hosted me at home for dinner one night a decade ago in Boston along with the former minister and campaigning journalist, Arun Shourie. The conversation was entirely about how business in India could truly be enabled to achieve its full potential. Jayant was elected to the Lok Sabha in the 2014 election from his father's[72] old constituency, Hazaribagh in Bihar, and was appointed minister of state in the Ministry of Finance in November 2014. Jayant is an intelligent, experienced business professional who knows what he is talking about when it comes to economic issues in India.

As the deputy to Finance Minister Arun Jaitley up until July 2016, Jayant was a prominent and effective champion for pro-development policies. He was given an opportunity to make a personal impact, and did so most of all in the area of the government's policy towards entrepreneurship. He had more space to operate than many ministers of state as Jaitley was stretched particularly thin in the early months of the Modi government, notwithstanding his capabilities and barrister's ability to handle a brief. Initially he was covering the Ministry of Defence in addition to finance, then had a period of poor health, and was often involved as fixer-in-chief in wider political issues across the government and the party.

Jayant was unexpectedly switched from minister of state in the Ministry of Finance to minister of state in the Ministry of Civil Aviation in July 2016. This was generally viewed in Delhi as a demotion for one of the emerging ministerial stars, leading to speculation that Jayant had taken a bit too much of the limelight and upset some in the system. His move was certainly a loss for those interested in government policy towards entrepreneurship. He would no doubt argue that by the time he left the finance ministry the new approach towards supporting entrepreneurship was already well developed.

---

[72] Yashwant Sinha, Jayant's father, was finance minister and then minister of external affairs during multiple BJP governments.

'I think that we can legitimately say that we have one of the most conducive policy frameworks for entrepreneurship in the world, especially post the Startup India event on 16 January,' Jayant told me when we met in early 2016, days before Narendra Modi's big launch event for the Startup India initiative. We were sitting in Jayant's wood-panelled office in the Lutyens grandeur of North Block in Delhi. The suit of old had been replaced by a politician's kurta, Modi style. His previous meeting had over-run. I had met Victor Mallet, then the *Financial Times*'s South Asia bureau chief, coming out of Jayant's room as I was ushered in. Jayant was in a feisty, combative, almost impatient mood, provoked perhaps by two Brits in a row asking impertinent questions. Victor certainly does not let his interviewees get away unchallenged and I wanted to explore how much of the rhetoric on promoting entrepreneurship was being translated to real policy and concrete changes.

'The government is fundamentally transforming the entrepreneurial ecosystem in India,' Jayant began. 'It is one of the topmost priorities to build out and strengthen India's entrepreneurial and innovation ecosystem. We have done that in many different ways, and the prime minister is going to be showcasing much of that on 16 January at the launch of Startup India. But we have already accomplished a great deal.'

Jayant's normal urbane charm flickered slightly when I asked what specific changes had actually been implemented. 'We've completely transformed the entrepreneurial ecosystem in India by carefully working through all of the recommendations that we've received on how to make this truly a flourishing ecosystem,' he asserted. He credited the Tarun Khanna Committee Report on Entrepreneurship and Innovation[73] with summarizing many of the issues and making cogent recommendations to address these. He then rattled off a series of initiatives already taken, including the Self-Employed and Talent Utilization (SETU) Programme and encouraging a domestic VC industry by allowing pension funds and insurance companies to invest in Alternative Investment Funds (AIFs). In many ways the headline

---

[73] 'Report of the Expert Committee on Innovation and Entrepreneurship', New Delhi: NITI Aayog, August 2015. The recommendation in the Khanna Report that caught media attention was the proposal to institute a series of 'Grand Challenges' with significant cash prizes to address a number of the major problems faced by India.

policy was the launch of the India Aspiration Fund, a fund of funds to put capital into other domestic VC funds to be administered by the Small Industries Development Bank of India (SIDBI).

The minister's phone rang and interrupted our discussion before I could question how, as someone from the VC world himself, he thought government funding of early-stage companies was going to make a major impact given the scale of private money already available for the right opportunities in India. It seemed Jayant was being summoned to a meeting with the finance minister in half an hour. He resumed at the macro level with his recently acquired political rhetoric. 'The encouragement of entrepreneurship is a centrepiece of our economic strategy. It will take 10 to 20 years but we're putting the building blocks in place now.' He argued that if India wanted to power through the middle income trap, GDP per capita in the range of $3,000–$5,000 per annum, the country absolutely needed a strong entrepreneurial base, including the creation of new corporate champions, 'the Apples of the world' as he termed them.

Before rushing away to join Mr Jaitley, Jayant concluded our meeting by discussing innovation. He began in his new political persona, 'India's manifest destiny is to be the entrepreneurial engine for the next six billion people on the planet. The kind of innovation and business models that are required at the design point that India represents are fundamentally different from the design points that are represented by first-world consumers. What works in Union Square, San Francisco, Times Square, New York, or Piccadilly Circus, London, doesn't work in Jhanda Chowk, Hazaribagh, or in other Tier 2 and Tier 3 towns in India.' Jayant's old persona of the precise, data-driven business consultant re-emerged. 'What we really want to focus on [next] is the innovation side. We want to make sure that we have the real innovation drivers, the great universities, the deep science base, the national institutes of health, which can really stimulate tremendous research that will lead to true innovation.'

#StartupIndia

The grand launch event of Narendra Modi's Startup India initiative, on 16 January 2016 – branded #StartupIndia – encompassed many of the points Jayant had described. The style of the event was classic Modi, familiar to those who have attended the Vibrant Gujarat Conclaves over his years as Gujarat's chief minister. A large invited audience was treated to a long string of foreign and Indian leaders explaining why things were now better and offering fulsome praise for Prime Minister Modi. The foreign guests were led by Travis Kalanick of Uber and Masayoshi Son of Softbank, and the Indian entrepreneurs featured most of India's entrepreneurial stars, including Sachin Bansal, Kunal Bahl, Bhavish Aggarwal, Vijay Shekhar Sharma and Naveen Tewari. The high point was the prime minister's speech in which he unveiled the 'Action Plan' on entrepreneurship.

The eye-catching announcement was the expansion of the SIDBI fund-of-funds by allocating ₹10,000 crore ($1.5 billion) to be invested into domestic funds focused on start-ups. The aim was to create a deep domestic VC industry and consequently 1.8 million new jobs. Other points in the Action Plan were an 80 per cent reduction in the cost of patents, three-year tax free status for qualified start-ups, easier compliances, including self-certification for start-ups and a simpler bankruptcy process. There would be 35 new incubators for small business and seven new research parks, similar to that at IIT Madras. As a package, this was impressive and generally welcomed, and the signalling effect of the prime minister seriously engaged with promoting start-ups and sharing a stage with young entrepreneurs was strong.

Inevitably, closer scrutiny of the proposed actions raised questions as to whether they would, in themselves, make a substantial difference. For instance, few start-ups are held back by tax considerations in their first few years, as they struggle to make positive cash flow, never mind taxable profit. Most regulations impacting smaller businesses tend to be the responsibility of local and state governments, rather than the central government in Delhi, so quite how the single window clearance and self-certification would work in practice was unclear. Most importantly, myriad questions remain on how the ₹10,000 crore fund-of-funds would be deployed to ensure true additionality.

In June 2016, the SIDBI chairman, Kshatrapati Shivaji, announced how the fund would be ramped up. It had, he said, received ₹500 crore ($75 million) of budget allocation in 2015–16 and ₹600 crore ($90 million) in 2016–17, and this would be increased over the next decade towards the headline commitment of ₹10,000 crore. So far, Shivaji reported, 95 funds had been supported with commitments of ₹2,576 crore ($390 million). He claimed that ₹1,065 crore ($161 million) had already been disbursed, which in turn had supported ₹9,520 crore ($1.4 billion) investment into 714 enterprises. These numbers and this timescale appear improbable. Had SIDBI already received its full budgetary allocation for both years (2015–17), and had indeed disbursed substantially all of that equity, it seems unlikely the funds receiving the cash can have deployed all of their capital already, given processing timelines.

More fundamental are concerns over true additionality and effectiveness. There is no real shortage of risk capital in India overall, as I explained in the previous chapter. The key challenge is one of allocation of capital. For the SIDBI fund to make a substantial difference it needs to enable sound investments that would not otherwise have been made. The investment is needed particularly in sectors which struggle to attract capital, such as ones with real technology content, and in businesses outside the main metros. There are sound economic reasons why the existing private-sector funds, foreign and domestic, have not chosen to make investments to the same degree in such areas. They often appear to entail a higher risk. The funds lack the capacity to assess that risk and monitor the investments. The business models appear less attractive in terms of scalability and are often more exposed to the operating issues represented by the chaos of India. It remains unclear how the SIDBI-supported funds are proposing to overcome these challenges.

To make a real difference, the SIDBI fund, and the funds it supports, require careful and professional management with the long-term perspective in mind. There should be adequate time to disburse funds sensibly without political pressure. The funds supported should be those that pursue different, longer-term strategies from those that most existing VC funds currently follow. In particular, supported funds should seek to invest in genuine technology in areas like biotech, materials, chemistry and energy. However, this type of investing requires different and more specialized skills. The government system in India has almost no track record and experience base in this, and there are too few private-sector fund managers in India who have travelled these tougher roads. Moving too rapidly is almost certainly a recipe for underperformance, as availability of money itself is not the key reason for the current market failure. Rather, as has been discussed, the incentives built into many VC funds and the lack of sectoral, technical and operational expertise in them explain the reluctance to invest in these more taxing sectors.

International experience of trying similar policies should make enthusiasts in the Ministry of Finance, NITI Aayog[74] and SIDBI pause. Josh Lerner's book *Boulevard of Broken Dreams*[75] chronicles the efforts of other governments, including in the US, Canada, UK, Israel, Europe, Taiwan and New Zealand, to intervene and support the more rapid development and financing of entrepreneurial businesses. He concludes that, overall, governments have failed in these policies, and such failure should have been predictable. The key reasons for failure are that governments are not good at allocating funds, tend to be too short-term focused, try to work against the economic incentives signalled by markets and change direction too easily.

Ease of doing business

While most specific policies designed to speed up entrepreneurship may have failed in other countries, the most vibrant entrepreneurial ecosystems, including Silicon Valley and Tel Aviv, have developed in large part as a result of government interventions, indirectly if not by policy design. Silicon Valley sprang out of California's role in defence and aerospace, with the Defense Advanced Research Projects Agency (DARPA) playing midwife to many of the early technologies. Tel Aviv has developed as a tech hub largely due to the Israeli defence requirements providing research support and an initial market. Similarly, for India to become a truly cutting-edge hotspot of entrepreneurship and innovation, it will require supportive government policy.

---

[74] National Institution for Transforming India (NITI) Aayog, the body created in 2014 to replace the Planning Commission.

[75] Lerner, Josh, *Boulevard of Broken Dreams: Why Public Efforts to Boost Entrepreneurship and Venture Capital Have Failed – and What to Do About It*, Princeton: Princeton University Press, 2009.

In Delhi, as in Gujarat before, however, Modi's broad-brush vision, policy campaigns and uplifting rhetoric needs practical translation into policy action by able civil servants. As in Gujarat, few ministers of ability thrive under the spread of the Modi banyan tree, as perhaps Jayant Sinha now appreciates. Amitabh Kant is typical of the confident, articulate and decisive civil servants Modi governed through in Gujarat, often cutting out the ministers theoretically in charge of departments. Earlier, Kant was behind the impactful 'God's Own Country' tourism campaign for Kerala and then the memorable 'Incredible India' campaign. He then spearheaded the Delhi Mumbai Industrial Corridor (DMIC) project under the previous government. Kant is central to implementing much of Modi's pro-business agenda. First as secretary of the Department of Industrial Policy and Promotion (DIPP) and then as CEO of NITI Aayog, the replacement body of the Planning Commission, Kant has ably managed the drive to make doing business easier, the promotion of manufacturing through the Make in India programme, and now the Startup India initiative as well.

The Indian business community has noticed, and appreciated, the change of tone and genuine intent from the central government, led from the top but dependent for implementation on able secretaries like Kant. Abhishek Lodha, Managing Director of Lodha Developers of the Lodha Group, the leading property developer in Bombay, admittedly from a family with BJP connections, said, 'The election of Modi is the election of Indian aspiration. He is very clear that his mandate is to get governance and development.' Anand Mahindra pithily remarked, 'I think this regime here finally gets it.' Ashok Wadhwa of Ambit said, 'I'd say the 1991 reforms were critical in many ways but the 2014 reforms are probably even more emphatic. Mr Modi has pressed the restart button; he has redefined how business will be done in India.'

Most new entrepreneurs, though less effusive than the established business leaders, also welcomed the newly positive tone of the government towards business and, in particular, the call for new business creation. According to most, the critical challenge for the government was to make doing business in India easier, to reign back the chaos of India caused, so often, by government action and inaction. Most agreed with Narayana Murthy that, 'The responsibility of the government is to reduce friction to doing business to zero so that entrepreneurs can grow their business rapidly and create jobs.' Nandan Nilekani, after years of working with Murthy, used similar words. He told me, 'The biggest thing the government can do is to remove the friction to starting a business, shutting down a business, to hiring, to access to capital, to access to markets. Just enable us, and I think entrepreneurs will figure out how to survive.' Kishore Biyani used blunter language: 'The government's intention is to create entrepreneurs and they announced an entrepreneurship fund for ₹10,000 crore. But I don't think it's the job of the government to run a fund like that. What they can do is to create a positive environment for business.'

Kunal Bahl, co-founder of Snapdeal, made similar points in an article in the *Economic Times*[76] just before the Startup India launch event. India was already buzzing with entrepreneurs, he argued, and the government policy initiatives were welcome. However, what India needed more than policy initiatives, was a simpler business environment. It was still taking 29 days in India to start a business, tax compliance was hugely complex, and closing a business often took more than four years.

For entrepreneurs, therefore, the government's drive to make India an easier place in which to do business is more important than the Startup India initiative. Progress is being made, and most business folk have noticed some improvement. Amitabh Kant announced in May 2016 that, having risen 12 rankings in a year to number 130 in the World Bank's Ease of Doing Business Index, India was now targeting rising into the top 30 countries in the index in three to four years. That would be a dramatic improvement indeed.

Sunil Munjal of the Hero Group has invested a great deal of his time over the years in working with the government in various capacities, including as President of the CII. 'I am very excited about this big initiative on ease of doing business,' Sunil told me. 'It's a very brave attempt and as an idea [it] is perfectly positioned in terms of timing as people are fed up with excessive red tape. We only want three things from the government. We want it made easier to start a business, easier to run a business and, God

---

[76] http://economictimes.indiatimes.com/small-biz/entrepreneurship/india-needs-more-entrepreneurs-and-less-policy-kunal-bahl-snapdeal/articleshow/50460830.cms

forbid if you need to, please make it easy to shut a business.' Sunil went on to recount how he had demonstrated the complexity of doing simple, everyday things to a group of ministers and officials. He chose three examples of everyday business activities, clearing an export consignment, getting a power connection and securing a loan. He took into the meeting the mounds of paperwork required for each of these. For one of these, 37 separate forms were required, compared to just three pages in Singapore. The officials got the message and, working with Sunil, reduced the 37 forms to seven.

Shailesh Lakhani of Sequoia Capital used a different example to illustrate the positive changes in parts of India's labyrinthine public sector. The Securities and Exchange Board of India (SEBI) regulates the capital markets. In 2012, Sequoia took 11 months to get approval for the IPO of Justdial. 'SEBI made us give all retail investors a put option, the right to sell the shares back to the company at six months at no profit, no loss,' Shailesh recalled. 'The stock doubled on the first day so no one ever needed that option, but the point is that they made us offer such a unique facility.' Now, Shailesh went on, Sequoia 'have a bunch of companies in registration [for IPO] and you get SEBI clearance in a few days. They have made things clear.' However, Shailesh concluded by saying that the positive changes in SEBI were an unusual example. In other areas, in his experience, there had not been enough real change on the ground to match the intent expressed by the prime minister.

The need for much more change

Here lies the rub for most businesses. The positive mood from the top of government and prominent policy initiatives are welcome. However, the experience of interaction with the myriad arms of the government, and in particular the agencies of state and local governments, has yet to alter meaningfully. For every good experience, like the RBI's slicker approvals for IPOs described by Shailesh Lakhani, there remain at least as many horrible interactions with the authorities.

Of the central government agencies, the Income Tax Department probably remains the one most complained about. One newly minted entrepreneur, who shall remain anonymous, told me, 'Some things have changed, obviously. But the physical environment in which we do business continues to be as challenging as before. We have been visited by two sets of taxmen already, each trying to extort us. It's tax terrorism. We don't know what it was like before because we were too small under the previous government, but we think – if anything – it has actually got worse.'

In some ways, the aggressive officiousness of the tax authorities is understandable. With its huge development needs and persistent budget deficit, the country desperately needs tax revenue. Only about 1 per cent of the population pays any direct tax, and there is a strong culture of tax avoidance and evasion. The black economy is massive onshore, and was the target of the bold demonetization of large denomination notes in November 2016 which aimed to drive the economy towards the use of traceable electronic payments rather than cash for transactions. Tax officials need to face this strong culture against paying tax. A recent amnesty for tax evaders saw 64,275 people come forward to disclose some $9.5 billion of undeclared assets, including a group of Bombay street food vendors who revealed $7.5 million of black money. Assessments of Indian black money in tax havens offshore vary hugely, but one recent estimate put the sum involved as anything between $180 million and $500 billion.

Yet, India must have the most complicated and unclear tax regime in the world. Almost everyone I know, however honest and scrupulous in tax compliance, has run into issues with the Income Tax Department. Most foreign companies cite tax compliance in India as an area of real concern in investing in the country.

The government claims it will no longer pursue foreign companies based on retrospective tax changes, as in the famous Vodafone case. Vodafone won its case in the Supreme Court over a $2.5 billion capital gains tax claim relating to its purchase in 2007, through a chain of companies offshore, of a majority stake in Hutchison Essar Ltd in India from Hutchison Telecommunications of Hong Kong. The transaction occurred in the Cayman Islands but the Income Tax Department assessed a tax liability in India on Vodafone, not Hutchison, for capital gains arising out of the change of control offshore. Following the Supreme Court ruling, the then finance minister very controversially changed the law in 2012 with retrospective effect to target Vodafone, a single foreign company. The matter is currently in international arbitration.

Even without such high-profile cases, many foreign companies struggle with Indian tax compliance. In the instance of one foreign company I know well, which operates in more than 100 countries, tax cases in India represent nearly half of all of the tax cases globally reported to the board. Domestic companies have similar issues. A prominent, and I believe honest, Indian company I was advising on international strategy stopped responding to my calls and mails for some weeks because of a series of tax raids across their network of offices. Compliance, even with every good intent, is complicated, expensive and uncertain. The scope for corruption is also consequently significant as the discretion of officers is wide to raise a claim, pursue it aggressively, including through tax raids on offices or homes, and then to settle.

The Foreign Investment Promotion Board (FIPB), which was charged with approving inward investment into the country, has over the years been another body with which many foreign investors have had issues. The government now claims that India has one of the most open inward investment regimes of any market, and the Modi government has taken further steps towards liberalizing some of the remaining controls, including in defence manufacturing and civil aviation. In the 1990s every investment had to go through the FIPB, even where the proposal was within policy and, consequently, there was scope for preference and corruption. I recall talking with one stunned director of a leading UK company on a flight to London in about 1994, who had, he claimed, been asked bluntly in Delhi for money to be transferred into a Swiss account in order to sanction increased investment in his Indian operation.

The opening up of the economy, the freeing of most sectors from any restrictions, the introduction of automatic approval within stated policies and much better administration progressively reduced the obstruction of the FIPB and the scope for protectionist lobbying by rivals and corruption. Eventually, the Union Budget of February 2017 announced the abolition of the FIPB.

The most important politically inspired mess remaining is the policy surrounding foreign investment in retailing. When Jardines secured FIPB clearance for three joint ventures in retail in India in 1996–98, the sector was as open as any other. The new BJP government in 1998 listened to its supporters in the trading communities and closed the sector to foreigners. Over the years, governments have tried to liberalize these restrictions, carefully navigating the opposition of traders, small retailers and unions. Arcane rules have been tried in order to allow partial liberalization, for instance, permitting 'single-brand retailing' but not 'multi-brand retailing', or introducing requirements for 30 per cent local procurement and minimum investment levels of $100 million. Foreign retailers and investors have responded by creating supply chain or cash-and-carry businesses that are not technically retailers but are linked with retail shops owned by a local partner. The grey areas resulting from these complex and shifting rules expose foreign companies to the risk of being judged to be in contravention, as Walmart found to its detriment when it was targeted for investigation in 2013. This policy dance has had a pernicious negative drag on the development of retailing, modern supply chains, the food manufacturing industry, farmer incomes and consumer choice.

The e-commerce companies that have emerged, at least in part, to fill the gap left by poorly developed modern retailing, have also evolved complex corporate structures to navigate the restrictions on FDI in retail. Many e-commerce players, including Flipkart, are incorporated offshore and are majority-owned by foreign investors. Lawyers and officials have an interesting debate as to whether e-commerce activities of such companies are compliant with India's opaque and evolving FDI rules. The FIPB clarified in 2016 that a marketplace, in which inventory is not owned by the e-commerce company, is not retailing, and so for them 100 per cent FDI is permitted. However, not more than 25 per cent of supply to such a business is permitted to be from a single vendor. Existing structures such as Amazon's partnership with Murthy's Catamaran Ventures to establish a supply chain for the consumer-facing marketplace may need to be reassessed for compliance with the new rules.

Such issues with central government policy and agencies such as the Income Tax Department, SEBI, RBI or FIPB, over-complicate matters for companies, add to cost and risk, and slow business growth. But they appear to be improving over time as the government tries to streamline administration, liberalize restrictions and apply IT solutions to improve service delivery. Often, however, the right long-term answer should be more profound deregulation. The abolition of the FIPB is a positive step, as long as a new bureaucracy does not assume its responsibilities. What policy issue, beyond protecting a favoured group to the detriment of consumers, is really involved in allowing a foreigner to operate a shop? Why is the process of filing an income tax return so fiendishly long and so much more complicated than in other countries? Why is an Indian resident restricted in his or her ability to invest offshore? India would grow much faster if many controls were not just streamlined, but abolished altogether.

Notwithstanding these gripes, my experience has been that where a regulatory hurdle does arise there is usually a proper and legal solution if you work at it. For instance, some years ago I was helping to set up the City of London office in Bombay. The RBI regulated such liaison offices and asked for a set of documents from the City Corporation in order to support the application. When I asked for these from London, I was told, rather grandly, that the City had none such foundation documents. The City pre-dated Parliament; it might be able to find a Charter from King Edward II (who ruled England from 1307 to 1327) but normally operated on the principle that 'we exist, therefore we are'. Explaining that to the RBI proved complex, but an impending visit from the UK prime minister, Gordon Brown, who wanted to announce the office while in India, focused official minds and a way through was agreed.

Shivakumar (Shivku) Ganesan of Exotel provided another example of the issues that can arise with government and its regulators as technology evolves. Shivku's trigger to become an entrepreneur was when, while trying to buy a second-hand fridge, he realized that India had no strong consumer-to-consumer marketplace, like eBay. He left his job with Yahoo and launched Roopit to try to fill this need, but the business did not take off. His experience with Roopit led to the insight that smaller businesses were in need of more cost-effective call-centre solutions, so he pivoted to creating Exotel, a virtual call centre using cloud-based technology. He secured funding from Mumbai Angels and Blume Ventures in 2011, and by 2013 was being written about by *Economic Times* as one of the start-ups to watch. However, the government suddenly intervened to question how he was supplying what looked like a telecom service without a telecom license. It took six months to persuade the Department of Telecommunications and the telecom regulator, the Telecom Regulatory Authority of India (TRAI), that Exotel was in fact not issuing telephone numbers but was, like with a conference call service, using legitimate telephone numbers issued by a licensed telecom provider to offer cloud-based value-added services. The eventual resolution of this uncertainty, which had arisen because the regulations were framed with older technology in mind, was to issue a new type of license called an Audiotext License. The delay while this solution was agreed on did considerable damage to the business, including triggering the departure of one of the co-founders. Fortunately for Exotel, by the time matters were clarified, a new business opportunity opened up. Shivku saw the need of taxi aggregators and similar service providers, for reasons of personal security especially for women, to be able to call a customer without the driver or delivery boy being able to see that customer's number. Exotel pivoted to focus on this new opportunity.

Much more invidious than issues with the central government are the cumulative impact of the state and local regulations, licenses, restrictions and taxes. Ajay Bijli at PVR explained that India's low screen count in cinemas, compared to China, was largely due to a series of government measures. State governments tax cinema-going; in Delhi, 40 per cent of a ticket price is tax, while in Bombay it is 45 per cent. In many states in the south, the state government regulates cinema ticket prices, keeping prices low. Pankil Shah, who runs a group of restaurants and bars in Bombay, told me that the impact of the various government entities on his business is considerable and the costs are high. He has to deal with multiple agencies, including the Mumbai Municipal Corporation, the police, the excise department and the fire department. Many of the regulations are completely outdated. There are multiple taxes to comply with, including corporation tax, service tax, and excise and local charges such as the Maharashtra Labour Welfare Fund. Pankil's sense is that the cumulative impact of these regulations is worsening, not easing.

Pankil introduced me to one of his suppliers, Gateway Brewing Co., who face an even more challenging task running their business as alcohol is a highly regulated and taxed industry. Navin Mittal, Rahul Mehra and Krishna Naik are the team that created Gateway Brewery Co., Bombay's first packaging micro-brewery. They met out of a shared interest in home brewing and connected through Navin's online brewing blog, and decided to set up a micro-brewery together. As they developed the concept, no one was able to advise them on what permissions they needed. Eventually, after they met the responsible minister, the excise department gave them a list of 15 clearances that would be required. One of these was from the Pollution Control Board, but that sanction was initially denied as, under a 1981 policy, fermentation was deemed a red classification activity and was therefore not permitted in the city of Bombay. Then they needed police clearance of all their trade partners, but the police official they applied to blocked the application for reasons that were unclear. Only when that official was transferred after three months did the excise permit come through.

The then existing brewery license system was developed for much larger operations so they had to work with the excise department to refine the micro-brewery policy and license to allow for packaging and self-distribution. The license they eventually secured covers kegged beer only, not bottled beer for retail distribution. A condition of the license, as with all breweries and distilleries in India, is that they need to maintain excise staff, in their case a sub-inspector and a constable, at their site in order to monitor production and issue an excise certificate for each shipment. Crazily, each of their customers, the bars, requires a separate sanction for each particular brand of beer carried and for each individual tap in the establishment. Moreover, in Maharashtra, each consumer requires a liquor permit to buy or consume alcohol (certifying, quoting from my own permit, that 'I declare that I continue to require Foreign Liquor and Country Liquor for preservation and maintenance of my health').

Navin went on to illustrate the hassle they continually have in operating: 'We have to renew our licenses every year. Last year, 2015, we put in our application in mid-March and we thought we would get our renewal in May or June. The excise department sat on the papers for six months, when suddenly the commissioner's office called us for a hearing. He said that the application was incomplete as Form 414, which we did not know about, was missing. We were given seven days to secure Form 414 from the sales tax department and submit it. The issue is that they are unresponsive, there is a lack of clarity on what is needed and the policy changes periodically.' Despite such complications, the team at Gateway has pushed ahead, to the benefit of all permit-bearing beer afficionados in the city.

Excessive bureaucracy and regulation, and wide discretion granted to officials, increases the risk of corruption. My own experience is that in India it is possible to operate without paying anything improper to anybody. Most of the entrepreneurs I interviewed said something similar, as you would perhaps expect on tape. Sometimes not offering to pay might mean a delayed project, sometimes it means walking away from an opportunity, but usually a way through can be found if you are determined and persistent. Being a foreigner might make taking this uncompromising position easier, but most good Indian companies, like Tata, also refuse to entertain any illicit payments. The harsh reality is, however, that many smaller business owners are more vulnerable to a corrupt official as they lack the protection of being a foreigner, having a strong corporate reputation or being able to access senior connections, government or otherwise, to help sort out an issue. Getting some agencies to issue permits without speed money is a battle beyond many small businessmen. Certain businesses that require much interaction with multiple departments are particularly vulnerable. The propensity towards seeking bribes varies widely between the central, state and local levels, between departments, between officers in the same department, and across the country between different states.

Typically, dealing with Delhi and its agencies is easier, and most agree that the current government has demonstrated a strict determination to stamp out corruption. Anand Mahindra, for instance, was very positive about the change in Delhi towards clean administration since Modi was elected. 'What is not getting enough attention,' he told me, 'is a complete wiping out of corruption at the top for large companies in Delhi. People don't understand how important for entrepreneurialism it is [for there to be no] corruption. That is a tectonic change in the climate here.' A retired senior British civil servant, who is invited occasionally to lecture at IAS courses, told me that his contacts in the civil service in India place responsibility for issues of corruption at the door of ministers. Appointing clean ministers, as Modi has tried to do, is much easier than changing the culture of millions of government employees at central, state and local levels.

The drive to remove any suggestion of corruption, which is very strong at the top of the present central government, dissipates further down the chain, particularly with local agencies. One interviewee, in a business which faces significant local regulation from state authorities, was entirely explicit, though he asked not to be named. 'The bribe levels have quadrupled in the last three years. You have no option but to pay as everyone does it. I just can't go on record saying that.'

India's reputation for corruption, nevertheless, is overdone by many foreign business people. The reality on the ground is that the situation is improving overall. The best comparative measure of the level of corruption in a country is the index published by Transparency International. In their 2016 survey, India was ranked at 79 out of 176 countries, equal with China and Brazil and just behind Turkey. Moreover, India's ranking had trended better over the past few years, from 94 in 2013, and was markedly better than its neighbours in South Asia. This data supports my own experience that India, while not perfect by any means, is not an impossibly corrupt location and better than many other comparable markets including the so-called other BRICS countries of Brazil, Russia, China and South Africa. No doubt the perception of India on transparency will be improved further by Modi's clampdown on the black money that fuels the dark economy through the abrupt withdrawal of large denomination notes.

Bribery is at one level a simple moral question. You should not pay, and if all did not pay the practice would wither. However, that determination is easier to make if you are wealthy, privileged and have the choice. The worst culprits are the wealthy and influential who bribe to gain a competitive edge or additional profit. Well-established companies such as Tata or Jardine, can and do take the clear position that paying a bribe is not just illegal, it is wrong. In Kiran Energy, we have taken the same approach and built an infrastructure business without paying. However, if you are poor and without a voice in the system, the question is less clear-cut. If you are an individual you might not get your passport issued, a gas connection, a tax matter resolved, or your house registered easily and fairly if you do not grease the system. If you are a small business you might not get a factory permit or your goods might be held at an octroi[77] inspection point if you do

---

77 The tax levied by the local government on goods brought into a municipality.

not pay. The challenges vary by sector; it is easier to run a clean business in software services, where interactions with government agencies are limited, compared to developing a bauxite mine, setting up a manufacturing unit or constructing a real estate development.

Minimizing corruption is possible through concerted government action, as the history of other countries, including developed countries such as the US and UK, demonstrates. Reducing bribery is often the flip-side of deregulation as the scope for official obstruction and discretion is reduced. Prosecution of cases of corruption by an independent and effective agency sends a strong signal to those who might give or take a bribe. Reducing corruption requires a strong tone from the top, ably supported by both appropriate ministerial and official appointees. The clear-headed identification of what governments need to control and license, and equally what they do not, and the definition of processes to deliver approvals in a set period, contribute. Computerization of records and processes makes a huge difference. India is making progress on most of these vectors of change, with positive results. However, the pace and seriousness with which this is being done needs to pick up. India needs deep deregulation to strip away the unnecessary, civil service reform to ensure efficient delivery of what the government legitimately should do, and privatization of those activities better done by others.

It is clear that changes in government policy, and better governance, have had a strong contributory effect on the sudden uptick in entrepreneurial activity in the country. The issue entrepreneurs and investors have with the government is not the intent or direction, it is the pace and achievement of specific concrete changes in the points of friction between business and government. Grand policy announcements are important and welcome. But real improvements in the way government agencies interact with business, the speed and clarity of their services, rulings and responses, matter much more. The drive to improve ease of doing business is much more fundamental and more difficult than announcing an action plan for Startup India.

The positive contribution that government policy and action has already made to the booming entrepreneurial ecosystem in India can be encapsulated in a single example. In many ways, Harsha Mahabala's Edutel, which offers schools additional teaching delivered through satellite broadcasting, illustrates what has been good and effective about government policy. The technology underlying Edutel was developed at a government college, M.S. Ramaiah Institute of Technology, and was initially commercialized drawing on grants from the Department of Science & Technology's National Science and Technology Entrepreneurship Development Board. The satellite platform that Edutel is carried on is a lower cost system developed indigenously by the Indian space agency, ISRO. The main customer and funder for Edutel's courses, which will reach 1 million children this year, is the state government of Karnataka, which provides the staff and equipment in each school and pays a fee to Edutel.

All of this has been positive and impressive. What has frustrated Harsha has been the time and effort required to get him to the current stage of development of Edutel, and the resistance from other state governments to adopt a proven model pioneered in Karnataka. Now that Edutel has a body of course content developed, a proven delivery model and independent measures of effectiveness and outcome, other government agencies should help to rapidly expand its current footprint to benefit not a million children but many multiples of that number. Government-funded rocket science got Edutel to where it is now; yet, it is not rocket science but good, honest and bold administration by a number of state governments that is needed to take it to the next stage in order to boost the education of millions of children from modest backgrounds in state schools.

Technology change has triggered opportunity, more readily available risk equity has supported people with ideas and the government has released the brake through better governance and liberalization. Underpinning much of the change in entrepreneurial verve in India, there have also been deep cultural changes in the Indian psyche, especially among the young. We now turn to discuss this fundamental cultural change in the country in recent years.

Creating New Consumer Brands
NEERAJ KAKKAR AND AMULEEK SINGH BIJRAL

I frequently used to be told that India was yet to spawn any power brands with international potential. With a rising middle class, and new entrepreneurs of great ability and ambition tapping into deeper wells of capital, this looks set to change. Srikumar Misra's Milky Moo has a long way to go from its base in Odisha to become national, never mind going overseas. But both Hector Beverages, the owner of the Paper Boat brand of tradition-inspired soft drinks, and Mountain Trail Foods, owner of the Chai Point tea chain, could create true international brands quite quickly.

I met Neeraj Kakkar, co-founder of Hector Beverages, in an old house near Whitefield in Bangalore which is his office. Neeraj gives the credit for his decision to become an entrepreneur to his time studying for an MBA degree at Wharton. His father was a manual worker at a Haryana State Electricity Board power station. He was brought up in a company town envying all of the privileges of the company officers' children. Two people changed his perception of the possible – Manmohan Singh by liberalizing the economy and Narayana Murthy through the IPO of Infosys, showing what could be achieved in India by people without connections or money. Without these examples, Neeraj told me, he would have become a government employee like his father. Murthy was to come back into his life later on, when Catamaran Ventures backed Hector Beverages.

When, after Wharton, Neeraj had declared to his family that he had decided to set up a business of his own, his father took it quite badly and did not speak to Neeraj for six months. 'Prior to this, in his social circle, I was a trophy kid because I did very well in my career and had a large house and a good car. Then I went to Wharton, one of the best schools, and seemed to throw it all away by going into business. Back then, the social status of an entrepreneur was not what it is now.' The ice between father and son was broken at last after Neeraj sent his dad a photo of himself with Murthy after Catamaran funded Hector Beverages.

Immediately after engineering college in 1995, Neeraj set up a small garment export business along with his cousins, possibly inspired by his grandfather's career as a tailor. When it did not work out, Neeraj went on to do an MBA at MDI Gurgaon. After sales jobs with Eveready and Wipro, he got a major career break in 2011 when he joined Coca-Cola. He recalled, 'Coke is where, for the first time, I started doing well in my career. Almost every year I was promoted into larger roles and then I got into general management, handling a bottling unit.' He met two of his three co-founders of Hector Beverages, Suhas Misra and Neeraj Biyani, at Coke. The fourth of the group, James Nuttall, is an American Neeraj met at Wharton.

James had worked at Dow Chemicals before Wharton and told Neeraj about flexible packaging and how that might be appropriate in India. This was the origin of the distinctive packaging which has become integral to the Paper Boat brand identity. Neeraj recalls his co-founder, now returned to the US, with affection: 'I told him that this is what we wanted to do and asked if he would like to come here and explore it. He is crazy… He had never visited India before, he had no money saved and had three kids with a fourth on the way. But he decided to come.'

Neeraj and team set up Hector Beverages in 2010. Initially they launched a product called Frissia, a protein drink targeted at gym users. Neeraj explained, 'It was protein powder. The hypothesis was that India is a vegetarian country and we can sell protein powder to Indians as so many have protein deficiency. We used to go to gyms in the morning to sell it, waking up at 6 a.m. every morning.' By late 2010 they dropped Frissia and launched Tzinga, an energy drink.

Neeraj's first pitch to secure external investment was to Narayana Murthy, who was introduced to him by a friend, Josh Bornstein of Footprint Ventures. 'We told him that functional beverages are growing at a fast pace around the world, but India is still dominated by carbonated drinks. We pitched that a similar functional beverage revolution was bound to happen in India, too.' When I told Neeraj that Murthy had been very complimentary about him and served Paper Boat drinks in his office, he responded, 'I think I am his distant son or something. He has had such an impact on my life.' Catamaran Ventures agreed to invest $3 million in two tranches. The company has subsequently raised a further $34 million in two follow-on rounds, bringing in Sequoia, Footprints and Hillhouse.

Hector Beverages made its breakthrough with Paper Boat: Natural, traditional and functional drinks, presented distinctively in James's flexible packaging. The idea for a range of traditional Indian drinks came when James's parents were visiting and he wanted to give them some aam panna, a drink made from green mangoes and thought to be cooling in the heat of summer. They could not find anyone who could supply authentic aam panna in Gurgaon, so Suhas's mother sent some over from home. James's parents' response to the drink triggered off the business idea. They began to research other traditional Indian drinks and identify their functional qualities, building a range including Sherbet-e-khaas, Jaljeera, Panakam and Ginger Lemon Tea, all offering functional benefits in addition to traditional flavours. The company also has occasional flavours launched for a particular regional festival. Word-of-mouth endorsement has been complemented by edgy and award-winning advertising on television.

Neeraj's ambition is to make the brand international, finding comparable traditional flavours in other countries around the world.

Chai Point is also centred on a traditional Indian drink, tea. Ginger tea – strong, sweet and milky – was served in small glasses brought round in a metal carrier to the conference room of Amuleek Singh Bijral's office in Bangalore when I went to meet him there. The flavour was redolent of chai drunk a thousand times on railway platforms or perched on string charpoys in dhabas (roadside restaurants) across the country. Amuleek was brought up in Kashmir, where his father, who was from a family which had migrated from Lahore in 1947, was a police officer. Amuleek studied engineering at Thapar University in Patiala, joining TCS on graduating in 1997 before moving to Microsoft in 1998. He credits HBS, where he was in the class of 2006, with opening his mind: 'I think HBS gave me the leeway, for the first time in my life, to think on my own from the very core. I was not really thinking on my own till then.' One of his HBS professors, Tarun Khanna, became a co-founder of Chai Point and helped Amuleek think through the concept, fund it and scale it up.

After HBS, Amuleek returned to India as the country manager of RSA Security LLC, an information security company. While visiting the technology parks in Bangalore and Gurgaon, Amuleek noticed that for all of the amenities within these campuses, people were still seeking the traditional chaiwala outside on the street, notwithstanding the heat, dust, traffic and suspect plastic cups. He began to chat with the chaiwalas and ask about their business and their tea, so much stronger and tastier than what came out of the machines in the offices. 'I am a technology guy and most of the literature I was reading and most of what my colleagues were talking about was technology. But suddenly I realized that chai is very powerful. Then I dug up the stats and I found the tonnage of chai versus coffee. I quickly correlated it back to the insights into Starbucks I had got from case studies at HBS.'

Despite family pressure against doing so, Amuleek decided to experiment with three chai stores, putting in his own money. At the same time, his friend Vikram Sharma, whom I knew as he had interned at Tata and declined the offer to join us after HBS, agreed to a trial tea stall in Pune. Vikram soon decided that the tea business was too difficult, but Amuleek persisted. With help from Tarun Khanna, he secured angel investment by the end of 2010, including investments from Pramod Bhasin, formerly of Genpact, D.S. Brar, the former Chairman of Ranbaxy and John Bilbrey, the CEO of The Hershey Company. With this capital he built a chain of 10 stores focused on the affordable end of the market. But it was very hard to make money at this price point. After a year, he and Tarun concluded that they needed to change their focus and, instead of affordability, they targeted office-goers, starting with a store at Infosys. The tea was the same, strong and milky, but the revised concept was to focus on white-collar workers. Very quickly they were outselling Café Coffee Day stores, with much higher repeatability.

After two rounds of angel funding, Chai Point raised a Series A round of about $2 million from Saama Capital and then a Series B round of $10 million from Fidelity Ventures.

The key to the business, Amuleek told me, was 'accessibility and convenience at work, and the provision of a consistent, authentic product. We need to own the ritual of chai as nobody wants a dip bag or a premix. They want authenticity; they want real ginger, not just flavours.' Amuleek warmed to his theme, picking up a fresh glass of tea. 'We never use lemon [lime, really] concentrate or ginger flavours. We are using six tonnes of lemon [lime] every month, and five-and-a-half tonnes of ginger.'

Chai Point now has more than 100 stores in eight cities and 700 chai and coffee dispensers in more than 150 corporate offices, serving in excess of 150,000 cups a day. At one large MNC campus they supply 1,200 litres per day. The company is innovating its model by developing an Internet-enabled leaf-tea dispenser, and offering home delivery in insulated disposable flasks. Another interviewee told me that at home they no longer make tea if they have guests, they order in from Chai Point.

There is a long way to go before Chai Point is a national chain, let alone an international one to rival Starbucks. But that is its rapid trajectory, achieved one cup at a time.

CHAPTER 7

The Opening Up of the Indian Mind[78]

'Actually, I didn't want to start this, I did not want the lifestyle of a businessman. That is why I had gone to IIT – I wanted to study science. Even though my brother, my father, all my father's brothers and sisters, my mothers' sisters and brothers, all of my extended family, cousins and everyone, have some sort of business or the other.'

Sachin Bansal, Co-founder and Executive Chairman, Flipkart

'What I find in India is, in spite of all the problems that we have, the current generation of Indians is very enthusiastic about the creation of new enterprises here. I get so many mails every week saying I have got this idea, I want to leave my job and do this.'

Narayana Murthy, Founder, Infosys and Catamaran Ventures

'In the last two years I have seen the best cohort of entrepreneurs that I have ever seen, the quality of people is phenomenal. India is becoming a bigger market with better people becoming entrepreneurs. It is going to be very exciting. You are going to see older folks as well, quitting their jobs and saying I want to go and start a company.'

Sasha Mirchandani, Founder and Managing Director, Kae Capital

---

[78] *The Closing of the American Mind* (Simon & Schuster, 1987) by philosopher Allan Bloom argued that, as the book's subtitle unequivocally states, 'higher education has failed democracy and impoverished the souls of today's students.' In my view, the experience in India has been quite the opposite.

Manoj Nair is probably the most naturally entrepreneurial person with whom I have worked. He bubbles with enthusiasm for his business, talks incessantly about every new thought to build the company, and seems to spend all night shooting WhatsApp messages at his team. RedGirraffe.com, which offers a better property rental experience to landlords and tenants by the application of technology, is his third venture. Just as the demonetization, which was unexpectedly announced by the government in 2016, squeezed the cash-based economy, he launched RentPay, a patent-pending product based on blockchain technology, to allow tenants to pay rent on their leased properties electronically. His story captures much about the massive cultural change that has swept India in recent years, most particularly among the young.

Manoj started from a very ordinary background. His father was an army jawan who took hardship postings like on the Siachin glacier in order to keep his family in their government accommodation in Delhi. Manoj recalls, as a small child, seeing his father on guard duty outside the house of a major general. This humble start in life has given Manoj a determination and drive to change things for himself and his family. He describes his memory as a child of not being able to afford the little things his friends seemed to take for granted, new shoes or a meal at Nirula's, a popular fast-food restaurant in central Delhi. While at college, he would work early each morning, delivering newspapers, and he claims that he can still toss a newspaper, tied with rubber bands, precisely to the fourth floor of a building. 'It taught me the value of money and discipline at an early age,' he says.

Growing up, he had no thought of becoming an entrepreneur and just wanted to get a secure job. After graduating in electrical engineering in 1996 from PUSA Polytechnic in Delhi, Manoj got a job as a salesman with Bharat Bijlee, an electrical engineering company that made transformers. After working for a little over a year he saw an opportunity in power-starved Delhi to sell large back-up diesel generators to housing compounds and industrial units. Barely 22, he left his job and set out on his own. His father was dead against this, fearing his son had made a major blunder. 'I was working at a salary of ₹3,250 per month. The day I left my job, my family got really worried; they thought that I was certain to hit a roadblock.' It took

Manoj six months to convert his first order, but that deal alone brought ₹7.5 lakh of profit, a huge sum for his family. Soon Manoj had a roaring business. 'At the height of the success of that first business, we were an 80-person organization and were supplying power units all over India. By 2001, I had bought good properties for my parents and my sister, and I was driving a nice car too.'

Manoj's career then took an unusual turn as he decided to sit for the intensely competitive UPSC (Union Public Service Commission) exam to become a civil servant and achieved a ranking of 157 nationally. His reason for trying for the civil service was partly because he saw his power business being squeezed by growing competition, and partly due to family influence. Members of his wider family extolled the attractions of a government job rather than the uncertain life of a businessman. 'They told me that if you are a civil servant, businessmen come and call you "sir",' Manoj recalls. He joined the Indian Revenue Service (IRS) in 2005.

From 2005 to 2012 he was an officer in the Income Tax Department, first as an assistant commissioner then as a deputy commissioner. He describes working on some of the most high-profile tax cases as 'a steep learning curve but cognitively demanding'. In 2012, he resigned from the IRS and moved to London to become the managing director of an asset management company.

Characteristically, Manoj simultaneously started studying for a Masters in Macroeconomics and International Strategy at the London School of Economics (LSE), juggling classes with travel and office work. By late 2014, as he graduated from LSE, he agreed to sell his stake in the asset management business and went to HBS for the one-year Program for Leadership Development (PLD). He graduated from HBS in 2015 with a clear business plan to create RedGirraffe.com. He had also persuaded four of his professors at HBS and one from LSE to join the founding team.

The idea for RedGirraffe.com was sparked by his own challenges in letting out the properties he had invested in and, in particular, the experience of dealing with unscrupulous estate agents.

The RedGirraffe.com platform presents a selection of screened properties to vetted tenants and has well-defined processes to manage the rental process from leads to property choices and through to the lease contract, the tenancy and renewal. The demonetization of large denomination notes in November 2016 provided a huge additional opportunity to digitalize the $60 billion annual property rental markets through the RentPay product, offered jointly with India's largest banks. Each morning the inbox on my phone bulges with overnight messages from Manoj on how RedGirraffe.com can seize the moment in this latest twist in unpredictable India.

Manoj has come a very long way from the child of an ordinary soldier who used to wonder nightly why he did not have the things that others enjoyed. Now he believes that entrepreneurship is the force that can change India and the lives of millions of young Indians. He told me, 'India is changing and is full of unbridled opportunity. In the next 10 years India is going to see enormous wealth creation. The world is going to gape at the unleashing of entrepreneurial energy as never witnessed before.'

New attitudes, new dreams

Manoj's journey from a humble background to being a serial entrepreneur, from Delhi's cantonment to a base in London's fintech hotspot, captures much of the economic and social change that is reforging India. The most striking change in India in the past decade is not the new suburbs sprouting in Gurgaon next to Delhi or Salt Lake on the outskirts of Calcutta, nor the explosion of shiny new cars on the roads replacing the lumbering Ambassadors of old, nor the swanky new airport terminals and glass office buildings. Rather, the critical reflection of the new India is a profound cultural shift in attitudes across the country, especially among the young. This fresh world view, similar to the confidence, impatience and ambition I saw in America when I went there for business school, is at the core of the upsurge in entrepreneurialism that the country is witnessing. While still anchored in a more traditional India, the young see the future differently and want to shape it for themselves.

Education is often key to the inception of opportunity. Experience of the West, especially the US, frequently acts as midwife to a sense of new possibilities. Role models in business who represent new ways of crafting a better life, endorse and spark new thinking. The media has also played a role by publicizing success. The outcome, especially among the young, has been a sea-change in attitude towards entrepreneurship as a life choice.

A safe job, advocated by the family as the natural, responsible step after a good education, has lost its totemic appeal as the only route to security, a good marriage, fulfilment of familial obligations and self-esteem. Now entrepreneurship is not only more appealing, in terms of financial upside and lifestyle, but its social status is higher than 'service'. It is even beginning to pass the 'father-in-law test' in the marriage market. Fear of failure has lost its suffocating hold over the aspirations of the young. The educated young have been brought up in a world of growth, year after year, in which getting a job is no longer seen as a challenge, even for someone who has tried and failed in business on their own. Rajeev Mantri of Navam Capital remarked, 'The degree of social transformation here is not fully appreciated.' This new sense of confidence, aspiration and drive among young people in particular was described aptly by Sanjoy Roy of Teamwork Arts, provocative as usual, as 'the Americanization of the Indian mind.'

Profound cultural change, as we have seen in India in the past decade, is always complex in its causes and spotty in its manifestation. Not every young person in India wants to be an entrepreneur, but many in increasing numbers each year do, and there are hotspots marked by education, cultural background and geography. Not every middle-manager is a frustrated entrepreneur waiting to jump ship into a start-up, but increasing numbers are. The causes of the changed attitude are multiple and intertwined. Economic growth and liberalization underpin growing opportunities. Technology has fragmented barriers to entry. Cable television, then the Internet, has seeped a different thinking about a world of opportunity into most homes across the country. Education plays a catalytic role, bringing young talent together, shaping it by formal teaching, but also allowing a million connections to be made on campus, in the new coffee shops and online chatrooms.

The result, as Sumant Sinha of ReNew Power put it, is that 'there is now a recognition that becoming an entrepreneur is better than working at McKinsey or at Citibank.' One survey of attitudes among young Indians, the Youth of the Nation poll conducted by Inshorts and Ipsos in September 2016, found that of the 51,629 respondees to the survey, 54 per cent would like to work in a start-up compared to 36 per cent who favoured working in a large company. Moreover, 45 per cent said they planned to found a business themselves in the coming five years. As an angel investor, Saurabh Srivastava, founder of the Indian Angel Network, has experienced this strong uptick in entrepreneurial interest, especially among the young. He told me, 'Being an entrepreneur has become fashionable. Five years ago, we would see 200 to 300 entrepreneurs a year, in 2016 we saw 7,000 entrepreneurs. There is a lot more self-confidence among these guys, possibly verging on cockiness and brashness with some of the younger ones.'

Repeatedly, I heard from the entrepreneurs I interviewed how going to college had changed their outlook on life and the choices open to them. All of the entrepreneurs I interviewed were college educated, most were engineers, and 27 per cent were from IITs. The most extreme concentration of entrepreneurial intent is no doubt in the premier technical and business colleges, especially the IITs and IIMs, but those who attended other institutions also echoed the importance of education in shaping their desire to work for themselves. Shashank N.D. of Practo described how, for him, going to college, in his case NIT Surathkal, was like being 'a bird released from a cage'. From a solid middle-class background in Bangalore, growing up, he had had no interest in a business career. 'It was always about engineering and getting a job.' College opened his eyes to so much, not only with the course content but also the clubs and travel away from home. Most of all, Shashank discovered the appeal of entrepreneurship. 'This whole entrepreneurship thing really got into me. I recognized this when I was at an event where there were four speakers from big companies whom I respected a lot, but they literally put everyone to sleep. And then enters this entrepreneur. His company is one-tenth the size of these big companies, but the way he spoke, he just cut through the clutter.'

One afternoon, in the calmer suburban surroundings of Niranjan Hiranandani's Powai, I had two conversations with graduates of IIT Bombay who illustrated the progression in attitudes towards entrepreneurship among graduates from their school. Rizwan Koita of CitiusTech, who graduated from the institute in 1992, said that 60 to 70 per cent of his graduating class from IIT Bombay went to the US to study further, and most stayed abroad. By contrast, Zishaan Hayath of Toppr, who graduated from IIT Bombay 13 years after Rizwan told me, 'When I was graduating in 2005 if you asked our class what they wanted to do, 40 per cent would want to do graduate studies in the US, 50 per cent would want to get a job, and 10 per cent would do something else, like the civil services. I think now the split is like 15 to 20 per cent want to go study abroad, 30 to 40 per cent still want to go for a job, and 40 to 50 per cent want to do a start-up.'

Other than the impact of college on aspiration, role models are a further major current in shaping a new, positive attitude among the young towards entrepreneurship. Many of my interviewees mentioned role models or mentors who inspired them to think differently. Among the older entrepreneurs, this tended to be through individual contact with an older person who guided them to take a different path. Uday Kotak and Kiran Mazumdar-Shaw were both encouraged by a mentor into setting up businesses for themselves. The influence of such mentors has, of course, continued for many entrepreneurs of the younger generation. Amuleek Singh Bijral of Chai Point described how important Tarun Khanna, one of his professors at HBS, was in shaping his organization, as well as the contribution of others among his angel investors such as Pramod Bhasin. Arjun Pratap, founder and CEO of EdGe Networks, attributes to a mentor the reorientation of the digital education exchange he had created, and which was not working out, into a smart recruitment tool which matched applicants with jobs. Such influential mentors help shape the thinking of many entrepreneurs lucky enough to have access to wise people. The really significant change, however, has been in democratizing such influence by the wider dissemination of the stories of role models attractive to young people through the media and the Internet.

In the 1980s and before there were fewer public role models of heroic business people, and indeed to many, businessmen were seen as grasping and probably corrupt. J.R.D. Tata was one beacon of rectitude, documented in books by R.M. Lala.[79] Then in the 1980s Dhirubhai Ambani burst onto the scene as a very different sort of self-made entrepreneur with the extraordinary success of Reliance Industries, first in textiles then in petrochemicals. Kishore Biyani talked about how Dhirubhai inspired him, and in his book he recounted, 'To me, Dhirubhai was a living proof of

---

[79] See, for example, Lala, R.M., *Beyond the Last Blue Mountain,* New Delhi: Viking Books, 1992.

my belief that, irrespective of one's background, it was possible to scale the heights of success.' By the 1990s, stories like that of Infosys were beginning to suggest to young people that starting a business was possible for smart people with no business contacts and a desire to operate without 'managing' the political system, a skill at which Dhirubhai seemed happy to acknowledge that he excelled. Narayana Murthy was cited as the inspiration in this period for a number of my interviewees, like Srikanth Velamakanni of Fractal Analytics and Neeraj Kakkar of Hector Beverages. More recently there has been an explosion of potential role models, with their narratives spread not just by personal contact and traditional media, but on the web and through social media. The new role models are younger, their success has been faster, and there are many more of them. More young people can imagine that they too could be a Sachin Bansal, Bhavish Aggarwal or Naveen Tewari.

As Radhika Aggarwal of ShopClues remarked, 'The young people of India have fundamentally changed, and the culture of any place changes by the role models. The role models are the heroes we can hold high [in our minds], the stories that you tell. India is now full of entrepreneurs.' At the colleges, at the IITs and IIMs, young people can see graduates from classes just ahead of them setting up businesses, getting funding and making a splash. Ashish Goel of Urban Ladder recalled the influence on campus at IIT Bombay of someone like Kashyap Deorah, who not only excelled academically and took a lead in various clubs and societies, but also set up a business and got it funded while still a student. Chandrakanth B.N., founder and CEO of Pairee Infotech, believes that role models play a more critical part in India than elsewhere because of the tradition of deference and respect to elders rooted deep in the culture. 'We hero worship, I mean as a country and a culture, we hero worship. This may reduce over time as people feel more confident and feel that they can be something on their own.'

I asked Sachin Bansal about how he and Binny feel about the responsibility thrust upon them when they became icons of the possible. He dodged a direct reply, just saying that the only thing he could do was work to ensure that Flipkart remains a successful company. But he was fulsome about the change he sees in the country, with entrepreneurship becoming mainstream. 'Young people are changing here, I think mostly it's about self-belief,' he told me. 'The Internet exposes youngsters to what is happening globally, they are much more aware. People are ready to think bigger and believe that things can happen soon.'

American connections

More significant than role models in the cultural shift in India has been the deepening influence of the US on evolving Indian attitudes. The American connection cropped up repeatedly and strikingly in the stories of the entrepreneurs I interviewed. They went to the US to study or work, their technical skills were developed there, their thinking was changed by exposure to the US and they raised investment for their Indian dreams there.

Among the 92 entrepreneurs I interviewed, the most important common factor, ahead of attendance at an IIT or coming from a trading community background, was time spent in the US. About 42 per cent of the interviewees had gone to study or work in the US. Others like Sachin Bansal or Bhavish Aggarwal had worked in India for a US company. The mindset of young people is therefore irradiated with American culture and business thinking, and many of them then become entrepreneurs. It is too early to speculate how this positive interaction between India and the US over decades may be changed by the advent of less generous, welcoming and outward-looking policies advocated by the new US administration of President Donald J. Trump.

Emigration to the US was the preferred option for the best in India for decades. As Abhishek Lodha of the Lodha Group pointed out, 'There are three to four million Indians in the US. They continuously export a set of values and systems back to urban India. There are few middle-class Indian families without a relative or a child in the US.'[80] Now, unlike earlier, those who go to the US to study are increasingly returning home rather than settling there.

---

[80] For a fascinating description of the Indian-American community and its economic success see *The Other One Percent: Indians in America* by Sanjoy Chakravorty, Devesh Kapur and Nirvikar Singh, OUP, 2016.

Kashyap Deorah, now on his fourth business, built his career of serial entrepreneurship straddling India and the Silicon Valley. He has always raised investment for his ideas from a network of angels and mentors in the US. Naveen Tewari of InMobi credited his time at HBS with changing his thinking and exposing him to entrepreneurs and VC thinking. He returned to India in order to set up a business and later raised his first serious money in the Valley, not Bangalore, after failing to persuade investors in India to back a nascent InMobi. The team at ShopClues met in the US, where they had lived for years, and conceived and angel-funded the business in California. Dhiraj Rajaram created Mu Sigma in a suburban house in Chicago. Pranay Chulet spent some years in New York, including doing his first start-up there before coming home to found Quikr, originally in association with eBay. Among investors, Vani Kola was an entrepreneur in California before returning to create a VC fund, Sid Talwar is himself an American, Sharad Sharma made his money in technology start-ups in the US before coming home to invest in indigenous start-ups, and Rajeev Mantri learnt the art of early-stage technology investing with a New York-based fund and brought the concept home with him. The LPs who have backed the VC funds have, to date, been overwhelmingly US-based.

Chandrakanth B.N. of Pairee Infotech, illustrates many of the facets of the Indo–US duality. When he graduated from Bangalore Institute of Technology in 1991, he left immediately for the US for further studies, like many at that time, and stayed there until 1995. As he recounted, 'When I was growing up there was sort of a doomsday mentality that nothing is going to work in India. The best thing you could do is get out of this country and work somewhere else, make money and be happy. But I think, after liberalization in the 1990s, things started to change and there was a whole social and cultural shift towards more positive thinking. The market opened up and we started to see brands which we had never seen in India. Our choices became greater. So, the kids who were of that generation started to sense that there was hope and opportunity in India.'

On his return to India, Chandrakanth experienced a culture shock as, 'I found a lot of older people complaining about India, the Indian government and the Indian system. I didn't want to complain, I wanted to come home and make a difference.' He secured a contract to set up an engineering development centre serving a former employer in the US and grew that until 2001, when the dot-com bust and the 9/11 attack punctured his market. Together with Sanjay Kulkarni, he then set up Theorum, a software services business focused on online advertising effectiveness largely for US clients, and developed that for a decade. He now finds the negativity he recalls from his childhood evaporated in the heat of the new India. 'The whole social and economic structure has started to change. I think kids today feel a lot more confident in this new world of India.'

From a different generation, Prashant Tandon, co-founder of Healthkart and then 1mg, an online pharmacy, was also profoundly influenced by his experience in the US. After IIT Delhi he joined Hindustan Unilever in 2002 and soon became a production manager. He then moved into brand development and innovation. While he enjoyed working at Hindustan Unilever, and the challenge of innovation in particular, he felt, 'I was climbing very fast up the wrong hill as I knew that this was not what I wanted to do long-term.' He went to Stanford Business School in 2005. 'Stanford completely changed my perspective... For the first time I [was] exposed to start-ups. It made me think that this is really cool and exciting, the idea of entrepreneurship.' On graduation, he spent some months in a start-up in India, MapMyIndia, but then joined McKinsey back in San Francisco. In California he increasingly 'felt pretty stupid to be wasting time in the US when the action was in India.' His choice of healthcare as a sector on which to focus was heavily influenced by what he had seen during his time in the US and he met his business partner, Sameer Maheshwari, in California. The two returned to India together in 2010, first trying a practice management software business, which did not work out, before identifying online health supplements as an opportunity with Healthkart.

A number of the entrepreneurs I interviewed, especially more recent ones, were older and in mid-career when they created their business. Kumar Ramachandran, founder and CEO of Farm Taaza, was in his forties when he became an entrepreneur. He also has a strong US weft in his career and business thinking. Like many from his class from the University of Madras in 1984, Kumar went to the US for further studies after graduating. He stayed in the US, first teaching and then working for EDS, Hitachi and, finally, Applied Materials. With a good job in the US, he had no interest either in a start-up or in India. He recalled, 'My wife was telling me, "Kumar, all your friends are working in start-ups, they all are doing very well, why don't you give it a try?" I said, "I don't think I'm a start-up guy, I'm a change guy."' From 2002 he started sourcing software services in India for Applied Materials and then moved to Bangalore to open the Applied Materials office there. He was surprised at how fast India was changing, and then management upheavals at Applied Materials triggered his exit from the company. In 2005, he founded Vignani Technologies, an engineering services company, with his friend from Applied Materials, Tom Rohrs, and they built it up until selling out in 2014.

Kumar's new venture, Farm Taaza, is founded on the sort of enthusiasm typical of young Americans, and now increasingly young Indians. The company seeks to replace the traditional inefficient and corrupt supply chain from farmer to retailer with a modern, technology-based and ethical alternative. The provocation for setting up a business in India with a social purpose came from his daughter, who was graduating from Stanford in 2014 as Kumar was thinking about what to do after Vignani was sold. He explained, 'My daughter was my main motivator. She said, "Appa, you're a born capitalist so I can't change you. But do something that makes money for your shareholders as well as gives something back to the community."' Kumar realized that his daughter was right, and despite all of his hard work until then, he had left no 'footprints in the sand' by making a real difference to anyone.

Kumar is now very excited about the change and the opportunity he sees in India, especially based on the skills and ambition of the young Indians he works with. He told me, 'When I first came back to India, I found there was a bunch of good, hard-working engineers but without much creativity or aggressiveness. Now [in Farm Taaza] I have got a lot of youngsters who have grown up in India. I am starting to see in this millennial generation the aggressiveness which I used to see in Silicon Valley.'

The confidence and sense of purpose which Kumar observes among the young people with whom he works was also very apparent among the younger entrepreneurs I interviewed. Shashank N.D. of Practo wants to change how healthcare is delivered while Tarun Mehta of Ather Energy thinks only the young can design a battery and a product around the battery that will truly change urban mobility. Abhinav Sharan of Aura Renewable Energy returned to India after schooling at Berkeley and Columbia to make a difference in water and energy challenges in rural areas. Akanksha Hazari, founder and CEO of m.paani, is a principled and deeply impressive young entrepreneur who, with every choice open to her after a stellar academic career at Princeton and Cambridge, decided to return to India to help improve life for the less well-off through the application of technology.

M.Paani offers a loyalty programme to very ordinary consumers at the bottom of the pyramid through mobile-based technology. Users build loyalty points redeemable at local stores or online. Akanksha had the idea in a year working in rural India for TechnoServe and developed the concept as a winner of the Hult Global Case Challenge while at Cambridge. She then relocated to India to roll it out, much to her mother's horror. Akanksha told me, 'I have the luxury of choice because I have had the benefit of a good education. People like me would not have come back in previous generations. My parents had worked so hard to take us to places where there was more opportunity and they were disheartened, very honestly, when I said I wanted to go back to India. If I look at my Indian peers at Princeton, possibly the majority are now back in India today running companies, and that's a fundamental shift.' M.Paani was piloted in partnership with Vodafone, and is now being scaled up after an investment from Blume Ventures.

Besides confidence and drive, two other key traits commonly associated with American business culture are fast developing in India. The first is a new attitude towards failure, and the fear of failure. The second is a level of ambition that is fresh and startling.

Junking the fear of failure

A repeated theme of my interviews was a changed attitude towards failure and the fear of failure. Globally, the majority of entrepreneurial ventures fail, and many successful entrepreneurs fail initially, sometimes repeatedly, before breaking through. The initial or previous failure rate I found among the 92 entrepreneurs I interviewed was 14 per cent, which seems low by most standards.

Among the very successful entrepreneurs I interviewed who had failed early on in an initial venture were Narayana Murthy, Ajay Piramal, Niranjan Hiranandani, Vijay Shekhar Sharma and Sharad Sharma. Earlier, in India, there was a deeply ingrained fear of trying a business and failing, which, possibly based on personal experience, both Ajay Piramal and Narayana Murthy called the 'stigma of failure'. In an inflexible, conservative and low-growth India still recovering from the Nehruvian ice age, the social attitude towards a failed business person was particularly negative. Moreover, very practically, if a young person did not take up a 'good job' early in his (normally his) career, he (normally he) would probably find it hard to get into decent employment, having tried and failed in business on his own account.

One of Ronnie Screwvala's key themes in his book, *Dream With Your Eyes Open*, is the importance of India learning to accept failure and not to fear it. When we met, he elaborated on this evangelism, advocating the need for a new attitude to failure. 'The fear of failure,' Ronnie explained, 'is there all the time. It's huge and deep. I want people to feel that it's actually cool to fail.' Interview after interview touched on a similar point, usually contrasting the earlier 'stigma' of failure with a new willingness to risk failure and to deal with the consequences of failure if that were the outcome. Abhishek Lodha summarized the point well when he told me, 'Acceptance of failure has changed and that allows more people to take risks. People are saying, what's the problem, I am 28, I will try this for three years and, if I don't succeed, what is the big deal? Parents, wives, husbands are now supportive of failure. If you take away the stigma of failure you really open up a set of creative energies.' I asked Akanksha Hazari about how she assessed the risk of failure in her venture; she replied simply, 'I don't know, I am not scared of it.'

A number of the interviewees were still working through the consequences of failure in a venture, and without exception spoke without despondency or regret. Moreover, they were determined to start again with a new venture. I had worked with Arvind Kothari on his start-up, Arjun's Direct, which offered connectivity to a modern supply chain for kirana stores. We failed to raise equity backing and consequently Arvind was bought out by Reliance. He told me that four of his top seven people, in the team he led at Reliance, were similarly entrepreneurs for whom things had not worked out. Arvind has now left Reliance and set up a new venture. Mahesh Choudhary's Microqual Techno (see p. 205, 'Picking Yourself Up to Do It Again: Mahesh Choudhary'.) was a more dramatic crash. Microqual was a very successful and prominent business for a while before it got over-extended and went into liquidation as the telecom market seized up after the 2G scandal. Mahesh is now working through the resulting mess and beginning to regrow some of the remaining pieces of the broken business.

EnNatura is another example of a good idea that did not work out. Sidhartha Kumar Bhimania and Krishna Gopal Singh were from IIT Delhi and worked on commercializing technology developed initially by Professor Ashok N. Bhaskarwar on the use of natural zero-volatile organic compounds (VOC) in printing ink. Other than having green credentials, zero-VOC inks offer health benefits, for example, in non-toxic printing for food-packaging or children's books. EnNatura secured grant support of $20,000 from the Department of Science and Industrial Research in 2008, and then raised venture investment in 2009 from Rajeev Mantri's Navam Capital, which resulted in a further grant from the government. The key issue the team faced was how to develop a way of using the inks in commercial printing machines at speed, but they only made slow progress as they did not have access to test machines of their own to tinker with the process. This slowed down the development as they had to pay for access to machines at commercial printers.

Sidhartha and Krishna were also open about the mistakes they made through inexperience. After raising equity, they ramped up their burn rate on salaries and premises too fast, with hindsight, and then were taken aback by the slow pace of commercial acceptance of their inks. They were close to raising fresh money twice, but, overconfident, they refused terms offered and then found no further proposals being offered. Sidhartha resisted the investors' proposal to hire a CEO with industry experience, thinking that he would grow into the role. Eventually the company simply ran out of money before sales efforts in India and the US delivered adequately to turn the cash flow positive. After they wound up EnNatura, both worked elsewhere for a while, Sidhartha for Snapdeal and Krishna teaching, but now they are back together and are crowd-funding for a new idea around ride-hailing.

As the entrepreneurial tide rises further, there will be many more failures, high-profile ones like Jabong, or a modest and largely unnoticed slide to death like EnNatura. Many young entrepreneurs will try a venture and fail, but many of those will learn from the experience and return with a better idea. The hoopla over start-ups in the press in the past few years might make admitting failure harder in some cases. The recent hype will no doubt normalize as failure is accepted as a natural part of the process. Nitin Gupta of Attero got it right when he told me, 'We should not be afraid of the collateral damage at all. The enthusiasm that start-ups have created for so many people in the country is fundamentally good. The country will change when millions and millions of people want to tackle problems that the government cannot tackle.'

The scale of ambition

A desire to change the country and the sheer scale of the ambition of many of those I interviewed was striking. Sachin Bansal wants Flipkart not just to lead the transformation of retailing in India by ramping up e-commerce to a $100 billion industry by 2020, but to go on to lead a revolution addressing the three billion underserved customers in comparable markets globally. Bhavish Aggarwal wants to change mobility in India, not just provide a taxi service in urban areas. Tarun Mehta and his colleagues at Ather Energy are building an electric bike with world-class looks and performance to alter commuting in urban India. Dhiraj Rajaram wants to change the way companies make decisions.

Shashank N.D. of Practo simply wants to 'help mankind to live longer and healthier.' He told me, 'I keep joking that if two kids can really change the way in which healthcare in India is delivered, people can do anything. Practo is seven years old; I want us to be a $100 billion company for 100 years.' Similarly ambitious is Naveen Tewari at InMobi who describes his aspiration as 'impacting 80 per cent of the global population, touching lives at a scale no other Indian company has, by being one of the best Internet companies in the world.'

With ambitions and capabilities like this, and now access to deep sources of funding, Minister of State Jayant Sinha's desire to see a company comparable to Apple emerge from India, serving the next six billion people, does not seem so far-fetched. These young entrepreneurs have watched companies like Facebook, Uber, AirBnB and Tesla become global players in their brief adult lives. There is no reason why a similar business could not be created in Bangalore, possibly with an initial focus on a non-Western consumer. However, India also needs millions of more modest, local and focused companies like Sharad Lunia's releaseMyAd, which aims to stay private and in a clear niche of traditional advertising, or Pankil Shah's Neighbourhood Hospitality which wants to offer good food and fine ale in Bombay.

Take the enormous success of Bangalore's Start-up Festival, organized annually over the past three years by Construkt, a media company that promotes the entrepreneurial spirit of Bangalore through events, radio and a blog. The festival has so far attracted 10,000 people, making it one of the largest start-up events globally. Where I come from, a start-up event might bring together a few score people in a conference room and 3,000 would be a respectable attendance at a rock concert.

Shashikiran (Shashi) Rao founded Construkt after earlier ventures in an educational start-up and an organic farm. Shashi's success demonstrates much about the coolness, immediacy and energy of the start-up scene in Bangalore. I first met Shashi when he organized a tour of the Bangalore start-up ecosystem for a youth conference using a fleet of speeding auto-rickshaws, much to the squealing delight of the young foreign visitors. We zipped between incubators and workshop spaces, weaving through Bangalore's notorious traffic. Later, we sat over coffee in the art-filled open space at the core of NUMA, the accelerator for entrepreneurs Shashi helps run. He looks the part of a trendy new age creative with his shades, shaved head and goatee. He wanted to tell me about his latest concept of hostels where young entrepreneurs can secure affordable, edgy accommodation while enjoying many of the social benefits of an incubator.

As Jerry Rao, taking a last drag on his cigar, pointed out, 'Socially, the pursuit of wealth or pursuit of business success is no longer considered a bad thing.' In fact, the social status of the entrepreneur is high, especially among the young. Entrepreneurs are cool, with the most prominent treated more like cricket or Bollywood stars than normal business people.

Cultural miles yet to go

'There is a lot of inappropriate conduct. I would get asked for meetings at inappropriate times – suggesting meetings at 9 p.m. on a Saturday, even asking for a date. I would say it happened with about 50 per cent of the investors I spoke to. You have to manage all of that.'

I was completely flabbergasted listening to Akanksha Hazari, founder of m.Paani, talking about what it can be like to be a female entrepreneur in India. Young and fashionable, with a slight American accent, she is very different from the intense tech entrepreneurs I had got used to interviewing. Pitching to investors is usually a difficult and frustrating process for founders, unless you have the luck, or the knock-out story, of Ashish Goel of Urban Ladder who secured a term sheet on his first pitch. But it had not occurred to me what additional issues a single female founder might face while trying to raise money. Akanksha was advised by a number of investors to get a co-founder, which is commonly a good practice, but it was stressed that the co-founder should be male. She also faced issues with recruitment as some techies did not want to work for a female boss. 'I think on the gender side, India is going through a big transformation,' Akanksha continued. 'I think it's one of the big transformations happening in parallel to this drive in entrepreneurship. It will take time to have it fixed in deeper parts of the country, but to me that's a second transformation that is happening now.'

In spite of the explosion of entrepreneurialism, India remains at an early stage in what will be a long process. One way in which the entrepreneurial ecosystem is still immature is the paucity of female founders. Only six of the 92 entrepreneurs, and seven of the 108 people in total, whom I interviewed, were women. I had expected that the acceptability of female entrepreneurs would have improved from the 1980s when Kiran Mazumdar-Shaw struggled with financing and hiring because she was 'a slip of a girl', as she put it. From the work on gender balance we did while I was at Tata I knew that there remain issues entrenched in Indian business related to gender, especially towards the top of organizations. In Tata, the manufacturing businesses, like Tata Motors and Tata Steel, tended to have poor representation of senior women, while software (TCS), hotels (Taj) and marketing businesses (Tata

Tea, Titan) did better. I was used to working with strong female leaders in various professions in India, including banking, legal and consulting. Many of the leading banks in India, including SBI and ICICI, are currently run by women, as is one of the largest law firms AZB & Partners (helmed by Zia Mody, one of my interviewees).

Once Akanksha pointed it out I realized that with a few exceptions, like Vani Kola of Kalaari Capital and Renuka Ramnath of Multiples, I had not encountered many women in the VC and PE world, other than junior associates. There are a number of well-known female entrepreneurs whom I did not manage to interview, despite my efforts in several cases, and a larger number among the younger group of early-stage founders. However, I suspect that 6 per cent is not far from the current female representation among entrepreneurs.

If women are under-represented among entrepreneurs, so are other sections of Indian society. Half of the entrepreneurs I interviewed were either from traditional trading communities (Marwaris, Gujaratis and Sindhis) or were Brahmins, only three were Muslim and none came from tribal or Dalit backgrounds. Stand-Up India, the parallel government initiative to Startup India, aims to spread entrepreneurship to less advantaged social groups like Dalits and Scheduled Tribes, with a target of encouraging 125,000 new Scheduled Caste/Scheduled Tribe businesses in three years. The Dalit India Chamber of Commerce (DICCI) estimates that there are already 8.7 million Scheduled Caste entrepreneurs in India, up from 1.5 million in 2001, representing about 15 per cent of all small businesses in the country.[81] However, these groups remain under-represented among Indian entrepreneurs, tend to be entrepreneurs of necessity, not opportunity, running very small enterprises that struggle to scale, and are largely excluded from external equity financing and often even from bank finance.

Other than family background and membership of a community whose culture encourages a bias for business, education is very clearly the best gateway to entrepreneurship of opportunity. By the nature of their educational backgrounds, in India and abroad, the entrepreneurs

---

[81] See, for example, Subramanian, N. Sundaresha, and Archis Mohan, 'Miles to Go for Dalit Entrepreneurs', *Business Standard*, 15 April 2016.

in my interview set were drawn from a small educational elite in India, whatever their social origins. Expansion of truly world-class education is a fundamental, if long-term, building block for democratizing and scaling entrepreneurship in the country. The government has been expanding the IIT network in recent years, but even after new IITs have been created in Indore, Jodhpur, Patna and Gandhinagar, there are only some 9,600 seats in each class at these premier schools. In 2016, 1.2 million students registered for the Joint Entrance Examination (JEE) for entry to the IITs and other leading institutes, of whom 200,000 were considered as candidates for the IITs. Only 1 per cent of the original registrants and 5 per cent of the short-listed pool eventually secured places at IITs.

Geographic disparities

In addition to social and gender biases, it was also clear that the start-up upsurge is, so far at least, geographically concentrated. There are, of course, entrepreneurs throughout India, in metros, small towns and rural areas. However, entrepreneurship of ambition is clustered in just a few cities, especially in Bangalore, Gurgaon and Bombay. These clusters result from the benefits of better-developed entrepreneurial ecosystems in these hotspots, the choice by entrepreneurs of where they want to live and the variation in the degree of business-friendliness of cultures and policies across the country. At Kiran Energy, we focused on a limited number of states, such as Gujarat, Rajasthan and Maharashtra, which were easier to operate in, had advanced policies and whose electricity boards were better managed.

There are other parts of the country where it is more challenging to run a business. Amuleek Singh Bijral of Chai Point, who was brought up in Kashmir, introduced me to his friend Amir Miraj, who is the station manager in Srinagar for Go Air and one of the best-connected and hospitable people in town. Over possibly the most delicious kebabs east of Lahore at Ahdoo's restaurant, Amir and his wife, Bobby, a gynaecologist, told us how difficult it is to run a business in Kashmir given not just the political and security situation, but also the poor work culture. Natural disaster had compounded the anti-business environment in the state. Amir and Bobby had lost their home and the pharmacy they owned in the devastating Srinagar flood of 2014; recovering the insurance and getting government compensation had not been easy, and they essentially had to rebuild their lives from scratch.

Kashmir may, sadly, be unusually tough for business, but other parts of India can also be very challenging. Only two of my interviews were based in eastern India, although three others were originally from the east and had chosen to live and set up their companies elsewhere. Both Sharad Lunia of releaseMyAd in Calcutta and Srikumar Misra of Milk Mantra in Bhubaneswar described how hard building a business in the east can be.

As an IT-enabled business, Sharad's challenges are less than those faced by Sri, who has to engage more with physical realities in building a consumer product business. Sharad has contended with the disruption owing to the frequent *hartal*s (strikes) in politically charged Calcutta and the relaxed work culture for which people from the state are famous, but these are to a degree offset by lower costs and lower staff turnover in a city with fewer employment options. Srikumar Misra has faced enormous challenges while creating a supply chain to collect fresh milk every day from small farmers in rural Odisha, building and operating a factory to process and package it, and then distributing the packaged milk and other products to the retail system. Sri found that even securing office space of reasonable quality in Bhubaneswar was not straightforward, and recruiting the right talent in, for example, brand marketing, is a constant challenge.

While such hostility to new business in areas of the country needs to be addressed as part of the drive to make doing business easier, clustering of start-ups in a small number of geographies with a more intense entrepreneurial ecosystem is, of course, a natural phenomenon. Even the US has hotspots of tech start-ups in California and biotech in Boston. The UK has concentrations of science-based companies in Cambridge and Internet-focused businesses in east London. Rajeev Mantri of Navam Capital argues, 'Clusters are normal and are no issue. You see this in the US and many European countries; even in China there are certain cities and regions that are far ahead of the others. I don't think we should be worried about clustering in India. It's easy for someone from Calcutta to move to Bangalore, why not? I come from Calcutta myself and there are all kinds of other issues in the eastern region, which is why business in general suffers there, so it's only natural that entrepreneurial activity will gravitate towards a few cities.'

There clearly is an economic rationale for clustering. Start-ups tend to spin out of larger companies or research centres. Pools of experienced people are more available, and might be reluctant to move to a remote location to join a start-up. Mentor networks, angel and VC investors and specialized suppliers all support the ecosystem. Entrepreneurs exit one venture and start another, or become angels and mentors to the next generation. Personal connections and frequent in-person interactions matter, even today, in the age of Skype and WhatsApp.

Bangalore has succeeded in creating a vibrant and fast-evolving cluster of entrepreneurial activity focused on IT, software services and now e-commerce. The government had a role in creating the conditions for its development by concentrating high-tech industries like aerospace in the city and supporting a good education system there, including the Indian Institute of Science and IIM Bangalore. The benign climate, greenery, relaxed culture, good schools and affordable housing make it a city of preference for many professionals who could have been located anywhere, such as the founders of Infosys when they left Patni Computers. As Sharad Sharma pointed out, in addition to the domestic IT companies like Infosys and Wipro, it was the choice of Bangalore in the 1990s by MNCs like GE, IBM, BT, BAE and Bosch for their India research and development centres that brought technology depth and rigour at scale. Many of the city's tech entrepreneurs had earlier worked in development centres for MNCs like Amazon, Google and Microsoft. A number of the entrepreneurs I interviewed, including Bhavish Aggarwal of Ola and Pranay Chulet of Quikr, had started their companies elsewhere, in Bombay in these two cases, but moved to Bangalore because of the depth of technical talent available there.

Bangalore as a cluster, however, differs in one important respect from Silicon Valley, Boston or Cambridge's Silicon Fen. These international clusters are all anchored by great research universities, Stanford, Berkeley, Harvard, MIT and Cambridge, and the start-up ecosystems have developed with strong connections with these universities. Google was conceived at Stanford while ARM Holdings developed with strong connections to Cambridge University. In Bangalore, by contrast, other than recruiting smart technical people coming out of the education system, the connections of the start-up ecosystem with the universities are much less intense and essential. India, in general, lacks truly world-class research universities, and the culture within academia is less open to the commercial potential of research and the importance of symbiotic relations with the business world than is the case in many places internationally, particularly in the US.

Clustering is no doubt a healthy and natural process, but India, given its size and development needs, requires more than just the Bangalore phenomenon. It needs multiple clusters, probably each with a different sectoral slant. The potential is there for more clusters to develop. Pune has many of the strands that could combine to create a cluster of engineering innovation and start-ups, Bombay could deepen its specialization in fintech and media start-ups, Delhi could create a hub of pharmaceutical activity. Intensity of private-sector activity would be the main drivers of such clustering, supported by a network of specialized role models, mentors, angels and VCs. More intensive ties between the entrepreneurial ecosystem and more outward-looking and commercially oriented universities are also required.

Yet, with the momentum towards entrepreneurship of ambition spreading, start-up activity is beginning to pick up in other large cities and smaller towns. I could have added to my interviews by meeting new entrepreneurs based in fast-growth Tier 2 cities like Jaipur, Hubli, Guwahati, Coimbatore, Chandigarh, Cochin and Vadodara. Chandrakanth B.N. of Pairee Infotech told me, 'I think what you see is most visual in let's say Bangalore, where the IT and the entrepreneurial ecosystem is great. But I have cousins in small towns who have tried different ventures, whether it's just owning a lorry or opening a retail shop.' Similarly, Neeraj Kakkar, founder of Hector Beverages with its Paper Boat brand, talked of the hope that success stories of entrepreneurship have given to people in small towns across the country, and the reduction of the sort of resistance he and many others faced from parents when he wanted to become an entrepreneur.

India's sheer size means that a globally significant trend in absolute terms can develop in parts of new India, yet the scale of traditional Bharat can average it out in relation to the economy and population as a whole. Rama Bijapurkar's concept of the great Indian rope trick, the impact of very large numbers, explains how India can have at the same time a globally significant start-up scene, a wave of entrepreneurship, and yet perform relatively badly when ranked on the Global Entrepreneurship Index, the GEI (98 out of 132 countries). As in the theory of quantum mechanics, in India there are often parallel realities, many versions of the truth co-existing at once, each equally valid.

India has become a boom country in terms of a new wave of entrepreneurship, in part if not in whole. But for India to become a global leader in entrepreneurship, and for business to lead the change possible for a large section of society, much more is required. The virus of the entrepreneurial dream needs to spread wider and deeper. The hotspots of start-up excitement, significant as they are even today in historical or international terms, are still swamped by the larger swathe of India, geographically and socially, that has not changed enough. Start-up Bangalore is not yet representative of Bharat. There are other Indias among the emerging middle class or the urban or rural poor, where the ambition to change the world through entrepreneurship seems distant indeed. There are millions of entrepreneurs in these Indias too, but typically they are not VC-fueled agents of a new India, but rather entrepreneurs of necessity, the street vendor and cobbler, or entrepreneurs of tradition, the traders and brokers.

The final chapter discusses the two most important ways in which the exciting yet immature upsurge in entrepreneurship in India needs to develop further to spawn the sufficient numbers and scale of world-class companies required to generate the wealth and jobs the country deserves. First, India needs more entrepreneurs in operating and manufacturing businesses and, second, Indian entrepreneurs need to be more innovative if they are to create truly world-class enterprises.

Picking Yourself Up to Do It Again
MAHESH CHOUDHARY

In 2012, Mahesh Choudhary felt as if everything were possible for himself and his company, Microqual Techno, which he had started in 1999 when he was just 19 years old. Microqual was a supplier of equipment to the rapidly growing telecom industry. Its turnover that year reached ₹810 crore ($123 million). He was operating not just in India but had followed his Indian customers in their international expansion to Nigeria, Kenya, Uganda, Tanzania and Bangladesh. He had just signed a term sheet to raise $72 million of equity to fund the next phase of expansion with the International Finance Corporation (IFC), New York Life and HSBC. That year, Mahesh gave an interview saying that he wanted to make Microqual a billion-dollar company within the next seven years.

On 2 February 2012, the Supreme Court ruled on a Public Interest Litigation case regarding the awarding of spectrum for 2G telecom licenses. The court found the awarding of the licenses 'unconstitutional and arbitrary' and 122 licenses issued by the government in 2008 were cancelled. The ensuing scandal, with accusations of corruption against the minister of telecommunications and multiple private-sector industry players, rocked the government. The expansion and investment projects of Mahesh's telecom customers, even those not caught up in the scandal, were frozen. He had taken a $30 million loan in order to get moving on his own investment plans in anticipation of the $72 million equity committed. The equity never came. Sales fell dramatically in 2013 to just ₹110 crores ($16.6 million). By 2015, Microqual, unable to service the debt, declared bankruptcy.

Mahesh comes from a traditional Marwari family in Bombay. His father and uncles were suppliers of dyes and chemicals to the leather industry. As a student, Mahesh used to spend time each afternoon in his father's office but he found it hard to settle into the conservative culture of the family business.

'He [his father] used to tell me, it takes decades or generations to build a company. The IT thing was just happening and I was seeing, right in front of me, Infosys, Wipro and other Indian companies on the first page of the *Economic Times* and filing for IPOs. I thought, why can't I be one of them?'

As a young man, Mahesh had an interest in telecom. A family friend introduced him to some contacts in the industry and he secured an opportunity to import some components. Mahesh recalled, 'There was no Indian company that was into radio frequency technology. We were dependent 100 per cent on imports. In China, the whole ecosystem of radio frequency was present. In India, the only people who knew wireless radio frequency technology [were] the military; there was no commercial company which was focused on doing it.' He started by importing splitters for Wireless in Local Loop (WLL) services, then offered by Tata and Reliance, replacing more expensive devices being imported from the US.

He found there was an untapped technical resource in the universities, especially IIT Bombay. 'I realized that there were many students doing PhDs or MTechs on antennas, splitters and combiners and I was shocked that these guys worked hard for four or five years to develop a paper and 97 per cent of these ideas never saw commercial production. They would get a hefty job in some foreign land and move out. I set out to convince these PhDs that I could give their theses a commercial angle and working along with me they would get to develop a commercial product, making their research all the more sexy.'

By 2002, WLL was a fading technology. Mahesh saw that a critical issue for the telecom providers was the quality of network coverage. By rejigging his splitters he could develop them into micro-cells to boost coverage for mobile phones. 'I realized these splitters could get good application in in-building coverage solutions. I just had to retune my frequencies: from 820 to 890 megahertz, 890 to 960 megahertz and 1710 to 1880 megahertz.' The telecom providers were delighted to see a low-cost solution to coverage issues, which boosted their revenue from high-yielding roaming customers. Mahesh explained, 'Early in my life I realized you can build a business on either pain-killers or energy boosters. I said I want to be a pain-killer. I don't want to offer an energy booster because there's a choice to take it or to not take it. A pain-killer is something that [the customer] will definitely take.'

The year 2005 was a watershed one for Mahesh. He achieved ₹13 crore of sales, exceeding the turnover of his father's company. And he enrolled in a part-time management course at S.P. Jain Institute of Management Research, where one of the professors, Dr D.D. Patel, opened his eyes to strategic ambition. Mahesh recalls Dr Patel telling him, 'Any Tom, Dick and Harry can become a ₹100-crore company. Only a guy with the ambition of [creating a] ₹1,000 crore plus [company] should attend my class; otherwise you don't need my class. Go out, sit in the canteen, have a good time, have some drinks and you will make it to ₹100 crore.'

In 2006, Microqual was recognized by Deloitte as one of the highest potential technology companies in the country. Mahesh was interviewed on the Young Turks programme on CNBC. That led to a call from Ernst & Young (EY) about a possible IPO, but instead the discussion with EY led to Microqual's first round of VC funding of $10 million in 2007. The funds supported a first manufacturing unit in Bangalore to make antennas, splitters, combiners and cables. The next step was to become an EPC contractor to the telecom industry.

By 2009, when Microqual raised its next $10 million from Headland Capital, it was a ₹350 crore ($53 million), profitable, high-growth company employing 1,000 people. This new funding led Mahesh to follow his customers overseas, and to plan a telecom tower infrastructure leasing business. 'I was getting a chance to spend time with Sunil Mittal and Mukesh Ambani. I was in newspapers and magazines. And that was the time we were raising $72 million from the round led by IFC.'

After the pride came the fall. 'In 2012–13, it was almost like a washout in India. The 2G scandal on the one hand. On the other side, the Vodafone tax case [elaborated on before] and Bharti facing a crisis in Africa [following their major acquisition of Zain's African assets for $9 billion in 2010]. There was no company who was willing to invest money; everything stopped, everything was on pause. People were not paying and customers did not want to give new projects or even complete agreed projects. So all the investors backed out and banks wanted us to repay their loans. We were caught by surprise. If all had gone right, in early March we would have had $72 million in the bank. We took on projects in anticipation of that $72 million, we started digging for a few projects in anticipation of $72 million and we made commitments based on $72 million.'

Sitting in a shabby office in Andheri, Mahesh looked back on the fallout of that time, the effect it had on his business and family. 'In the 16 years of my career, I have seen 12 years of success and four years of struggle, failure, whatever. The learnings from the years of failure are 10 times more.' He is determined to rebuild his business and to pay back the last of his creditors. And he has a new business in mind. 'I am a special child of God. I am religious, and I know whatever God has done to me is for a special purpose. Today I am 36, next week I will be 37. How many 37-year-olds have seen what I have seen? Now, when I bounce back, I will be able to become much larger, much more solid – the organized corporate that I always envisioned.'

CHAPTER 8

Something Yet Lacking

'If you take a 10- to 15-year view, India will become as vibrant an idea ecosystem as any other place in the world, absolutely. For that to happen, many things need to happen in parallel. Lots of investors need to come in, of whom some will make money, some lose money. Lots of entrepreneurs need to come in with good ideas, some of which will fail badly. But there will [be] many who will become real success stories.'

Ashish Goel, Co-founder and CEO, Urban Ladder

'There is massive scope for improvement. IT is just scratching the surface of things to do.'

Dhananjaya Dendukuri, CEO and Co-founder, Achira Labs

The Ather S340 electric motorbike is a sculpted thing of beauty. Its smart design is all smooth curves. Placed in the picture window of Ather Energy's Bangalore office, it attracts a crowd outside on the pavement. Tarun Mehta, the co-founder of Ather Energy, is an intense young man with professorial glasses and a shy grin, and when he finds me looking at the bike he eagerly demonstrates its features. The large, touch-sensitive instrument display offers not just control information but also navigation. It has a driving range of 60 km and 80 per cent recharge of the battery takes an hour. The pick-up performance is similar to a petrol scooter: from 0 to 60 kmph in 12.1 seconds. The price is yet to be announced as the commercial launch is now scheduled for 2018.

This new automotive brand is the creation of two young engineers still in their twenties, Tarun Mehta and Swapnil Jain. They met at IIT Madras, from where they graduated in 2012. While at IIT they worked together on several research projects and applied for a number of patents. On leaving college both took jobs, Tarun at Ashok Leyland and Swapnil at General Motors. Tarun told me, 'I realized that what I really wanted to do was to focus on engineering and start up a product company, as did Swapnil. But, while we worked on a bunch of ideas, nothing seemed big enough to spend the next 20 years of our lives working on.'

Batteries loomed in Tarun's mind, given the potential transformational impact of the major reduction in cost expected in the next few years; projections suggest that battery costs should fall from today's $600–$700 per kWh to $300 per kWh by 2020. Elon Musk's Tesla is talking about achieving $100 per kWh at the huge scale of manufacturing they envision. Tarun is dismissive about the understanding of batteries in India: 'Most people who build battery packs in India are caught in an older technology. Knowledge of lithium-ion packs, battery management systems and production processes is limited. Young designers have as much a shot at excelling as someone with years of lead-acid battery experience. A small team can have a disproportionate impact with good design work. So we decided we could build a better battery.'

The pair resigned from their jobs and returned to IIT Madras in the autumn of 2012 to work on battery design. Dr Krishna Kumar R., their old professor, was very supportive of two former students wanting to return to do development work, and provided space on campus, accommodation and a bit of work to help with costs. They decided to extend from batteries to designing a whole vehicle, built around a better battery, which could meet market expectations of range, performance and charge time. The work was funded by an angel investor, Srini Srinivasan of Aerospike, and a grant from the Technology Development Board.

By mid-2014 they had only $7,000 left from their funding, despite their low burn rate of $2,000 a month. Conversations with other angels and VCs were not encouraging. Tarun recalled that they had the same feedback from multiple meetings. They were told, 'You are wrong about starting an automotive company. You just graduated and you are making all the classic mistakes. You are saying that you will do it all yourselves, the design of everything except the motor itself. Instead you should finish all the design work and hand it over to Tata or Mahindra, let them do the assembly and distribution.' All of this was very logical and Tarun had no good answers to many points, except, 'I knew [that] what I was doing was the only way to do it.'

After VCs showed no interest in backing Ather, a mentor, Achal Kothari, advised them to approach non-traditional investors to find someone who would be excited about the idea of developing the complete chain, from battery to sales point. Tarun secured a meeting with Sachin Bansal of Flipkart to ask for his advice. Tarun remembers, 'Sachin told me, "I would really like to help you guys." He smiled and said, "I'd love it if you'd let me do the entire round."' Sachin and his partner Binny put in $1 million between them. Then, presumably after a nudge from Sachin, Tiger Global got in touch a few months later and agreed to invest $12 million in May 2015.

Ather Energy has now moved out of IIT Madras to an office in Bangalore, and is building a plant at Whitefield on the outskirts of the city. The open-plan office is buzzing with young engineers fired up to create something truly new. The design looks excellent and the claimed performance is impressive. Twenty-six patents have been filed, in addition to 50 proprietary designs. With the product finalized, Tarun is now facing the challenges of building a full process-driven organization from scratch, creating a supply chain, establishing the assembly unit and putting in place a distribution and service infrastructure. When I last spoke with him, the prototypes were in test, the assembly facility was under development and a commercial launch was expected in 2018.

In October 2016 Ather Energy announced that Hero, the world's largest two-wheeler manufacturer by volume, was investing up to ₹205 crore ($31 million) for a stake of up to 30 per cent, valuing the company at more than $100 million pre-revenue. Like the performance of the bike itself, that's impressive acceleration from a thought on campus just five years ago to attracting investment at that valuation from the industry leader.

Ather Energy is a rare example of a young company with many of the facets that the burgeoning entrepreneurial ecosystem in India yet signally lacks and will need to strengthen if it is to develop to its full the potential it has to change India for the better. In sum, the key weaknesses are a paucity of true innovation and a neglect of manufacturing. While the S340 bike looks good, its real market edge lies in its performance on parameters about which customers truly care. This comparative advantage derives from innovation in the battery which is the outcome of development work done at one of India's leading technical universities, IIT Madras. Rather than selling or licensing the technology, Tarun and Swapnil have been determined to build the whole bike themselves and to do so at scale. This chapter explores what needs to be done to encourage more young companies to have the determination to seek true innovation and to have the confidence to see manufacturing as a potential source of advantage.

Make in India

India's fast-developing but immature entrepreneurial ecosystem is currently skewed towards sectors other than manufacturing. Of the 92 entrepreneurs I interviewed, the largest number, 37, were in IT or e-commerce and 21 were in financial services; only nine were in manufacturing. This broad picture of sectoral distribution, with a bias towards sectors like IT and finance, is confirmed by the VCCEdge database of private equity capital investment in India. In 2016, 31 per cent of the $15 billion invested went into financial services and 22 per cent into IT and related businesses, despite IT-related investment halving compared to 2015. Only 20 per cent of investment went into industrial and manufacturing businesses.

My earlier discussion on the VC industry, 'The Money Men', explained why, from an investor's viewpoint, it appears to make sense to prioritize investment in sectors other than manufacturing, or indeed other areas like infrastructure or biosciences. This is partly because of the perceived ease of profitable scaling in sectors such as IT and e-commerce, and the consequent capital efficiency and higher anticipated returns. It also reflects an unwillingness to assume implementation risk in sectors like manufacturing or infrastructure or technical risk involved in product development.

From a policy perspective, the bias towards a few sectors at the expense of others is a concern. Successful businesses in IT and e-commerce are of course to be celebrated, but economic development and job creation demand much more. For India to spawn the next Apple, Tesla or Intel, an ecosystem conducive to the development of products and intellectual property is needed. India desperately needs better infrastructure, but if entrepreneurs are not motivated to face the challenges of developing projects in India, given issues of land, permits and payment, and investors are not excited to put up a substantial part of the $1 trillion required to fill the infrastructure deficit, India's power, roads, ports and airports will remain inadequate. Most importantly, to create the jobs needed – 1 million a month – and address India's balance of trade gap, $120 billion in 2015–16, growth in manufacturing is essential.

Coming from a background in manufacturing, distribution and infrastructure businesses, and now having been exposed to technology-oriented start-ups, my belief is that sound investment opportunities are being neglected by the current propensity among both entrepreneurs and VCs to favour certain sectors. The most pressing neglected sector is manufacturing, where there is a huge and growing opportunity in India.

Prime Minister Narendra Modi has recognized the critical need for manufacturing in the country if growth, poverty alleviation and job creation are to be achieved. He launched his 'Make in India' campaign in September 2014, soon after assuming power, to encourage both domestic and foreign investment in manufacturing in India. Manufacturing currently represents just 16 per cent of India's GDP, compared to 43 per cent in China. India's growth in recent years has been principally driven by the rapid expansion of services. The government's target is to reverse the relative decline of manufacturing and to restore it to 25 per cent of the GDP by 2025, creating 90 million jobs.

'Since the industrial revolution, no country has become a major economy without becoming an industrial power,' Lee Kuan Yew, Singapore's first prime minister, remarked in Delhi in 2005.[82] The Economic Survey of 2014[83] made the case for boosting manufacturing to achieve long-term prosperity. Essentially, industrial output drives productivity in the economy, which

---

[82] The Jawaharlal Nehru Memorial Lecture in New Delhi, 2005.
[83] http://indiabudget.nic.in/es2014-15/echapter-vol1.pdf

in turn underpins long-term economic growth. India has so far taken a different path of economic development from Japan, the tiger economies of East and South-East Asia (South Korea, Taiwan, Hong Kong and Singapore) and China. Because of its inward-looking, protectionist policies from 1947, and its inefficient infrastructure and complex regulation, manufacturing for export has not developed in India to the same degree as elsewhere in emerging Asia. To sustain growth and absorb the millions of new job seekers who will come into the economy in the years ahead, an improved manufacturing performance is essential.

I am a firm believer in India as a manufacturing location, and I have seen many superbly managed operating businesses in India returning 20–30 per cent on capital employed. Within a factory in India it is possible to operate at world-class levels of cost and productivity, largely due to the quality and affordability of staff available. Tata had a range of such strong manufacturing businesses in sectors from automotive to metals to watches. When I ran the dealership for Mercedes Benz in western India I used to frequently visit the assembly plant in Pune which was consistently rated as one of the best in Daimler Benz globally. Similarly, JCB now has five world-class factories in India that produce back-hoe loaders and other machines for both the domestic market, in which JCB's market share exceeds 50 per cent, and for export. JCB has continued to invest in a new capacity in India because of the quality, productivity and cost achieved by its Indian plants.

I am a director of Coats, the world's leading thread supplier, for whom, similarly, India is a major manufacturing hub and supply base for grey thread to feed Coats dyeing and finishing facilities globally. Because Madura Coats is an unlisted subsidiary of Coats, UK, it has a low profile among MNCs in India, but it remains one of the largest foreign manufacturing employers in the country. Coats thread is an integral if anonymous part of Indian life, the 'Intel Inside' of a high proportion of garments stitched in the country, but also for more socially significant celebrations like the symbol of marriage, the mangalsutra, and the hugely popular sport of kite-flying.

The challenge holding back the enormous potential for manufacturing in India is the external environment in which a plant operates – the chaos of India. Within the facility everything can be of global standards, and the quality and cost of technical and operating staff contribute to a competitive advantage. Yet, the reliability and cost competitiveness of supply from the plant are all too frequently eroded by inefficiencies arising from excessive regulation, high taxes and unreliable and costly infrastructure. These are the issues that need to be addressed to make the aspirations of Make in India a reality.

Textiles provide a good illustration of the friction holding back manufacturing in India. The country has a long history of textile production, both of traditional hand-woven material and, from the late nineteenth century onwards, also a modern, mechanized industry based largely in Bombay, Gujarat and Coimbatore. Coats has been spinning and finishing thread in India since 1883, while Jamsetji Tata established the Empress Mill in Nagpur in 1874 as his first enterprise in what would grow into the Tata Group. Given this textile tradition, as well as abundant low-cost labour, one would have expected India to have emerged as a major part of the global supply chain for garments when, from the 1980s, clothing production migrated from the West to the East. But it was China, not India, that emerged as the dominant force in ready-made garments.

Global clothing brands and their major contracting suppliers perceive India as a less competitive and reliable source of supply, despite the fabric supply base and low labour rates. India has draconian state-level labour laws that regulate and complicate hiring and firing in units employing more than 100 staff, meaning it is extremely hard to close a factory or even remove an individual unproductive employee. Moreover, the supply chain is rendered inefficient, unreliable and expensive by clogged ports and roads. Government action, or inaction, worsens matters by slowing customs clearance, imposing multiple taxes and frustrating factory operations by myriad license and inspection regimes.

As China has in more recent years become a more expensive source of products like clothing, with rising wages and an appreciating currency, supply has switched increasingly to countries like Bangladesh, Vietnam and Indonesia, but not India. The bras I used to make at Courtaulds for Marks & Spencer in Bristol in the late 1980s are now stitched in Sri Lanka, not India. In 2015, China exported $185 billion worth of clothing, Bangladesh

$34 billion, Vietnam $23 billion and India only $16 billion.[84] Concerted action could reverse the perception that India is a less attractive location for thin-margin assembly operations, like garment stitching, which are relatively mobile and gravitate to locations with pools of available labour and lower costs. If India could match the success of Bangladesh in textiles exports, up to 4 million jobs could be created quite rapidly. Initially, the necessary dramatic change in ease of doing business, and upgradation of infrastructure, could be focused on specific areas designated for export units, as was the case early in China's transformation to an industrial superpower.

India's superb engineering skills mean that it is typically already competitive in batch-style, engineering-intensive manufacturing like earth-moving equipment, but less competitive in manufacturing of lower-margin volume products like clothing or mobile phones. Yet the gap is narrowing. When I looked at sourcing from China for the Tata Group a decade ago, on average China was about 20 per cent cheaper than India for manufactured goods, with a greater edge in volume products and less advantage in more engineering-intensive items. In 2014, when Avalon Consulting, with whom I was then partnering, examined the automotive component sector, they concluded that for most such products China was about 5 per cent cheaper than in India. This remaining advantage will be swiftly eroded as China's costs rise, the rupee weakens and the disadvantages of India, largely poor infrastructure and government-related friction, reduces.

There are many entrepreneurs who recognize the potential for manufacturing in India, though not an adequate number, and they find it harder to secure funding for their businesses. This is a situation that needs to change.

Micromax launched its mobile phone business sourcing the product from China, partnering with contract suppliers like BYD Company Ltd and Foxconn Technology Group. Starting in 2014, the company has invested in new manufacturing units in Rajasthan and at Hyderabad. Vikas Jain explained that to remain competitive long-term they decided they had

---

[84]   Analysis from Coats Group plc based on data from USITC, EUROSTAT and The Statistics Bureau, Japan.

to manage manufacturing themselves, and while costs in India were still higher than in China they expected that to reverse by 2020. Micromax's belief in India as a location to assemble a low-margin, high-volume product like a mobile phone was vindicated by the Department of Telecom's announcement that, in the year to October 2016, 38 new factories making phones were opened in India with a combined capacity of 248 million handsets. Foxconn, the Taiwanese contract manufacturer and a major Apple supplier, announced in 2015 a $5 billion investment programme for India, including 10 assembly plants, though only four of these facilities appear to have been created so far.

Auto-components often have characteristics similar to textiles or phones as a volume-oriented, labour-intensive manufacturing process with great reliance on supply chain efficiencies. K.R. Sundaresan (Sundar) is a great advocate of the potential of manufacturing auto-component products in India. Sundar spent years in Ford, and ended up running a procurement function that developed new external suppliers and drove global sourcing of parts from India. He saw the huge opportunity for auto-components in India as the car industry grew rapidly so, in 2007, he left Ford and tied up with Magal Engineering from the UK to move the manufacturing of a number of simple products including jacks, pedals, connecting rods and clutches from Europe to India. Later, in 2009, he joined a team turning round an aluminium casting business, which was eventually sold to Rockman Industries, part of the Hero Group. Now he has left Rockman to pursue other ideas, such as a start-up precision machining company, Integral Component Manufacturers (ICMPL), which supplies critical components to car companies in India and overseas.

Sundar's experience is that the key challenge to developing a scaling auto-component business is not establishing globally competitive manufacturing, but access to capital. World-class manufacturing can be developed at low cost in India, but requires investment. Sundar has found PE investors cautious about the sector. He told me, 'Frankly, for manufacturing, private equity [funds] till date are not showing interest. They all look at services as a better option to invest in for the returns that they expect.' With assets to offer as security, Sundar has used bank leverage to build his plants but the process was consequently slow and involved.

Milltec, the manufacturer of rice mills discussed earlier, is more representative of the sort of manufacturing in which India has traditionally excelled. The company produces low volumes of many different designs of large machinery, playing to India's advantage in engineering and low labour costs. Unlike Sundar, Ravindranath has successfully raised PE investment but only when the company was already at the scale and profitability to source growth capital, and funds were required to buy out the partners who had invested early on in the history of the company. Ravindranath believes he would have had little chance in interesting VC investors early on in his concept of designing and building rice mills more appropriate for Indian customers than those being offered by the international suppliers.

Despite the clear potential in manufacturing as a sector, which will improve as the friction on business in India reduces, investors remain cautious about early-stage plans with a manufacturing bias. So too are many entrepreneurs. Few start-ups have the boldness that Tarun Mehta of Ather Energy showed in defying the apparently sage advice of potential investors and insisting on building and controlling his own integrated manufacturing base. Like most investors, the majority of entrepreneurs favour easier sectors. Jerry Rao illustrated this with a story about his students at IIM Ahmedabad. Jerry told me, 'There are about 60 kids in my class at IIM, and about 10 say that they want to start their own thing after school. I usually take them out for a cup of tea and ask about their plans. Not one of them wants to start a factory; it's all dot-com, data analytics or something in IT.'

Jerry told me a story that paralleled my own experience of helping Arvind Kothari source point-of-sale terminals for Arjun's Direct from Shenzhen in China. 'One of my students at IIM Ahmedabad showed me a small device he had developed which can control the intensity of lighting all over the house from your phone. I said, "Very nice, at least you are making something, everybody else is doing analytics." He started smiling and said, "I only make the outer case in Hyderabad, all the circuits come from China." He had gone to China on a three to four week visa and had all his meetings with suppliers in the hotel coffee shop. Their only question was did he want 100,000 pieces or half a million. In fact, he didn't think he could sell more than 2,000 pieces. But the point was that given such responsive suppliers, why bother creating some shed in Nasik or somewhere [else] to make things yourself with all of the hassles involved?' There are two essential answers to the question as to why entrepreneurs and investors should look hard at manufacturing in India. First, manufacturing offers the opportunity for sustained attractive returns in its own right, as I have seen across multiple sectors. Second, manufacturing is often an integral part of the competitive advantage of a business and hence should be seen as an essential strategic competence. Micromax's decision to bring manufacturing in-house was motivated by both of these considerations. The company could have continued to follow the Apple model of designing and marketing in-house while outsourcing production. But Vikas Jain and his colleagues took the longer-term view, provoked at least in part by the rising costs of supply from China, that investing in manufacturing in India was the best route to maintaining a market edge in the cut-throat mobile business.

Any investment decision needs to be made based on clear strategic thinking and hard economics. There are a series of reasons to believe that increasingly smart operators and perceptive investors will, like Micromax, see the advantage of India as a manufacturing hub.

The government has, for policy, social and fiscal reasons, targeted a resurgence of manufacturing in India. To achieve its ambitious goals will require significant changes to the operating environment in India. Progress is already clear on a range of parameters including easier regulations, lower corporate taxes and the introduction of GST as a national value-added tax. More challenging will be to improve the physical infrastructure, but there are early signs of greater investment in better roads and an improving power-supply situation. Changes to politically contentious laws around land acquisition and labour will take more time.

Second, India is a growing market so local production will be increasingly required for many categories of goods. When Ardeshir and I started Kiran Energy there were only a few Indian solar panel manufacturers but they were more costly and had older technology than the international suppliers from the US, Japan or China. We chose to source the equipment for our plants from international majors with assured quality and technical acceptability to the banks who financed the projects. As India becomes one of the largest solar markets in the world, local production of equipment will become economic and be preferable to importing with consequent logistics costs and timescales.

Most importantly, the nature of manufacturing is changing, not least due to the digitalization of the supply chain. Saroja Yeramilli's Melorra only manufactures a product, using a 3D printer, once an order is placed. Increasingly, manufacturing equipment will become linked to the total supply chain allowing more rapid response to smaller orders. As setup times fall with digitalization, flexibility will increase and scale economies will fall. Manufacturing may, therefore, be more distributed as transport costs and time become critical elements in the economic mix. These trends, of course, have implications for employment as more tasks will be robotized but, equally, productivity levels will be much higher and the total value-add much greater, so the number of jobs in the economy as a whole will still grow.

Anand Mahindra of the Mahindra Group, pointed out that India missed the manufacturing boom in Asia from the early 1990s caused by liberalization, the search for cheap labour and lower freight costs. Now, with the government finally serious about enhancing the ease of doing business, a growing domestic market and the transformational impact of new technologies, manufacturing in India will become increasingly attractive. Moreover, manufacturing will be deeply entwined with the overall strategy of many companies as a result of digitalization of the whole value chain. These changes will throw up myriad new opportunities for India's burgeoning entrepreneurs. Tarun Mehta's insistence on manufacturing his electric bike in India, rather than buying from China, and in-house rather than contracting to a third party, will increasingly look like the path more trodden.

Innovation, not just jugaad[85]

A deeper issue for India and the future prospects of the ambitions of its growing army of aspiring entrepreneurs is the underdevelopment and

---

[85]   Hindi for making do, a fix. See Radjou, Navi, Jaideep Prabhu and Simone Ahuja, *Jugaad Innovation: Think Frugal, Be Flexible and Generate Breakthrough Growth*, New Delhi: Random House India, 2012.

neglect of innovation as a source of business advantage. Entrepreneurship and innovation are conjoined twins, as Peter Drucker identified when he defined entrepreneurs as those who 'create something new, something different'. While there may well be demand for another pizza parlour, tea stall or e-commerce website, sustainable long-term business which achieves superior returns and true scale must ultimately be based on offering something different and better to the customer. As my interviews progressed I became increasingly concerned that too few of the entrepreneurs I met placed a sufficiently high priority on innovation. Most innovation I encountered was around the business model rather than the product and was often offering novel features that could readily be replicated by the competition.

Questioning the underlying innovation culture of entrepreneurial India provoked a number of my interviewees. Vani Kola of Kalaari Capital suggested that I was taking an overly Western view of what constitutes innovation. She rightly argued that innovation is less frequently about fundamental research and technology breakthroughs. More often, innovation is incremental and is often related to better service standards or addressing a previously unmet consumer need through improvements to the business model. Dramatic product breakthroughs, the equivalent of a new class of drug in the pharmaceutical industry, are rare and their achievement is highly uncertain. While of course such fundamental breakthroughs would be welcome, innovation tends to be less dramatic. As with Moore's Law in chip speed, or the improvement in solar panels over many years, customer-focused innovation in great companies that survive in the long run tends to happen in frequent small steps, and then occasional big jumps as major new products or technologies are introduced.

As examples of sound process innovation, Vani cited the cash-on-delivery service for e-commerce pioneered by Flipkart, important in an under-banked society under-penetrated by credit cards, or a two hour order to shipment cycle offered first by Myntra. Similarly, Kiranbir Nag of Saama Capital took Chai Point as an example of the multiple innovations possible in the seemingly mundane, but actually non-trivial, challenge of offering an authentic, predictable cup of tea at volume through multiple delivery channels. Chai Point started with street outlets but has moved to augment its offering with in-office supplies of tea and now home delivery. They have had to create new ways of machine-brewing leaf tea with fresh ingredients to a reliable and high standard, as well as keeping it hot in distribution without degradation of flavour.

While such examples are impressive, they remain too few and inconsistent. Very few Indian businesses, small and large, embed into their operating muscle a cultural imperative to innovate constantly with the innovation process focused firmly on an appreciation of their customers' needs. Among the entrepreneurial ventures I encountered, too few spoke of innovation being at the core of their being. Many were, of course, founded to address an unmet need but then too often they appear to have become distracted by the everyday challenges of running a business and the fruits of success to insist on constant and continuing innovation. Jugaad, low-cost, frugal innovation, has been much discussed and admired in recent years and is seen as a particularly Indian approach to the challenge of innovation. Where jugaad represents true incremental innovation and value engineering, almost Japanese *kaizen* (continuous improvement) in its thinking, it can be a source of competitive advantage. However, lazy faith in a perceived Indian ability to come up with a last-minute fix, like go-faster stripes on an Ambassador car, will not survive open competition in today's informed and demanding marketplace.

Milltec developed rice milling machines better suited to Indian rice and operating conditions, resulting in less breakage of the rice, not through any single breakthrough but with a series of small improvements of tried and tested technology. Ravindranath is now focused on integrating the generation of power using the waste husks from the milling process into the complete plant designs he offers, thus reducing operating costs. Micromax's phone with a battery life of up to a month met a real customer need in power-starved rural India, and was achieved through a series of relatively simple steps in battery selection, simplification and power management. These are good examples of effective jugaad and incremental innovation.

Dhiraj Rajaram of Mu Sigma set out to rethink business decision-making, combining multiple disciplines, consulting, computing and statistics, to trigger new insights. Dhiraj argued, 'We still talk only about Make in India, why not also Thought in India? The biggest manufacturing happens in the manufacturing of the mind, right? I've a lot of respect for Sachin at Flipkart, Kunal at Snapdeal and all of those guys. But they still make in India something thought in the US. Amazon was thought in the US while this is the Amazon of India adjusted for the Indian masses. There is innovation in the why, how and what. These companies that are the Amazon of India, the Uber of India or the Expedia of India are based on innovations of how, not innovation of why and what.'

The e-commerce entrepreneurs I interviewed argued that their businesses were replete with innovation and rejected the implication of their being desi imitations of Western models, the Amazon of India or the Uber of India. Ashish Goel of Urban Ladder talked of 'bucket-loads' of innovation in his business, like the stair-climber which effortlessly takes a sofa to a high-rise flat in Colaba. Bhavish Aggarwal of Ola explained that, 'We do a lot of innovation in our business processes to create value-add. The paradigm of mobility in the West always meant owning a car. We look at mobility in a very broad sense and seek ways to improve mobility in the modern age for India.' Sachin Bansal defended Flipkart's record on innovation, arguing that solutions to payment challenges were examples of innovation for the needs of the Indian market, first cash-on-delivery and now the application of UPI payment gateways. While extending the concept of aggregation from taxis to rickshaws or offering cash-on-delivery in e-commerce were bold moves providing an initial edge, they can be copied by others, including foreign majors. In the US, Amazon would not deliver on a cash-on-delivery basis but, responding to Flipkart and others, now does so in India.

To maintain an edge over competition, innovation needs to be a constant process because it will be copied or leapfrogged. The success of India's IT services companies was originally based on labour arbitrage, but more recently has rested on process innovation in the creation of the global delivery model. TCS innovated global delivery, yet international majors like IBM and Accenture have now copied it, becoming huge employers in India with some 280,000 staff between them. The Indian IT majors are very aware that they need to evolve further, probably to offer more innovation of value-add or product development.

Sharad Sharma of iSPIRT has doubts about the ability of IT services companies to achieve product innovation. He argues that across industries it is the holder of the product IP, rather than companies in service delivery, which capture the value. The profits of the top 20 IT services companies are less than that of Microsoft, even in its diminished state. A similar pattern can be seen in telecom, aviation and pharmaceuticals, with the bulk of the profit pool being captured by the product innovator rather than those in the distribution chain. Sharad doubts that companies whose mentality and competences are honed to offer services will easily be able to develop the organizational muscle required to develop product. Innovation of product, he argues, requires a different type of culture, process and incentive. Of course, some companies may be nimble enough to make the transition. Parth Amin of SLK Software asked me to switch off my recorder when, over lunch in his office, he began to describe the very exciting product development programme he has initiated, designed to move SLK Software beyond services and into product. Parth's new product development is being carried out by a different team, away from his core business. He believes it will deliver a paradigm shift in the way that software is developed and delivered.

The explanation for the muted drive towards innovation in too many businesses in India, large or small, is not straightforward but has deep roots. In the years of the license raj there was little incentive to innovate as there were few producers of each product and restricted competition. Once the market began to liberalize, exploitation of a cost advantage over international competition has been the favoured strategy for most Indian companies, rather than seeking to compete on innovation. There may also be cultural factors at play. Innovation often emerges from a challenge to accepted thinking, yet Indian culture traditionally values respect towards elders and collective decisions rather than individualism. The intensely competitive education system embeds further conformity and rewards rote-learning, rather than the creative thinking encouraged by less structured education systems as in the US. Shiladitya Sengupta, who has now founded three biotech ventures in India as well as one in Boston, overstated his case to make a point when he told me, 'The biggest challenge in my space [biotech] is that we don't have enough people with ideas in India. We are still doing me-too business, copying anything that is successful in the US or in global markets and adapting it for India. We lack innovation because we are very conservative as a society and prefer to play it safe.'

While these historic and cultural factors have no doubt played some role in the underdevelopment of the innovative gene in too many Indian businesses, the most critical motivator for change and innovation is a reaction to strong competitive pressure. People and businesses do not tend to change unless they have to. Effective innovation is typically a response to a threat, or is driven by strong leadership that anticipates that things cannot continue as they are. While a cost strategy remains viable in India, many businesses will persist in relying on that advantage even though they know it will dissipate with time. Naveen Tewari at InMobi, pitched against the mighty Google in mobile advertising, talked convincingly of the existential need to innovate in order to survive. He told me, 'If you don't innovate in technology, the cycle will kill you. I think what we have to do is to achieve tectonic innovation to reinvent advertising. We have embarked on some massive projects of product innovation, which will take us years to deliver. We launched one of them last year, hopefully we will launch one more this year.'

There are examples of companies in India which have embedded innovation deep in their DNA and operating processes, but the country needs many more. Kiran Mazumdar-Shaw of Biocon recalled that she began to seek innovation from the earliest days of her start-up enzyme plant in her garage. 'I started developing microbial enzymes and fungal enzymes apart from the papain I was selling to Ireland,' she told me. 'I had to get an excited, young R&D team together and we set out to develop novel enzymes and new production technologies.' Initially, she focused on solid state fermentation enzymes as these were not produced by her Irish partner and were being imported from Japan. 'The Japanese had a coveted proprietary technology and I had to use my scientific understanding to create comparable processes. Then we started looking at fungal strains and microbial strains, mutating them, genetically engineering them. It was the first time that such stuff had been done in the country.'

Kiran has continued that focus on innovation, shifting the company away from enzymes and towards biotechnology in the 1990s. Her heavy investment in R&D, 15 per cent of sales, has caused discomfort to many market commentators. She explained, 'Each biosimilar costs almost $100 million to develop, and then putting up a facility is an even bigger challenge as in bio-pharmaceuticals you need to have a global-scale manufacturing setup. That's what makes it expensive. So between my manufacturing and R&D, I've spent almost a billion dollars over the last 10 years. Which Indian company is willing to spend that kind of money? In the last two months alone I've filed two biosimilar dossiers.'

Kiran has followed a different path from most in the highly successful pharmaceutical sector in India which has been built principally on so-called generic drugs, producing off-patent drugs or innovating around patents to offer the same efficacy as patented, branded drugs. Among the established pharma companies only Glenn Saldanha of Glenmark articulates drug discovery as a core strand of strategy, though Sun Pharma has a separate subsidiary, Sun Pharma Advanced Research (SPARC), for research and development.

Over the years, some have tried to develop new molecules. Dr Yusuf Hamied of Cipla explained that his withdrawal from attempts at drug discovery resulted from biases in the Indian system against indigenously developed drugs. Indian doctors and patients, he argued, preferred global brand names even if an Indian drug was as, or more, efficacious. Ajay Piramal tried to develop a drug discovery business based on his 1998 acquisition of Hoechst's Indian research centre. He explained that the strategy failed after the costs of trials were escalated by higher standards of approval in the US, and he felt they had not adequately invested in global talent. The critical point was made by G.V. Prasad of Dr Reddy. He bluntly explained that in simple economic terms the returns from investing in generics were far superior to those from attempting the long, uncertain path of fundamental drug discovery.

As in other sectors of the economy, a long-term reliance on a cost advantage must be a high-risk strategy. This is as true of pharma as of IT or engineering. Costs can rise over time with exchange rates or labour inflation, and while the cost advantage is there foreign companies can invest to access it just as easily as domestic players. Indian business in general needs to make the transition from relying on cost as a principal source of competition to an innovation-based strategy. However, experience suggests that large companies find such a transition difficult. Globally, most innovation comes from smaller, more entrepreneurial businesses. That is why it is especially vital for true innovation to be demonstrated in India's start-up ecosystem.

Biotech innovation in new ventures is at a very early stage in India. Shiladitya Sengupta has created three drug discovery businesses in India, of which two, Vyome Biosciences in dermatology and Invictus Oncology in cancer care, were initially supported by Rajeev Mantri of Navam Capital, with whom I work. Shiladitya is based at Harvard and the basic scientific insight is founded on his research work in Boston. The formulations are developed in India using the talented professional research staff available at an attractive cost. Vyome is focused on the treatment of drug-resistant acne and other antibiotics targeting drug-resistant bacteria and has just gone into trials with the US Food and Drug Administration (FDA) for its first molecule, VB-1953. Invictus Oncology is developing supramolecular therapeutics to fight cancer and its first platinum-based molecule will soon go into FDA trials. Both companies, chaired by Professor R.A. Mashelkar, the doyen of the Indian scientific community, are VC-funded, initially by Navam but now including a number of Indian and international funds.

Shiladitya and N. Venkat, the CEO of Vyome, see themselves as pioneers in the sector, lacking a supportive ecosystem and specialized investors. Shiladitya contrasts this with what he has experienced in Boston around MIT and Harvard, where academics straddle university careers and for-profit start-ups and VC funding is widely available for the commercialization of good science. Venkat argues that India's challenge is less about the shortage of fine scientists and entrepreneurs with good ideas and more about the lack of capability to take an idea to scale given the ecosystem, most especially the paucity of investors with the skills and confidence to back drug discovery through the development process. He told me, 'There are about 200 pharma start-ups according to DBT [Department of Biotechnology] statistics. But there are hardly any companies that have scaled up. We don't yet have enough start-ups and the scale-up ratio is far too low.' Both Vyome and Invictus are now doing their FDA trials outside India and are seeking the next rounds of investment from specialized investors based in the US rather than from India-focused funds.

Vyome and Invictus are early movers in drug discovery and it will take time to develop a mature and supportive ecosystem in the sector, as has developed around IT connected companies in Bangalore. Kiran Mazumdar-Shaw argues that there are positive early signs of medical research beginning to spawn new businesses in India. She mentors a number of small companies including OncoStem Diagnostics, which has developed a novel and cost-effective diagnostic test system for breast cancer, and Bugworks which is working on antibiotics for drug-resistant bacteria. There are about 16 start-ups in the accelerator in the Biotech Park at Bangalore's Electronics City. However, her huge frustration is with the attitude of too many researchers in Indian universities who still seem to disdain business. Their bias makes them head straight for publication rather than first patent their findings. 'I've told them patent first, publish later, that should be your mantra. That is our biggest weakness in India, there should be academic excellence in research through a patent culture. Once you achieve that, you'll then have a start-up culture blooming because then scientists will be encouraged to start up companies.'

The limited contribution of academic and research institutions is the biggest lacuna in the Indian start-up ecosystem and a strong contrast to comparable entrepreneurial hotspots globally. Silicon Valley is closely entwined with great research universities like Stanford, while Boston's biotech start-ups could not exist without Harvard and MIT. The Silicon Fen phenomenon in East Anglia is the result of academics spinning out of Cambridge University. Minister of State Jayant Sinha identified stimulating world-quality research in India's universities and encouraging collaboration between universities and entrepreneurs as the next priority agenda item for the government's development policy. India's universities vary in quality and funding for world-class research is often a challenge. Most global rankings place India's best research universities like IIT Madras, IIT Bombay, University of Delhi and IIT Kharagpur lower than a ranking of 200 in world standing. However, given its sheer size, India overall does better on rankings of quantum of R&D spend (some $66 billion) or numbers and citations of research papers (India ranked seventh on one measure of output from research).[86]

Clearly, there are elements of world-class research in Indian universities

---

[86] SCImago Journal & Country Rank.

and other research institutions and they could be developed far more with greater funding. I sit on the Circle of Advisors for India for Cambridge University. Cambridge has pursued a series of research partnerships with Indian institutions over the past seven years, including in crop sciences (with the University of Delhi and Punjab Agricultural University), drug-resistant tuberculosis (with National Institute for Research in Tuberculosis, Chennai) and novel cancer drugs through the creation of the Centre for Chemical Biology and Therapeutics at Bangalore with joint funding from the government and Cambridge. This experience with Cambridge shows that the talent and skill to do pioneering research work that meets world standards exists in India, but the funding and incentives are still missing.

Most importantly, India lacks a culture of universities and business working together. There are a range of organizational and cultural issues holding back the commercial exploitation of research undertaken in Indian institutions. Too many of the best brains still leave India for more research freedom and better pay at international universities. There is no tradition, in recent years at least, of private funding or endowments of Indian universities. Ratan Tata, who has created the Tata Centre at IIT Bombay along with MIT, found the process hugely complicated compared to his experience of establishing centres at Harvard or Cornell. He believes that the system of research grants being given to university departments rather than individual research teams, as elsewhere, is a major deterrent to ground-breaking work. The culture within universities tends to be strictly academic and, as mentioned earlier, often anti-business. Kiran Mazumdar-Shaw stressed the lack of patenting, while Rajeev Mantri noted that universities in India do not have Technology Licensing Offices to manage collaboration with private business. Few venture firms have deep connections with academia or the staff to assess the commercial potential of research ideas.

There are some tentative early signs of change in academia and some examples of technology spinning out of the research base into the commercial world. Professor Balram Bhargava from All India Institute of Medical Sciences (AIIMS) is a colleague on the Circle of Advisors for Cambridge in India. Balram is not only a leading cardiologist but has also pioneered the creation and then the commercialization of affordable biomedical devices, resulting so far in more than 20 patents. Among the entrepreneurs I interviewed a few based their business on technology developed and incubated at a university. Harsha Mahabala's Edutel is based on an algorithm developed in college. Tarun Mehta's Ather Energy is built around battery technology conceived at IIT Madras and the company took shape in the on-campus incubator. The chemistry for Aniruddha Sharma's Clean Carbon Solutions was derived from work at IIT Kharagpur and further developed at the Institute of Chemical Technology in Bombay (see p. 233, 'Innovating Globally: Aniruddha Sharma').

Other businesses are built on technology conceived at an international university and transplanted to India for commercial development. Vyome and Invictus derive their technological insights from Shiladitya's laboratory at Harvard which are then developed systematically by the companies in Delhi. Dhananjaya Dendukuri, the founder of Achira Labs, backed by Narayana Murthy's Catamaran Ventures, is applying science he developed while at MIT. Achira's device offers the testing of blood samples on a 'lab-on-a-chip'. The advantage is that small distributed labs can do the blood work cheaper and quicker as compared to the current system of larger labs which have more investment and logistics issues to manage.

Dhananjaya graduated from IIT Madras in 1999 and decided to study overseas, as did 210 students from his class of 360. Initially, he did a Masters at the University of Toronto, then a PhD at MIT, both in chemical engineering. Dhananjaya told me, 'MIT is very strong in terms of seeing academic ideas get out in the market through start-up companies. My lab colleague and I co-invented a technology which has now become very well known in microfluidics, a technique called flow lithography, which we patented and it was then commercialized.' He came back to India in 2007 and joined Connexios Life Sciences where he hoped to apply his specialization in microfluidics, originally for drug screening and later for diagnostics. By 2009, Connexios decided that the microfluidics work was non-core so Dhananjaya spun his technology into a separate company, Achira Labs. He secured funding from the family office of N.S. Raghavan, one of the Infosys founders, who was also an investor in Connexios. Raghavan was subsequently taken out by a ₹18 crore ($2.7 million) investment from Catamaran, Murthy's fund, with the equity stretched by various grants including one from the government (under the Biotechnology Ignition Grant Scheme, BIRAC) and from Grand Challenges Canada.

It has taken six years to take the concept to a commercial product, a time span that few investors in India would tolerate. Nevertheless, Achira Labs shows that cutting-edge science can be developed in India into an exciting product targeted at a very large opportunity in the Indian and international market. The company holds 25 patents. While Dhananjaya has seen a number of twists along the road, including two changes of shareholders with delays caused by each search for new money, he has been able to develop a breakthrough product supported by private shareholders with the patience to see through such a long-term project.

Nitin Gupta of Attero Recycling similarly credits unusually patient and supportive VC investors for allowing him to develop the breakthrough technology upon which his business is based. As Nitin told me, 'For us to build a billion-dollar company, we needed real technical innovation.' Nitin and his brother Rohan had the idea of recycling the metals in electronic circuit boards when Rohan tried to dispose of his old laptop and could not find anyone to take it. They raised $6.3 million from DFJ in 2008, and have subsequently raised another $20 million. The business is based on the green but compelling economics that it is 40 per cent cheaper to recover metals from old phones than mine new metal out of the earth, and the energy used to do so is 70 per cent less.

Attero has invested heavily in their own proprietary process for recycling, with 205 patent applications made over the past eight years. Their technology requires much lower capital expenditure per tonne of capacity of the plant, $2,000 versus a global standard of $17,000 per tonne. This means that plants can be smaller and more distributed. Furthermore, the Attero process has reduced the amount of collector metal required in the smelter from 10 tonnes per tonne of recycled circuit board metals to just 0.45 tonnes. This gives Attero a big cost advantage on a global basis, which Nitin describes as a 'tectonic shift' in industry economics. Nitin believes that this competitive edge will make Attero a global leader in recycling.

Promoting more innovation in Indian business is a critical challenge, and probably the most important question facing the entrepreneurial ecosystem as it develops further. This will require leadership from entrepreneurs to emphasize the criticality of offering something different and better. The innovation imperative should be hard-wired into the genetic core of start-ups from their earliest days. It will require a different mindset and time horizon from at least some specialist VCs. Above all, much deeper connection and collaboration between research institutions and business, supported by VCs, is required. Indian philanthropists and corporates need to revive the historic tradition of private support for universities and other research institutions, typified by the Tata Group's endowment for the Indian Institute of Science or the Tata Institute of Fundamental Research. The government has a role in terms of funding research of real quality and encouraging academics to support, and benefit from, the commercial exploitation of their work. The entrepreneurial ecosystems developing in Bangalore and elsewhere need to add a further dimension as their roots need to entwine with the country's best research institutions.

Anand Mahindra captured the need for Indian business to up its game around innovation. He told me, 'My motto is "from jugaad to jhakaas". We have got to move on from jugaad, which is to make do, to fix something. Now we need disruption, or jhakaas, meaning wow, something superb.'

Innovating Globally

ANIRUDDHA SHARMA

'India is a country where nobody invests in a technology company,' Aniruddha Sharma complained as we drank tea at the Institute of Directors in London, oil paintings of naval battle scenes looming above us. Aniruddha and his partner, Prateek Bumb, had moved their company, Carbon Clean Solutions (CCS), from India to the UK after winning a Global Entrepreneurship Programme grant of £3.6 million in 2012. 'If you open a website which is selling used shirts, you will raise a million today or tomorrow. If you are saying I am going to save the world, here is the technology, and, you know, we actually won three prominent awards, no one is interested. People say, you should do this in the US. In India, they don't want to understand the technology as the mindset is too short-term.'

CCS, with the technology application principally led by Prateek, has developed solvent technology that increases energy efficiency and lowers the cost of carbon capture and reuse within energy-intensive industrial processes. CCS claims that its chemicals save 80 per cent in cost over a life-cycle of investment in operating plants like power stations, compared to the current solutions from the likes of Dow and BASF. 'Their price is a little less than [that of] our product,' Aniruddha explained, 'but when you look at the life-cycle of the operations, we save a lot of money for the customer. There is no corrosion so they don't have to change the heat exchanger, the piping or the pump.'

Aniruddha had just closed a new $5.2 million funding round led by Eldon Capital which will help in commercializing the product in large, heat-intensive operations in Europe, the natural-gas industry in Germany, and hopefully back home in India. Government pressure, especially in the European Union, for industry to reduce carbon emissions gives CCS a major opportunity.

The origin of CCS was a conversation in their hostel at IIT Kharagpur between Aniruddha and his neighbour Prateek, about their summer internships in Europe. Prateek had worked on a carbon capture project in Italy. The two realized that no one in India was doing world-quality work on carbon capture. They decided to create a consulting company, Code Green, to advise on de-carbonizing large facilities like power plants. Their idea won the business plan award at the Pan-IIT Business Conclave at IIT Madras in 2008.

One of the judges was Dr Martin Haemmig, who was then teaching at Stanford. Martin invited the pair to the Cleantech Forum in San Francisco in February 2009, which they accepted even though it meant bunking their exams at IIT. Martin also arranged for meetings with investors in the Valley. Aniruddha and Prateek were evolving their thinking from a consulting model to building a demonstration plant. It was a meeting at Kleiner Perkins with Wen Hsieh that provided the bedrock of their current business model. Rather than investing in plant and equipment, he suggested, why not focus on the chemical inputs required to capture carbon?

After leaving college in 2009, Aniruddha and Prateek managed to raise $60,000 of angel funding for their idea. They then needed a laboratory to develop the molecules. After months of fruitless discussion with the National Chemical Laboratory in Pune, they found a home at the Institute of Chemical Technology (formerly the University Department of Chemical Technology) in Bombay. Professor M.M. Sharma, the former director of the institute, was interested in their ideas and the department had a lot of the kit they needed, though it was all a bit rusty. With $15,000 it was upgraded to what they required. With the molecules under development, and interest in collaboration from Tata Power arising from their desire to reduce emissions, CCS was able to raise a seed round of funding from Blume Ventures in 2010.

CCS sought grant funding from the Government of India under the Technopreneur Promotion Programme (TePP). 'We applied for that. It was ₹5 lakh of funding in the first phase and then you had to demonstrate progress over a period of time, and then it was another ₹25 lakh. But it was a tonne of paperwork and the first time they lost it in Delhi and we had to send it again. We travelled to Delhi every time, spending lakhs to get a grant of ₹5 lakh. We realized that this was not going to work.' CCS would quickly need an industrial-scale plant to prove the performance of the molecules, which grant-funding of this sort was not going to support.

For the next step, to validate the compounds they had developed in the lab, they needed a real operating plant and an independent testing agency, all of which required more capital than they could raise in grants or the angel and seed system in India. Tata Power was reducing its spend on green technology experimentation given operating pressures at the time, and so was unwilling to invest in the technology. Aniruddha had a chance meeting with James Graham of the United Kingdom Trade and Investment department (UKTI) at the beginning of April 2012. James mentioned the Global Entrepreneurship Programme, but the deadline for applications was 29 April, later in the same month. To make an application, Aniruddha had to assemble partnerships with both UK universities and industrial partners in a few short weeks. Working frantically, he managed to tie up with two universities, Imperial College and Sheffield University, and two power utilities, Scottish & Southern Energy Plc and E.ON. CCS completed its application just in time and was one of the winners. This paid for the validation process at TNO, the Dutch applied-research agency, which had the required facilities and the reputation to certify the effectiveness of the CCS molecules. Later, CCS also won a further $3 million grant from the Department of Energy in the US to work with the US National Carbon Capture Center.

Aniruddha believes his technology has both strong economics and the capacity to make a compelling contribution to global reduction of carbon dioxide (CO_2) emissions. He told me, 'Bill Gates says that there are five things that can save this planet from CO_2 emissions. One of them is carbon capture. He says if that's not going to happen we will never be able to decarbonize industry.' CCS started as an Indian company but had to go overseas to secure the funding to support the development of its technology outside the lab at an industrial scale. Aniruddha believes that the company's products, nevertheless, will enjoy a major market back in India, as industry faces obligations to reduce emissions and hence slow down global warming.

CONCLUSION

The First Five Miles of a Marathon

'Entrepreneurship has become mainstream.'

Sachin Bansal, Co-founder and Executive Chairman, Flipkart

'The spark has been ignited. How much time it will take to become a big fire is something that we will have to see.'

Narayana Murthy, Founder, Infosys and Catamaran Ventures

In August 2016, the Turakhia brothers, Bhavin and Divyank, sold Media.net, an online advertising technology business founded by Divyank Turakhia in 2010, for $900 million to a consortium of Chinese investors. Earlier, in 2014, they had sold their web presence business for $160 million, meaning that the two brothers have realized more than $1 billion in cash in the previous two years. Forbes and Hurun both reported that each brother was worth well in excess of $1 billion.

Bhavin and Divyank had created their first start-up, Directi Group, an Internet domain registration company, in 1998 when they were aged 18 and 16; today Bhavin is 36 and Divyank is only 34. The Turakhia brothers have built their online empire without outside capital, except a ₹25,000 ($600) initial loan from their father in 1998, which was repaid in the first month. In September 2016, the brothers announced investment plans for four new Internet-based businesses, as well as their intention to acquire 100,000 square feet of office space in Bangalore for expansion of their India-based start-ups. The world will be hearing more from the Turakhia brothers.

At the same time as I interviewed Divyank, I was talking to Colonel Vijay Reddy about the future of his business, Footprints Collateral Services. Vijay is in his sixties, a precise, correct army veteran who never expected to be an entrepreneur. After retiring from the army, he joined United Breweries Group's (UB Group) software business and was relocated to the US to run the administration of staff moving there to service clients. Based on this work, he created an employment-background verification business in Pittsburgh to offer to other clients the same services he had delivered for the UB Group. Family pressures, ageing parents and property issues led him to relocate himself and the business back to India. Footprints is now one of the leading verification service providers to large employers, principally IT companies, checking job applicants for identity, educational qualifications, previous employment references and criminal records. Much of this work still requires follow-up with individual sources, rather than simply accessing databases, as there are still no complete digital records for university qualifications and police First Information Reports (FIRs).

Divyank and Vijay are a generation apart in age, and more so in attitudes. One had expected to spend his whole career in government service, as had previous generations of his family, and became a businessman almost accidentally. The other saw the opportunities of the Internet as a boy, never considered seeking employment, and became a millionaire while still at school. Divyank's business is online and global, Vijay still needs, all too often, to send a representative to a police station in a remote part of the country to check their physical records. Vijay drives to his farm outside Bangalore every weekend and switches off his phone; Divyank spends his weekends enjoying adventure sports like flying, wake-surfing and diving.

Different in many ways, Vijay and Divyank are both, nevertheless, examples of the legion of new entrepreneurs who have sprung up in India in the past few years. They represent different aspects of the upsurge of entrepreneurship that has changed much in India already and promises to change India fundamentally in the next decade and beyond.

India is on the cusp of something truly exciting as it progressively emerges as one of the most exciting entrepreneurial societies in the world. Many factors have aligned, at last, to position the Indian economy on a swelling wave, with plenty of fetch to build up the surf ahead. The cumulative and combined effect of changes over the past 25 years in government policy, technology, finance and culture has triggered an extraordinary upsurge in entrepreneurship in the country. Most importantly, the change in attitudes in the country towards business and entrepreneurialism has been striking. The entrepreneurial ecosystem is as yet immature and patchy and there will be reversals and disappointments but, looking ahead, there are myriad reasons to believe it will strengthen, deepen and spread.

This book has chronicled these developments, most importantly through the eyes and narratives of more than a hundred participants in the entrepreneurial ecosystem, 92 of whom are first-generation entrepreneurs. By their very nature, such people tend to be boundlessly optimistic and determined to drive profound change. They talk a good game. Even discounting this, the picture that emerges from a tour of the entrepreneurial front line in India is hugely encouraging. India is witnessing what I would like to term as 'an entrepreneurial insurgency' and there is much more yet to come.

Why then the question mark in this book's title? Why is *Boom Country* followed by a question mark? Am I not fully convinced by the evidence I have assembled that India is seeing a new wave of enterprise that will transform the country and the lives of its people? The answer is clear from the evidence I have chronicled and the narratives of the entrepreneurs themselves. The fact is that I am a cheerleader for what has changed in India and a firm believer in the enormous upside of what should pan out in the decades ahead. A long-term boom in the economy from the boom of entrepreneurship is developing and strengthening. Yet, I cannot ignore that significant risks and fragilities remain.

First, the new entrepreneurship we are witnessing in India is at an early stage of development. Vani Kola of Kalaari Capital called it 'mile five of a marathon'. I have identified a spectrum of weaknesses in the ecosystem today, including the reality that India remains a challenging operating environment for business, the need for further evolution in government policies and practices, lacunae in the VC-funding system, and shortcomings among the entrepreneurs themselves. The most alarming failing of too many of India's entrepreneurs is the endemic neglect of the criticality of innovation as the fuel at the core of the entrepreneurial reactor. No doubt these issues are improving and will continue to do so, but to address them in full and bring about a significant and effective change will demand much hard work, bold leadership and significant capital.

Second, the hard learning from my 35 years of experience in India has been that, despite the massive and glaring potential, the country too often seems to underdeliver on its full promise. In 1982, when I first visited, India was on a par with China in terms of economic development. In the ensuing years, notwithstanding its manifest advantages, India has underperformed as compared to China by a significant margin both in terms of economic growth and human development. Where there have been mini-booms, a bust has almost certainly followed. The key explanation for this unrealized potential and oscillating performance has lain, historically, with a failure of political courage and leadership in the intensely febrile politics of democratic India. Reforms and changes are hard things and tend to deliver over a wavelength longer than the electoral cycle. Tough political choices have, until recently, typically been made in times of crisis. Otherwise, shorter-term electoral calculations, woolly thinking residual from the time India was a socialist economy and the shrill voices of vested interests have smothered the imperative to change things for the better. The indications remain broadly positive that Narendra Modi is determined to be different, but he too needs to remain in power long enough to see through his economic agenda and resist the seductive advice to pander to shorter-term political temptations that set back reform.

Third and last, the Indian economy is not isolated from global trends and there are clear risks over the next few years that the benign economic conditions from which India has benefitted since 1991 may be at threat. Globalization and liberalization are much in India's interests. India's relationship with the US, in particular, has been a critical thread of the changes that have occurred socially and economically. The agents of change who have led the entrepreneurial upsurge, the entrepreneurs and investors, have become used to moving easily in both directions between India and the US, benefitting from American education, work experience, investment and markets and applying them to India. India's growth companies, most notably in IT, require markets to which to export. India still depends on the availability of capital from overseas, both in terms of FDI and PE and

VC investment. Looking forward, there are worrying scenarios in which the fluidity of people, ideas, goods and capital could become more challenged, to the detriment of both the US and India.

Even if these risks do not crystallize, the remaining weaknesses and fragility in the entrepreneurial ecosystem in India will certainly result in reversals and setbacks even as the secular, underlying trend remains tremendously positive. After the over-hyped exuberance of 2015, 2016 was a much more challenging year for many entrepreneurs. Funding sources tightened. The restructuring and consolidation of a range of leading growth companies has yet to fully play out. Creative destruction is part of the entrepreneurial process and failure is the inevitable shadow of entrepreneurial success, so we can expect more high-profile bankruptcies, reversals and mergers.

India's entrepreneurial boom is so far only partial, restricted by geography, social group and sector. NASSCOM ranks India in the top three countries for technology start-ups, ahead of Israel and China. At the same time, India's ranking in the GEI in 2016 was a lowly 98 out of 132 countries, reflecting the vast scope for democratizing and enhancing the start-up wave wider into the vast country. For India to match China, ranked at 60 in the GEI, it would require only a ten-point, or 30 per cent, improvement in India's performance – which is so perfectly achievable. China enjoys significant advantages as a business location, including far superior infrastructure, effective government and scale of demand. In the past decade, China, has hugely outperformed India as a location for scientific research, whether measured by R&D dollars or patents filed. Reflecting these advantages, China has attracted a much greater quantum of investment, including PE and VC money, than has India. Yet, India enjoys significant advantages in its private-sector economy and education system, which means that the potential to match or outperform China as an entrepreneurial ecosystem is very much there and readily achievable.

A partial boom, a boom overly focused on a few sectors, groups and locations, and a boom that contains risks of periodic deflation, can and should certainly strengthen and mature to forge a genuine boom country. India can move from 'mile five' towards a 'half-marathon' by matching where China is today, and then onwards towards the achieving real leadership in new business creation. The prognosis for Indian enterprise is very good if the right actions continue to be taken. India can quite rapidly become a true boom country for new enterprise

As Karl Marx observed, 'The philosophers have only *interpreted* the world, in various ways. The point, however, is to *change* it.'[87] Or, as Vladimir Lenin asked, 'What is to be done?'[88] Let me offer three recommendations each for aspiring entrepreneurs, investors and the government which would help realize the dream of India as an entrepreneurial boom country.

Three Recommendations for Aspiring Entrepreneurs

I have quoted extensively from my interviews with the 92 entrepreneurs I met researching this book. Many of them are brilliant, inspirational leaders with unique capabilities and drive. However, the majority are all too human, with foibles and fears just like the rest of us. The over-riding message I believe they would want to impart is that you too can be an entrepreneur, if you so choose and if you really want it.

- **Do it, when it feels right.** There is no single path to entrepreneurial success. Nor is there a correct time to become an entrepreneur. Some of those I interviewed created their businesses while they were still students, others became entrepreneurs after years of working for others. It is less risky to try a start-up early since, if it goes wrong, you can more readily do something else, losing little and gaining experience. On the other hand, an older entrepreneur sacrifices more in terms of income and position, but his or her wider experience may increase the chances of success. Among those I interviewed, some consciously planned ahead and built a base of experience and contacts to launch a start-up, choosing educational options with this in mind and then seeking specific employment experience for a limited time before leaving to create a start-up. Most of those I interviewed, though, relied more on intuition and

---

[87] Marx, Karl, *Eleven Theses on Feuerbach*, 1845.
[88] Lenin, Vladimir, *What Is To Be Done? Burning Questions of Our Movement*, 1902.

serendipity, feeling their way forward without a long-term game plan.

Ambitious people who want to change things should seek a range of interesting and challenging experiences, often outside their natural comfort zone, and opportunities will crop up. I worked in banking, manufacturing, government, luxury branded goods and two diversified conglomerates before taking the plunge to try something of my own, and I did it 4,500 miles from home in a culture with which I was comfortable but which was not my own. The decision to create a business grows inside and you will know when the time has come.

- **Persistence pays.** Entrepreneurs are pioneers, creators, disruptors and explorers. They take risks, and risks may go wrong. They try something new, which may take time to work out. Most new ventures fail; many great entrepreneurs failed initially, sometimes multiple times, before the stars aligned and things went right. Doing anything exciting and new is hard work, especially in the chaos and rapid changes in a market like India. Stretch your ambitions, dream, but be realistic as to what it takes to build something, how frustrating that can be, and how you might need to change direction along the way or even to start again from scratch. You may be surprised how quickly and easily things turn up. Many of the entrepreneurs I interviewed struggled long and hard, while a few were more quickly favoured by success. As Napoleon said, 'Give me lucky generals,' though it has also been said that you make your own luck.

- **Follow a path less travelled, but don't travel alone.** Most businesses are originally derivative of others; only a few start with an original idea or genuinely new technology. However, truly great businesses shift gears as they gain traction and generate differentiation through innovation. I have argued earlier that dedication towards innovation is an essential determinant of sustained success. Whatever the business and its strategy, entrepreneurs think for themselves, listen to customers, assess competitors and plough a furrow of their own rather than following received wisdom. Innovation often comes from a paranoid obsession with the need to be better, faster and cheaper than others.

Most entrepreneurs do not achieve their dreams by working alone. With some notable exceptions, entrepreneurs trying something different work best with co-founders who share the thinking and the stress, and complement each other's skills. The importance of the selection of a founding team, and the dynamics within that team as the business grows, was a frequent theme in my interviews. Some founding teams drift apart; others explode with massive damage to the business. As with a marriage, relationships within a founding team demand hard work, openness and honesty. And, as with a marriage, when it works well, as in many of the cases I have covered, it is a source of real strength to the business. When it goes foul it can be terrible for everyone. Selecting your co-founders with care and working hard at maintaining their trust is a requirement for success.

Whatever the founding team, any entrepreneur needs to attract and retain a great second line of talent, as no single person or leadership team builds a business alone. Your success will be built to a large degree by the team you craft.

Three Recommendations for Investors

A significant increase in investment available to back start-up, early-stage and growth companies has played a central role in the upsurge in entrepreneurship in recent years. Nevertheless, it is clear that the VC industry in India is at an early stage of its development and needs to mature in critical ways. Having been on both sides of the table, as an investee entrepreneur and working with investors, I am convinced that an increase in the quantum of funds deployed is not the only vector along which the venture industry needs to develop further.

- **Be different, be disciplined.** Initially, Indian venture funds were generalists by necessity. In the past few years, we have seen the development of funds at different stages of the investment cycle and the beginnings of funds with focused and selective investment theses. However, the venture industry still moves too much as a herd, susceptible to shared mood swings and following investment strategies which are excessively generic. In the 2015 gold-rush, the disciplines of investment criteria seemed to warp as investors from hedge funds, sovereign wealth funds, growth funds and family offices scrambled for participation in early-stage companies in the e-commerce sector in India. Investors without the skill set required for venture investing piled into the sector. The result was a clear market distortion and a ramping up of valuations and expectations, which have done real damage both to some companies which were over-funded and certain investors who joined the bubble late. Immunity from the contagion of groupthink across the industry and discipline in investing strategy are essential; superior returns come from crafting an investment strategy different from the market, sticking to it, being early on a trend and shaping the portfolio to reflect a strong view of opportunity, not from mirroring the enthusiasms among others. Presenting such differentiated strategies to Limited Partners and Investment Committees, particularly if they are remote from India, requires courage of conviction and strong, persuasive communication skills.

■ **Know more about less.** To have confidence in making differentiated choices, funds need deeper insight into the competitive dynamics of sectors of interest than many currently demonstrate. This lack of specialization and focus among funds is the most striking difference between the Indian venture market, which is still dominated by generalists, and the more sophisticated and deeper venture system in the US. The Indian venture market has developed sufficiently in a decade so that more funds are now developing that prioritize a few sectors, and increasingly some will focus on a single sector. Deep sectoral knowledge has a range of advantages. It helps in assessing opportunity and risk better; it will boost proprietary deal-flow as discussions with entrepreneurs will flush out opportunities that are not already part of a banker-led auction process; entrepreneurs may prefer to work with a fund with real insight into their business, from which they can see potential additionality beyond the commodity of capital.

- **Contribute more than just money.** Investors in early-stage business should be able to offer more than just capital and governance oversight. Vigilance and challenges from investors are, of course, required as founders can sometimes make poor decisions, find themselves beyond their natural expertise or comfort zone or can simply be tempted into fraud. Any well-functioning board builds in reviews, controls, checks and balances to ensure operating managers are complying with policies and lines of delegated responsibility. However, the function of an investor and director, especially in an early-stage business with less-experienced leadership, is also to guide and support the founders. Striking the right balance between the role of director as guardian of shareholder interests and as support to management, without transgressing the line between executive and non-executive, is a fine judgement that everyone gets wrong occasionally. At the same time, shareholders' representatives who say nothing are as unhelpful to founders as those who interfere excessively, sound off with easy, ill-informed opinions or demand constant streams of unnecessary data.

Through being smart and good with people, some investors intuitively achieve the right balance for any situation. However, international experience in more mature venture markets like the US or Israel suggests that adding real industrial and technical expertise to the fund team, either as an operating partner or nominee to a specific board, is an effective way of ensuring that more value is added during the investment cycle and relations with the management team are kept constructive. While some funds are run by people who have business experience outside consulting and finance, many industry practitioners in India do not have wide managerial experience or specific sectoral knowledge. Too few India-focused funds have hired senior team members with operating experience, partly because of fund size and hence economics, but also in some cases because fund managers think they do not need such expertise. Funds that recognize this issue will, I suggest, tend to outperform others over time.

Three Recommendations for the Government

Government action over a long period has played a major, positive role in triggering and supporting the surge in new entrepreneurship in India. The new priority placed on entrepreneurship by the administration of Prime Minister Narendra Modi, including the Startup India initiative, is well timed and welcome. While such announcements help at the margin, they are not in themselves truly transformational. International experience is that governments do not create entrepreneurial ecosystems, though they can certainly help by nurturing an environment conducive to entrepreneurship. The policy measures needed from the government by Indian business are widely understood, and indeed encouraging progress has been made in recent years, yet swifter and more radical implementation is still called for. The three proposals below will surprise no one, yet, given my background as a former policy advisor to a British Conservative prime minister, some may deem them too market-oriented in tone for India. Nevertheless, experience in the years since Margaret Thatcher started the global shift to market-based policies across the world, and most especially in India, demonstrates that encouraging open markets and free competition delivers growth through business, while government meddling and protectionism does not.

- **Ease of doing business.** Above all, entrepreneurs want to be able to operate their businesses as simply and cost-effectively as possible within a clear, predictable and efficient legal and regulatory regime. The government has made a sound start on improving ease of doing business, but there is much further to go, especially in state-level agencies. A new crusade is required to change the way government works, drawing on best practice globally. Using outside expertise and referencing benchmarked information from other governments, each process in which government interacts with business should be identified, mapped, measured and challenged. In each case, the process should be reviewed in detail, benchmarked against best practice in other countries, to establish why the government is carrying out this task and, if it is indeed required, how best to fulfil it. Many requirements of business in India from the government could be scrapped altogether, following the FIPB process into the dustbin of history. Residual rules restricting FDI, including in retailing, should be among the first to go. Where there is a legitimate rationale for the regulation or process, ways in which the activity can be carried out faster, cheaper and with more certainty should be identified.

Other governments have found a toolkit of measures that work dramatically to improve service delivery by government agencies. These include separation of policy formulation from service delivery, with services delivered by separate agencies focused against quality and cost targets. Quality standards can be set for government services with performance independently audited and published in league tables. Service delivery can be outsourced on competitive tenders that specify quality, and not just cost. Government activities which generate a profit, from banking to coal-mining, insurance to power generation, oil and gas to engineering, should be fully privatized; as Prime Minister Modi said, 'government has no business to do business'. Where investment is required to improve standards, in IT systems or staff, fees can be increased to pay for a better service. Where things go wrong there should be clear redressal systems and swift arbitration. Senior roles in government service should be advertised and private-sector experience brought in to leaven the civil service culture, inject fresh thinking and improve service delivery.

Central government agencies are progressively less of an issue for business than state-level policy and regulation. While the government in Delhi can direct its agencies to reform, state governments can be encouraged to follow suit through audited league tables, with comparative performance published. Competition between states will have an impact quite swiftly and politicians will be motivated to be bolder in administrative reform.

■ **Infrastructure.** The pressing need to upgrade India's infrastructure has been long recognized. For 25 years, governments, including the current government, have prioritized improving infrastructure, especially roads, railways and power, but the results have lagged behind expectations. The reasons are myriad and complex, including budgetary limitations, underpricing, property rights and land acquisition issues, environmental regulations, difficulties in contract enforcement, the selection of least cost (L1) bids without adequate consideration of quality, political interference and questionable public-sector management. Despite progress in some sectors like airports, ports and telecom, Indian infrastructure remains atrocious compared to that in similar countries. This adds significantly to the cost of doing business and hence diminishes India's global competitiveness. Poor infrastructure reduces the chance of small companies succeeding and skews investment towards sectors that are infrastructure-light and penalizes manufacturing. More radical solutions are needed than have been politically acceptable previously.

International experience suggests that government, in principle, should not operate infrastructure and that private businesses, properly regulated, deliver better results for customers. The transformation of Indian airports under private management in recent years supports this contention. While 'disinvestment' has been controversial in India, a government determined to transform India should not shy away from the sale of assets, grant of long-term management contracts and competitive tendering. The UK experience of privatization, which I saw up close as a member of the Number 10 Policy Unit, proves the benefits of transferring ownership and developing competitive markets for services that previously enjoyed a monopoly. Even a capital intensive, intrinsically loss-making natural monopoly like the railways can benefit from private management, with government committing investment and subsidy funding as part of the bidding process.

Taking outside assistance, such as from the World Bank, McKinsey or Goldman Sachs, the government could review each infrastructure sector and set clear targets for delivery of improvements over 10 years. Investment should then be committed at levels adequate to achieve this, leveraging private capital and management. Existing operating assets could be sold to defray the cost of new investment, as well as to improve their operations. In complex greenfield projects, government should take a strategic role, for instance securing land and permits and then bidding out complete packages to private-sector operators. Truly independent regulators can ensure natural monopolies are not abused by private concessionaires. Contracts need to fairly apportion responsibility and risk, and where government pays or regulates payment for the service, the stream of revenue needs to be assured and not subject to delay or political interference.

As in China in its early days of growth, a small number of areas can be prioritized for investment in order to create hubs of international business with world-class infrastructure. India should create three business zones akin to Guangdong's Shenzhen, where export-oriented manufacturing businesses can flourish.

■ **Universities and research.** India has the makings of a globally competitive research base, but currently the output is not consistently world-class nor are the connections with the business world adequately developed. There are patches of excellence, as ISRO, the space agency, has demonstrated, and as foreign universities such as Cambridge have discovered in seeking research partners in India. The limited role of the leading research institutions in the entrepreneurial ecosystem is the most marked difference from international experience.

Improving the quality of research output, protected by patents, and encouraging deep links with business, will be essential to cementing India as a global leader in entrepreneurship and start-up success. The leading research institutions need to be permitted to operate independently, reporting to their own boards, and not be subject to political interference. Funding of research grants should be increased and tied to individual teams, not the institution. Universities should be free to hire the best staff, including from overseas, and pay as they wish for the best people.

Research collaborations with leading universities globally should be encouraged, along the model pioneered by Cambridge and others in India. Universities should be free to seek private donations, both in order to build endowments as well as for specific programmes, with investment in research collaborations from industry sought for world-class research centres.

Learning from best practice at MIT or Stanford, leading Indian universities should set out to spin knowledge out to business, licensing intellectual property to private-sector partners and permitting academics to create companies with sharing of the IP according to set rules. Individual universities with world-class skills in specific sectors should be encouraged to build incubators and research parks focused on that sector, and fully participate in the creation of cluster ecosystems with sectoral slants.

Peter Drucker's comments about the US 30 years ago could clearly refer to India today: something 'quite different', 'a profound shift', is indeed happening in the economy and in the 'attitudes, values and ambitions' of the young people of India. India's young are increasingly seeing the future in new ways and have intensely different ambitions. The sheer size of the pool of talent India possesses, young and ambitious, confident and impatient for change, is the chief reason to believe that India's entrepreneurial time has come. Entrepreneurship is replete in the promise it offers the country and the world to create new products and services, generating wealth and employment and reducing poverty and the tragedy of fractured lives. The boom that India offers now to a few can, and should, go viral across swathes of the economy to transform India into a true 'boom country'.

Kiran Energy was my first entrepreneurial venture and I am now involved in a range of other new ventures. Surfing the waves of the surging tide of the boom in new business in India will be, over the next 10 or 20 years, one of the most exhilarating experiences possible as entrepreneurship changes the contours of the possible and of countless lives in India. I intend to remain engaged with this entrepreneurial insurgency as it changes so much for the better.

APPENDIX

List of Interviews

Abhinav Sharan, Aura Renewable Energy
Abhishek Lodha, Lodha Developers, Lodha Group
Adi Godrej, Godrej Group
Ajay Bijli, PVR Cinemas
Ajay Piramal, Piramal Group
Ajay Sethi, ASA & Associates LLP Chartered Accountants
Akanksha Hazari, m.Paani
Amuleek Singh Bijral, Chai Point
Anand Mahindra, Mahindra & Mahindra
Aniruddha Sharma, Clean Carbon Solutions
Anita Patel, Tania-Tapel Events
Ardeshir Contractor, Kiran Energy
Arjun Pratap, EdGe Networks
Arvind Kothari, formerly Reliance Industries
Ashish Goel, Urban Ladder
Ashok Wadhwa, Ambit Holdings
Bhavish Aggarwal, Ola Cabs
Chandrakanth B.N., Pairee Infotech
Danny Carroll, Alchemy Solutions
Deep Kalra, MakeMyTrip
Dhananjaya Dendukuri, Achira Labs
Dhiraj Rajaram, Mu Sigma
Divyank Turakhia, Directi Group
Ganapathy Venugopal, Axilor
Gautam Ghai, SourceFuse Technologies

Govindraj Ethiraj, PING Digital Broadcast Network
Gurcharan Das, writer
Harsha Mahabala, Edutel
Ireena Vittal, formerly McKinsey
Jacob Mathew, MAPE Advisory Group
Jaithirth (Jerry) Rao, VBHC Value Homes, formerly Mphasis
James Crabtree, *Financial Times*
Jayant Sinha, Honourable Minister of State for Civil Aviation, Government of India
John Elliott, journalist, formerly *Financial Times* and *The Economist*
John O'Sullivan, *The Economist*
Karthik Reddy, Blume Ventures
Kashyap Deorah, HyperTrack
Kiran Mazumdar-Shaw, Biocon
Kiranbir Nag, Saama Capital India Advisors
Kishore Biyani, Future Group
K.R. Sundaresan, formerly Rockman
Krishna Gopal Singh, EnNatura Technology Ventures
Kumar Ramachandran, GS Farm Taaza Produce
Kumar Shiralagi, Kalaari Capital
Mahesh Choudhary, Microqual Techno
Mahesh Ramakrishnan, Nanobi Analytics
Manoj Nair, RedGirraffe.com
Mark Hannant, Magenta
Mark Runacres, SQN Partners
Mohandas Pai, Aarin Capital
Mukesh Bajaj, CreditCheck Partners
Nandan Nilekani, formerly Infosys and Unique Identification Authority of India (UIDAI)
Narayana Murthy, Catamaran Ventures, formerly Infosys
Naveen Tewari, InMobi
Navin Mittal, Gateway Brewery Co.
Neeraj Kakkar, Hector Beverages
Nelabhotla Venkateswarlu (N. Venkat), Vyome Biosciences
Nigel Lang, Flitabout

Niranjan Hiranandani, Hiranandani Group
Nitin Gupta, Attero Recycling
Pankil Shah, Neighbourhood Hospitality
Parth Amin, SLK Software
Pramod Bhasin, formerly Genpact
Pranay Chulet, Quikr
Prashant Tandon, 1mg
Prashanto Das, PING Digital Broadcast Network
Praveen Sinha, formerly Jabong
R. Ravindranath, Milltec
Radhika Aggarwal, ShopClues
Rahul Mehra, Gateway Brewery Co.
Rajeev Mantri, Navam Capital
Ratan Tata, RNT Associates, formerly Tata Group
Rehan Yar Khan, Orios Ventures Partners
Rizwan Koita, CitiusTech
Ronnie Screwvala, Unilazer Ventures, formerly UTV
Rushabh Desai, formerly JobInsight
Sachin Bansal, Flipkart
Sanjay Nath, Blume Ventures
Sanjay Sethi, ShopClues
Sanjoy Roy, Teamwork Arts
Saroja Yeramilli, Melorra
Sasha Mirchandani, Kae Capital
Saurabh Srivastava, Indian Angel Network
Shailesh Lakhani, Sequoia Capital
Sharad Lunia, releaseMyAd
Sharad Sharma, iSPIRT
Shashank N.D., Practo Technologies
Shashikiran Rao, Construkt
Shiladitya Sengupta, Vyome Biosciences
Shivakumar Ganesan, Exotel
Siddharth Talwar, Lightbox India Advisors Private Limited
Sidhartha Kumar Bhimania, EnNatura Technology Ventures
Srikanth Velamakanni, Fractal Analytics

Srikumar Misra, Milk Mantra
Srinivas Vishnubhatla, Mosaik Risk Solutions
Suhas Baliga, Innove Law
Sumant Sinha, ReNew Power
Sunil Bharti Mittal, Bharti Enterprises
Sunil Kant Munjal, Hero Group
Tarun Mehta, Ather Energy
Tejpreet (TP) Chopra, Bharat Light & Power
Uday Kotak, Kotak Mahindra Bank
Vani Kola, Kalaari Capital
Victor Mallet, *Financial Times*
Vijay Reddy, Footprints Collateral Services
Vijay Shekhar Sharma, One97 Communications/Paytm
Vikas Jain, Micromax Informatics
Zia Mody, AZB & Partners
Zishaan Hayath, Toppr

ACKNOWLEDGEMENTS

My biggest thanks go to those 109 people who agreed to be interviewed for this book. As ever in India, senior and busy people were incredibly generous with their time, open with their thoughts and blunt with an outsider. On many occasions they strayed beyond what sensibly they should have commented on tape, so I trust I have got the balance between honest disclosure and discretion broadly right. My partner in Kiran Energy, Ardeshir Contractor, has been a critical companion on my own entrepreneurial journey.

The conclusions and opinions, and any errors, are mine and no doubt many will take issue with them.

I am also grateful to the staff at many of the interviewee's companies who juggled dates and times for me. Dilnaz and Deepthi at Tata were especially persistent in syncing diaries as Ratan seems busier in retirement than as Group Chairman. I have lost count of how many changes we had with Flipkart due to Sachin's impossible schedule. Some interviews did not work out despite best efforts, including Snapdeal, Suzlon, Apollo and Essel, but thank you for trying.

Friends, and interviewees, were tremendously kind in introducing me to others with a view to be interviewed. Thank you for those referrals. Roger Pereira, Sasha Mirchandani, Kashyap Deorah, the team at Blume Ventures, Rajesh Ranavat, Kumar Shiralagi and Sandeep Naik were especially helpful.

Patrick Foulis, Rajeev Mantri, Subrata Bhattacharjee and Chris Bogan were kind enough to read and comment on the first draft. Patrick's critique was especially thorough, demanding, encouraging and helpful.

I received help beyond what I could have reasonably asked from Xavier Raphael, my driver of nearly 20 years, now an entrepreneur himself. Clare Birch and Jaideep Prabhu at Cambridge University, Rajesh Mehta at Everstone Capital, Jeannie Burton and Judith Wettach at Coats and the team at Datamatix who did my transcriptions, were also very kind in giving me support. I am grateful to the VCCircle Network for allowing me to refer to data from their database, VCCEdge. Paul Abrahams and Anie Begum of RELX Group kindly helped me with a search on LexisNexis.

Broo Doherty, my old friend and now agent, got me into this. The team at Hachette India, led by Thomas Abraham and Poulomi Chatterjee, have been remarkably encouraging from our first lunch a year ago. The most difficult issue we had was agreeing on a title that captured what I wanted to say with their sense of the market.

My family has put up with my obsession with all things Indian, and more recently, in particular, Indian entrepreneurs. The travel needed to research this book and the toll it has taken trying to make sense of what I learnt has impacted them greatly. My thanks and love to them all and particularly to Shahilla for her invaluable help and support.

INDEX

CLICK!: The Amazing Story of India's E-commerce Boom and Where It's Headed

Jagmohan Bhanver and *Komal Bhanver*

A sharp study of the evolution of the e-commerce sector in India and how it is reshaping the way we do business

For a population with severe trust issues with online payments, Indian consumers have embraced e-commerce with phenomenal enthusiasm in the past few years. In turn, an incredible number of e-commerce companies operate here today, the more successful among them disrupting business paradigms and changing the way products and services are bought, sold and consumed in the country.

Through the stories of eight players that have experienced the incredible highs and lows that the industry has witnessed – Flipkart, Snapdeal, MakeMyTrip, Pepperfry, Just Dial, redBus, InMobi, Paytm – this book unravels the incredible story of the evolution of e-commerce in India. *Click!* provides a long view of where the industry is headed and presents an incisive vision of it that is both inspirational and cautionary.

ISBN 9789351950271

HARDBACK

Rs 499

Frugal Innovation: How to do Better with Less
Navi Radjou and *Jaideep Prabhu*

Corporate India's guide to reclaiming global leadership in frugal innovation

In the global business landscape, increasingly defined by trends such as the sharing economy and the maker movement, companies the world over are facing pressure from consumers, employees, and governments to create and deliver first-rate, affordable and sustainable products and services using less energy, less capital, and less time. This has led to the development of a new model for business success: FRUGAL INNOVATION, or the ability to do more – and better – with less.

In this inspiring and significant book on a revolutionary worldwide phenomenon, innovation experts Navi Radjou and Jaideep Prabhu show how 50 of the world's top companies across sectors – including American Express, GE, Novartis, PepsiCo, Renault-Nissan, Siemens and Unilever – are achieving great success by embedding frugality into their business models and corporate culture.

ISBN 9789351950653

PAPERBACK

Rs 399

The Elephant Catchers: Key Lessons for Breakthrough Growth
Subroto Bagchi

'Unlike an operation to catch rabbits, trapping an elephant calls for expertise over enthusiasm. Those who hunt rabbits are rarely able to rope in elephants.'

Many organizations, even those that may have a brilliant start, falter in their attempts to achieve transformational growth in their later phases. In *The Elephant Catchers*, Subroto Bagchi distils his years of on-the-ground learning to explore why this happens, and what such organizations and their people must do to climb to the next level and beyond.

Through a combination of engaging anecdotes from his experiences as co-founder, and subsequently Chairman, of Mindtree Ltd, and insightful stories from our everyday world, Bagchi demonstrates a crucial point: Organizations with real ambition to get to the top need to embrace the idea of scale and then ensure that it systematically pervades every aspect of its functioning.

ISBN 9789350095836

HARDBACK

Rs 499

The Modi Effect: Inside Narendra Modi's Campaign to Transform India

Lance Price

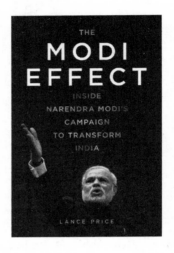

How did a 'chai wallah' who sold tea on trains as a boy become Prime Minister of India?

On 16 May 2014, Narendra Modi was declared the winner of the largest election ever conducted anywhere in the world, having fought a campaign unlike any before.

Political parties in Britain, Australia and North America pride themselves on the sophistication of their election strategies, but Modi's campaign was a master-class in modern electioneering. His team created an election machine that broke new ground in the use of social media, the Internet, mobile phones and digital technologies. Their pioneering techniques brought millions of young people to the ballot box as Modi trounced the governing Congress Party led by the Gandhi dynasty. In *The Modi Effect*, Price lifts the lid on a whole new box of tricks, where message-management and IT wizardry combined to create a vote-winning colossus of awesome potency.

ISBN 9781473610910

PAPERBACK

Rs 499